WHAT REALLY WORKS
IN Secondary Education

This book is dedicated to Col. (Ret) Rance Farrell
Rance is Wendy's stepfather and left us way too soon in 2014.
Rance led soldiers, as well as students, and he knew what really worked in his field. He exemplified leadership. He was trusted and respected as a role model and as a leader. He educated others: on the battlefield, in the classroom at West Point, in his role as Division President of the Association for the United States Army, and at home with his children. We were all in very good hands.
Rance, we will miss you.

WHAT REALLY WORKS
in Secondary Education

Wendy W. Murawski
Kathy Lynn Scott

Editors

CORWIN
A SAGE Company

FOR INFORMATION:

Corwin

A SAGE Company

2455 Teller Road

Thousand Oaks, California 91320

(800) 233-9936

www.corwin.com

SAGE Publications Ltd.

1 Oliver's Yard

55 City Road

London EC1Y 1SP

United Kingdom

SAGE Publications India Pvt. Ltd.

B 1/I 1 Mohan Cooperative Industrial Area

Mathura Road, New Delhi 110 044

India

SAGE Publications Asia-Pacific Pte. Ltd.

3 Church Street

#10-04 Samsung Hub

Singapore 049483

Acquisitions Editor: Jessica Allan

Associate Editor: Kimberly Greenberg

Editorial Assistant: Cesar Reyes

Production Editor: Veronica Stapleton Hooper

Copy Editor: Beth Hammond

Typesetter: C&M Digitals (P) Ltd.

Proofreader: Dennis W. Webb

Indexer: Jeanne R. Busemeyer

Cover Designer: Gail Buschman

Marketing Manager: Amanda Boudria

Printed in the United States of America

A catalog record of this book is available from the Library of Congress.

ISBN: 978-1-4833-8665-2

This book is printed on acid-free paper.

15 16 17 18 19 10 9 8 7 6 5 4 3 2 1

Contents

Foreword

I remember it like it was yesterday. My first day of teaching, that is. It was September 1996 in Room 323 at John Burroughs High School in Burbank, California. I was ready to face my very own class of real live tenth graders and teach them the mysteries of English. My seating charts, the ones I spent a ridiculous amount of time perfecting, were beautifully printed out. The walls papered in sunny colors with eye-catching posters tacked artfully here and there. In my arms, a sheaf of terrifically important, hot off the copier, papers ready to pass out. On me, a polished, smart-looking outfit with sensible, made-to-last-all-day shoes. I had a megawatt smile and enough enthusiasm to fill a dozen classrooms. I was SO ready. By second period, my naïve ideas of preparedness met the gritty reality of classroom dynamics, and I was exhausted just trying to keep up. By third, I was terrified; by fourth exhausted; and by sixth, ready to walk out and never return.

If you would have asked me, on the eve of my first day as a real teacher, if I was ready, really ready, I'd have given you a hearty yes. And that's the strange magic of teacher preparation programs. I left mine certain that I'd done the important work of becoming ready to teach. I'd had experiences and opportunities and assignments that had truly shown me not just how to teach, but how to teach skillfully and well. At least, that's what I thought. And I wasn't wrong. You DO walk in ready, but an actual classroom is a remarkable and very real crucible that has its own lessons for you, lessons you cannot learn until you are the teacher.

And here's what's utterly wonderful about being the one in charge in the room. No matter how ready you are, how prepared you feel, you don't really know a thing. But you learn, and you learn fast.

You see, the growth curve in our profession is enormous. You are better at 10:00 a.m. than you were at 8:00 a.m., and by 2:00 p.m. your lesson is amazing. On Tuesday, you're much better than you were on Monday. And Friday? Friday is a gift you give your students . . . you're that good. And don't get me started on the first day of your SECOND year of teaching. On that day, you are truly the rock star teacher you've grown to be. Naturally, as is the order of things in teaching, in walk your new students and a completely new dynamic presents itself. All the skills and talent you brought with you don't seem to work the same magic on these kids, and back to square one you go trying to figure it all out. It's alarming and wonderful at the same time, which is why our job forces us to stay on our toes every single day.

After 18 years of this, there's only one thing I know for certain, and it's this: I don't know very much for certain. There has not been one way to teach my classes or one strict set of ideas or procedures that worked every year or with every group of students. There just isn't.

What I do know is that I have needed to fill my metaphorical teacher toolbox with every possible tool, tip, technique, idea, and strategy possible so that when new situations in my classrooms arise, I have a deep set of possible options from which to grab as I try to teach my way through. The idea of the teacher's toolbox coupled with the gritty determination to grow and get better by staying open to new ideas and best practices are what turns good teachers into great ones.

And that's where this book comes in.

In the pages ahead, you'll learn from some of the country's best educators about what REALLY works in classrooms. From their experiences comes wisdom along with a whole host of tried and true, practical, hands-on solutions for you to use in your classroom. That's another one of the perks of our professions—our close proximity to other practitioners and our easy access to the greatness that exists in the classrooms right down the hall.

I don't know where I'd be if I didn't have Traci, Karen, Stefanie, Joe, Jim, or Alex to call on for ideas, hope, inspiration, or even just a shoulder to cry on. I am who I am because of the collection of ideas and skills I've gathered from my peers, filtered through my own philosophy and sensibilities, and put to use in my classroom. In that sense, I'm a patchwork quilt of all the great things I've learned from other teachers, but how I patched those pieces together makes me the unique teacher I am proud to be. That's how we grow. Your growth into greatness simply depends on your community of support. This collection of great ideas about what REALLY works in classrooms is another great tool to add to your toolbox; perhaps it's the greatest tool of all. That you can decide for yourself, but it's important you have it as you set out to create or transform your classroom into the vibrant and engaging learning space for all of your students.

I wish I'd had a book like this before I stepped into Room 323 all those years ago. I'm glad I have it now.

Rebecca Mieliwocki

2012 National Teacher of the Year

About the Editors

Wendy W. Murawski, PhD, is the Michael D. Eisner Endowed Chair and Executive Director of the Center for Teaching and Learning at California State University, Northridge. She is a tenured Full Professor in the Department of Special Education, as well as the past President of the Teacher Education Division (TED) of the Council for Exceptional Children (CEC). Wendy is proud to have been the Distinguished Teacher Educator of the Year for the state of California (which is a pretty big state!). She has authored numerous books, chapters, articles, and handbooks in the areas of co-teaching, collaboration, inclusion, and differentiation. Wendy owns her own educational consulting company (2 TEACH LLC), loves to travel and speak nationally and internationally, and is a frequently requested keynote speaker. Wendy would like to publicly admit that, though she is keenly aware of the research on child development and best practice, she allows her 10-year-old son Kiernan to eat way too many sweets. She's working on that.

Kathy Lynn Scott, PhD, is the Center Administrative Analyst for the Center for Teaching and Learning at California State University, Northridge. Kathy was trained as an "old school" darkroom photographer, but she fell in love with all things to do with education. After conducting research on art education and adult education in England and coordinating research on learning disabilities in New Jersey, Kathy jumped from coast to coast, finding a new home with the CTL where she gets to do a little bit of everything related to education. When not acting as the "glue" for the CTL (as Wendy calls her) and when she finds the time, she collects passport stamps at National Parks. But more often than not, she's just relaxing at home, eating something with entirely too much garlic, watching *Jeopardy!*, and shouting out the (not always correct) answers.

The CSUN Center for Teaching and Learning (CTL) is the research and professional development hub of the California State University, Northridge's Michael D. Eisner College of Education. The CTL was created through a generous endowment by the Eisner Foundation in 2002. The CTL's focus continues to be improving the education of all learners through the betterment of preservice and inservice teachers, counselors, administrators, educational therapists, and other educational specialists. The CTL provides local, state, and national professional development across a variety of topics and is dedicated to bringing the best evidence-based practices to educators in a practical manner. The CTL is committed to "what really works" in education!

About the Contributors

Making Math Meaningful

Ivan Cheng, EdD, is an Associate Professor at California State University, Northridge, who has taught at both the middle school and high school levels for over 23 years and was among the first secondary math teachers to be National Board certified. There are three things he likes to do besides being with his family and teaching . . . Disneyland, wine, and . . . well, maybe just two things (unless you count coffee . . . but that's actually a daily necessity). He has actually been spotted on more than one occasion at Disney's California Adventure grading papers (or writing chapters in a book) with a glass of wine (or two).

Rewarding Reading Practices

Mira Pak, PhD, is on faculty at Cal State Northridge's Secondary Education Department where she teaches credential and MA courses. Her areas of academic interest include reading across the content areas and differentiated instruction. Every day she fights the urge to buy clothes for her dogs.

Teaching Writing Right

Kathleen Dudden Rowlands, PhD, teaches in the Department of Secondary Education and Directs the Cal State Northridge Writing Project. When she can sneak away for a few days, she enjoys camping and hiking in Death Valley or Joshua Tree, spoiling her grandchildren, or checking up on the school of Humuhumunukunukuapua'a (reef trigger fish) that live in Shark's Cove on Oahu.

Successful Social Studies

Greg Knotts, PhD, is an Associate Professor of Elementary Education and the Director of the Queer Studies Program at California State

University, Northridge. He has published and presented extensively on social studies, the arts, and LGBT (Lesbian, Gay, Bisexual, and Transgender) issues in elementary education. He dreamed of being a *Solid Gold* Dancer; okay . . . he's still dreaming . . . but now it's for *So You Think You Can Dance.*

Joyce H. Burstein, EdD, is a professor of Social Studies Education and the Director of Community Engagement at California State University, Northridge. She is the recipient of the university's Distinguished Teaching Award and author of several works on social studies and arts education. After hours, you can catch her in her role as party mixologist.

Sensible Science Strategies

Stacey E. Hardin, PhD, is an Assistant Professor at Illinois State University. Her primary goal is to save the state of STEM and special education one word at a time! This being said, she has written a few articles in both areas and plans to keep combining the two areas to hopefully become famous with science and special education teachers around the world.

Nanci Hanover, EdD, has been with the Los Angeles Unified School District for 25 years, most recently as the Secondary Science Specialist. Her job is to work with administrators, teachers, and community science partners in integrating the Next Generation Science Standards into the secondary schools. Additionally, she is a Core Adjunct Professor for National University. When not doing those things, Dr. Hanover is out chasing mountain lions.

Awe-Inspiring Arts Instruction

Mary Wolf, PhD, is the Director and Assistant Professor of Art Education at Daemen College. For 20 years, she's taught art and advocated for the arts at a variety of levels in a variety of settings including elementary, middle, high school, magnet school, alternative school, home school, adult education, higher education, and at international, national, state, and local conferences. She secretly wants to teach and represent the arts as a professor on the sitcom *The Big Bang Theory.*

Rachel Lyons currently teaches art at the Buffalo Academy for Visual and Performing Arts and has taught visual art education in Buffalo, New York, for 17 years. She's been involved with two Professional Development for Arts Educators grants serving as a facilitator and mentor. As she works to keep up with her talented and energetic students, she slowly replaces her blood with coffee.

Tuning in With Technology

Lisa A. Dieker is a Pegasus Professor and Lockheed Martin Eminent Scholar Chair at the University of Central Florida. In addition, she directs the doctoral program in special education and is one of the creators of the virtual classroom TeachLivE. She has no spare time these days even as an empty nester, but when she does, she enjoys her two crazy cats (one will ignore you and the other will attack you)—noting her failure in behavior management with her pets.

Lauren Delisio is a doctoral candidate in Exceptional Education at the University of Central Florida. She is a native New Yorker with 9 years of teaching experience in both general and special education classrooms. Her areas of research interest include identifying effective academic interventions for students with disabilities in inclusive classrooms, especially in STEM content areas. A true Type-A personality, Lauren enjoys creating to-do lists, cleaning, and waiting on the prince of the house, her tiny, pampered Pomeranian.

Caitlyn A. Bukaty is a doctoral scholar of Exceptional Education at the University of Central Florida. A native of Buffalo, New York, she's still thawing out! As a professional educator and former ballet dancer, Caitlyn infuses her passion for the arts with her commitment to students. She is especially interested in postsecondary transition for students with disabilities. The rest of Caitlyn's time is consumed by catering to the every whim of her two rescue dogs, Giselle and Bukets.

Perfectly Positive Behavior

Brittany L. Hott, PhD, is an Assistant Professor of Special Education at Texas A&M University-Commerce. While Dr. Hott spends much of her time focused on developing and testing interventions to support secondary students, with or at-risk for learning and behavioral disabilities, she has been observed running in circles—literally! Dr. Hott is a Boston and New York marathon qualifier and multiple ironman finisher.

Dodie Limberg, PhD, is Assistant Professor at the University of South Carolina in Counselor Education Program. Dodie has worked as a counselor in Florida, Switzerland, and Israel. She is passionate about showing how school counselors make a difference in kids' lives. Dodie enjoys traveling and going out to dinner with friends but loves making macaroni and cheese at home.

Classy Classroom Management

Rebecca Mieliwocki is a seventh-grade English teacher in Burbank, California, and the 2012 California and National Teacher of the Year. Honored for her teaching by President Obama in a White House ceremony, Rebecca almost had more fun shooting the breeze with Secretary of Education Arne Duncan and Barack Obama than receiving her award. Typical middle schooler: always socializing instead of paying attention.

Cool Cooperative Learning

Scott Mandel, PhD, has been a classroom teacher for 30 years. A National Board Certified Teacher, he has written 11 teacher education books, including *Cooperative Work Groups: Preparing Students for the Real World* and *Improving Test Scores: A Practical Approach for Teachers and Administrators.* He wants to write a book about champion sports teams in his hometown of Cleveland, but he's still waiting for material.

Unique Universal Design for Learning

Tamarah M. Ashton, PhD, is a Professor in the Department of Special Education at California State University, Northridge, and a frequent presenter for the Speakers Bureau through CSUN's Center for Teaching and Learning and with 2Teach LLC. When not running the graduate program in Special Education, Dr. Ashton is on stage in numerous theatrical productions waiting to be discovered. Still . . . waiting. . . .

Incredible Inclusion

Erin Studer, EdD, is the Executive Director of CHIME Institute in Los Angeles, California. CHIME is a national model for inclusive education and serves over 700 children from the Los Angeles area each year. Mr. Studer has taught special education and general education in K–12 and also has taught preservice educators at the university level. He hails from the great state of Iowa and, like many from his native state, spent many years wrestling. Though he no longer grapples, he enjoys wearing his wrestling shoes around the house because of how cool they look.

Amy Hanreddy, PhD, is an Assistant Professor in the Department of Special Education at California State University, Northridge, where she teaches classes related to inclusive and collaborative practices that benefit all students. Amy has worked as a special education teacher and an administrator at an inclusive school and has presented on a range of topics related to inclusive education with a particular focus on students with significant support needs. When she is avoiding deadlines, Amy is busy posting cat and kid pictures on Facebook.

Creative Co-Teaching

Wendy W. Murawski, PhD, is the Executive Director for the Center for Teaching and Learning at California State University, Northridge. She travels and speaks on co-teaching nationally and internationally. For some strange reason, she is recently very into homicide detective shows. Dr. Murawski's idol is Reese Witherspoon in *Legally Blonde,* and her goal is to prove to colleagues that wearing pink does not inherently decrease one's intelligence or abilities.

Amazing Assessment

Brooke Blanks, PhD, is an Assistant Professor of Special Education at Radford University. She is particularly interested in inclusive classrooms in rural schools. When she is not teaching, writing, or supervising interns, Dr. Blanks enjoys running (slowly) and learning to play more than three chords on her guitar.

Great Gifted Education

Claire E. Hughes, PhD, lives her life in twos: She is an Associate Professor at the College of Coastal Georgia in a dual-certification Elementary/ Special Education teacher preparation program and received her doctorate in both gifted education and special education from the College of William and Mary. She specializes in twice-exceptional children; lives on St. Simons Island, but works in Brunswick on the mainland; and has two children, two dogs, two cats, two fish and is one half of a two-parent team.

Engaging English Language Learners

Shartriya Collier, PhD, is currently an Associate Professor, Director of the Los Angeles Times Literacy Center, and Graduate Advisor in the Department of Elementary Education at California State University, Northridge. Her publications and research passions include TESOL methods, English language learners in elementary contexts, immigrant family literacy, writing workshop, and male teacher preparation. When she is not teaching students or working with families in the community, she is a professional deejay and backup singer at local lounges and events in and around the Los Angeles area.

Addressing Autism Spectrum Disorder

Emily Iland, MA, is an award-winning author, advocate, filmmaker, researcher, and leader in the autism field. She travels extensively conducting training in English and Spanish on almost every autism-related topic. When she is not exhausted from doing all that stuff, she loves to research family history, which is not as boring as it sounds, honest!

Developing Deaf Education

Flavia Fleischer, PhD, is currently the Chair of the Deaf Studies Department at California State University, Northridge. She is an activist who is very interested in fighting against oppression of all minorities, especially oppression of Deaf people through her research and teaching. When Flavia is not handling department needs, teaching, or presenting, she is either out on her crazy training runs or in the kitchen experimenting with new recipes.

Will Garrow, PhD, is from upstate New York, where he was first introduced to the Deaf Community through his career as a professional snowboarder. As a faculty member at California State University, Northridge, his teaching mainly focuses on how oppression works in American society, Deaf Culture, and ASL Linguistics. When Will is not teaching, he can be found either on the snow in the mountains or splatting balls on the racquetball court.

Rachel Friedman Narr, PhD, is a Professor in Special Education/Deaf Education at California State University, Northridge. She's published and presented nationally on reading with DHH students and parent-to-parent support for families raising DHH children. She's best known for her truthiness and well . . . her husband's amazing skills in the kitchen.

Superb Social Skills Instruction

Michelle Dean is an Assistant Professor in Special Education at California State University, Channel Islands. She received her PhD from the University of California, Los Angeles. Michelle's research focuses on the social engagement of children with disabilities at school. At home, Michelle changes diapers, plays "I'm gonna get you," and cooks in real and pretend kitchens. Prior to becoming a professor and a mom, Michelle was a special education teacher for the Los Angeles Unified School District.

Fantastic Family Collaboration

Mary Anne Prater, PhD, is the Dean of Education and Professor of Special Education at Brigham Young University. Mary Anne has been a special education teacher or professor for 30 years. She enjoys traveling, counted cross stitch, and reading children's books that include characters with disabilities. While traveling for business or pleasure, Mary Anne loves to visit museums, if not for the exhibits, then for the gift shops!

Nancy M. Sileo, EdD, is Professor and Assistant Dean of the College of Education and Behavioral Sciences at the University of Northern Colorado. Nancy has worked in the fields of special education and teacher education for 25 years. She has the unique experience of publishing and presenting at professional conferences with her parents (retired professors of special education) and her sister, who is also a professor of special education. Nancy enjoys traveling, and to ensure that her administrative skills remain up to par while away from the office, Nancy practices by nagging her teenage daughter.

Introduction

What you have at your fingertips is a compilation of chapters written by individuals who not only know the theory and research in their various fields of expertise, but also know teaching *and* teachers. They are in classrooms across the nation, learning and adding to our knowledge of what really works—and unfortunately what does not work—with students today. There are so many experts nationally and internationally who write about and study different areas of education. What was important to us as we invited authors to write for this book is that they provide us with work that is timely, practical, to the point, and written so that you would want to pick it up and use it time and time again. We asked authors to talk to you, not to preach or write as if this were a research journal. We wanted humor and realism throughout the best practices and substantive content. And we think we got it!

You may notice that there are some areas of redundancy. For example, many authors ask teachers to stop talking so much, to give students more choice, to individualize and differentiate, and to connect with parents. Rather than pulling these items out, we left them to help emphasize and highlight tips that experts from differing frames of reference share. On the other hand, you might notice some discrepancies among chapters. While person first language (e.g., "the boy with the learning disability" as opposed to the "learning disabled boy") is important for many of the authors (and honestly, for us as the editors), we respected the fact that fields such as Deaf education and gifted education don't use person first language and instead refer to the Deaf child or the gifted student. We left those also to depict the variety in the field.

How do you use this book? That's up to you. You can read it from beginning to end or you can pick and choose. We organized it so that our content areas are first, followed by instructional strategies and pedagogy. In the third section, we include information on special populations. While some chapters may be more or less relevant to you and your teaching, we hope you consider reading them all. You may be surprised what you pick up in a chapter on working with English language learners, even if you haven't yet had any of those students in your class yet!

We'd also like to point out that we have interspersed quite a few "Making Connections" boxes throughout the chapters. This is so you can see how all of these chapters interrelate and support one another. If you want, you can make this a "Choose-Your-Own-Adventure" book and follow the Making Connections boxes throughout the text! Want to keep learning? We certainly hope you do. If so, please look at the plethora of references our authors have included and cited from. In many cases we also provide a "Recommended Readings" section but be aware, if an item was cited in the References section, it is not in the Recommended Readings section as well. We hope you will know the author recommends it by the fact that it was important enough to reference.

We must thank each and every one of our authors for their hard work on this book. When we approached them and said, "We want you to write a practical chapter on your topic, but please keep it mainly focused on bulleting the Do's and Don'ts . . . oh right, and keep it really short," we had mixed responses. Some replied, "Heck yeah! I could do that in my sleep," while others said, "Just a few pages? On this huge topic? Are you crazy?" But they all took up the challenge and came through! They, like us, felt this book was important enough to get out there. They, like us, knew that teachers are busy and are understandably looking for something short and sweet that boils down the key information in a quick to grab format. They, like us, are passionate about education and improving what we are doing for all kids. All of them. So we thank our authors. (And yes, we owe you all a drink!)

We must also thank the Eisner Foundation for creating and supporting the Center for Teaching and Learning (CTL) at California State University, Northridge (CSUN). Their vision of ongoing professional development for urban education has enabled us to create this book in the first place. Our Dean at the CSUN Michael D. Eisner College of Education, Dr. Michael Spagna, also continues to constantly encourage us to pursue cutting-edge practices in education and to remain the professional development and research hub of the college. We would like to make a "shout out" to Rick Goldman, Marcia Rea, and Amy Sheldon, who were with the CTL when we first conceptualized "What Really Works." We hope you three are proud of where we've come! Last, but never ever least, we both would like to thank our CTL student assistants, Ashot Nikoyan, Timothy Nang, and Michelle Jones, for their incredible support as we worked diligently on this text (while trying to concurrently run about 17 other projects and events). Special thanks to CTL student assistant, Sam Garley, for providing indispensible behind-the-scenes help. You four are amazing, and we are grateful you have joined our CTL family.

Wendy W. Murawski and *Kathy Lynn Scott*

SECTION I

What Really Works in Content

1

Making Math Meaningful

Ivan Cheng

California State University, Northridge

WHAT REALLY WORKS IN MATH IN THE SECONDARY CLASSROOM

How to Teach Them Math (Even When They Don't Want to Learn)

The bell rings. Students "quietly" begin working on their warm-up problems. After 10 minutes, it's time to go over the homework from last night. As predicted, the students all had trouble with the even-numbered problems from the book. Not wanting to leave any child behind, you patiently go over the procedures for solving those problems again . . . and again . . . and again. And that was just for students who actually didn't quit when the problems got hard.

At this point, there are only 20 minutes left in the period (barely enough time to go over the new lesson, let alone the hands-on activity you wanted to try). So the lesson quickly turns into a brief lecture where the new homework problems are demonstrated on the board. Luckily, it's an easy procedure to learn, so the students actually have 5 minutes to practice a couple of problems before the bell rings. Period 1 ends and it seems like the entire rest of the day will be the same—another day of reviewing yesterday's lesson and barely squeezing in a short lecture before the bell. This scenario was often *my* typical day when I started my teaching career decades ago. Unfortunately, this scenario is still all too common in math classrooms today.

In contrast, the new *Common Core State Standards for Mathematics* (National Governors Association Center for Best Practices & Council of Chief State School Officers, 2010) and the book *Principles to Actions* from the National Council of Teachers of Mathematics (2014) both paint a picture of a new kind of classroom—one where students actually "make sense of problems and persevere in solving them" (California Department of Education, 2014, p. 6). In this new math classroom, students will need to "reason abstractly and quantitatively," "use appropriate tools strategically," and "attend to precision." Just those few standards alone suggest a radically different type of classroom where students learn mathematics as a part of making meaningful connections, rather than endlessly practicing procedural skills to prepare for a multiple choice test. After nearly two decades of relentlessly focusing on improving test scores, however, most students are not accustomed to learning math as a part of sense making and problem-solving . . . and neither are their parents or teachers. In fact, many teachers probably have forgotten what it means to teach math beyond a collection of procedures.

Making Connections

Check out Chapters 9 and 10 on Classroom Management and Cooperative Learning

Seem impossible or at least, unlikely? It's really not. In searching for a better way to reach students (who really didn't want to learn math), a group of teachers and I collaborated to design learning activities that guided students to make mathematical connections on their own. By having students *develop* their own understanding and discover possible solutions, our classrooms were transformed to places of learning and student success. The focus of this chapter will be on ways to help make the *mathematics* make sense for students and ways to design learning activities that engage all students (yep, even when they don't want to learn).

WHAT DOES IT MEAN TO TEACH MATH EFFECTIVELY?

What does it mean to teach effectively? At the most basic level, it is the ability to help a student learn. Period. If the goal of a lesson is for the student to learn a particular procedure, then an effective teacher will be successful in helping the student learn that procedure. If the goal of a lesson is to learn how to solve a problem, then an effective teacher will be successful in helping the student learn how to solve a problem. However, before discussing what effective teaching strategies might actually look like, a few ideas must be clarified first.

It is important to note that "good teaching" should *not* be thought of simply as how well a teacher explains or how well she keeps students engaged. *Engagement* should *not* be interpreted as how productive students are in completing their assigned tasks successfully. *Success* should *not* be thought of as how quickly and accurately students can complete a set of problems using prescribed procedures. With the new Common Core State Standards, effective teaching needs to be redefined in terms of how well students can *connect* and *apply* a range of mathematical concepts and procedures to *solve* abstract and numerical problems. In order to help students do these things, a few guiding principles need to be explained.

First, think of mathematics as *tools* to be used, not merely as topics to be covered. Huh? Let me explain. Learning procedures should not be an end in itself. Instead, they should be thought of as tools to help provide understanding and for solving problems. For example, solving equations involves procedures that reinforce key mathematical properties. Solving equations for their own sake does not automatically generate understanding of those properties. We've all had students who could follow steps without having any idea what they were doing or why, haven't we? Nor does fluency in solving equations necessarily mean the students can *apply* those procedures in solving problems. Some teachers focus all of their energies on showing students how a procedure works and never really give students a chance to use the procedure. This is like explaining how all of the buttons on a calculator work without giving the student a chance to solve any problems with the calculator. Mere familiarity with the operation of the calculator is not enough for a student to know how to *apply* it in unfamiliar situations.

Being able to solve unfamiliar problems is called adaptive reasoning (Bransford, Brown, & Cocking, 2000) and is one of the main areas of emphasis within the Common Core Standards. Thus, the second thing that teachers should realize is that they must focus on both *instrumental* understanding and *relational* understanding (Skemp, 1976/2006). Instrumental understanding refers to knowing the mechanics of how a procedure works. For example, knowing when and how to apply a particular rule to carry out a procedure is an example of instrumental understanding. Relational understanding, on the other hand, occurs when a student knows why a rule might work and how that connects with other rules or other concepts. Recognizing the connection between the "constant" terms in linear and quadratic equations (i.e., the "b" in $y = mx + b$ and the "c" in $y = ax^2 + bx + c$) would be an example of having relational understanding. Furthermore, having a relational understanding of mathematics gives students the power to experiment with and choose different possible strategies in solving a problem (Harris, 2011).

Third, teachers need to remember that all people learn new ideas through *progressive formalization* (Bransford et al., 2000). In other words, students must first develop and build upon their intuitive understanding of a concept before they can formalize that understanding into abstract representations. For example, in order to understand the meaning of slope beyond just a formula (that is basically arithmetic), a student must first grasp the idea of a constant rate of change represented numerically, graphically, in a table of values, and in the context of realistic situations. In other words, *the ideas have to make sense first* before mathematical symbols can have any meaning for the student. See? Progressive formalization sounded scary and overwhelming, but it's not. Too often, students are merely taught just the mechanics of a procedure without any real understanding of what that procedure means or how it might be applicable to other problem situations. In my own experience, the result of this approach was that my students could do the problems in the "A" section of a chapter that focused on a discrete procedure but had no idea how to use that knowledge to solve the word problems in the "C" section that focused on application of the procedure.

Finally, remember that many students are not intrinsically interested in learning math unless they first see the *immediate relevance* of what they are learning. In other words, these students won't care about learning the math until they are either intrigued by a problem or interested in using an application of a concept. When students do not think the math is worthwhile (or relevant), they will often tune out. This then leads to inattentive or disruptive behavior. For some students, learning math might be meaningful because they see it as a necessary step toward higher aspirations (such as going to college). For many others, however, the perceived lack of relevance or meaning is what keeps them from making the effort. The key to effective teaching, then, is to find ways to help students see the *worthwhileness* of learning the math. Thus, designing appropriate *learning tasks* is where effective teaching begins. Such learning tasks must provide **immediate relevance**, use **progressive formalization**, and help students develop **relational understanding**. With these principles in mind, the following section provides some tips for designing effective learning tasks that engage students in learning.

⬣ STOP OLD HABITS THAT NEED TO GO

Teachers

- ✘ **STOP focusing on "procedures without connections"** (Stein, Smith, Henningsen, & Silvers, 2000). Learning procedures are important; learning procedures in isolation and without clear connections to contexts, multiple representations, or application problems makes learning math a mindless chore. As a result, students will arrive in the next grade level "knowing nothing."
- ✘ **STOP "going symbolic" before students have had a chance to grapple with the concept intuitively** (e.g., giving students the formula for slope before they recognize the relationship between

points on a line and the constant rate of change represented by those points). More important, students need to see how those points on a graph represent "real life" contexts.

✗ **STOP confusing the** *representation* **of a math concept with the concept itself.** For example, the concept of slope is often mistakenly thought of as synonymous with the incline of a hill. As a result, students develop an erroneous understanding of what slope really means. An incline can have a slope if the change in its vertical distance over its horizontal distance is constant. But, mathematically, the incline itself is *not* the slope. Such a misrepresentation can prevent students from recognizing a negative slope situation when an object is physically rising (e.g., the distance between a hiker and the summit over time as she hikes *up* the mountain at a constant rate).

✗ **STOP** *over-***scaffolding the learning process, which reduces learning to simply following directions.** Students need a little bit of challenge to really learn the math. Telling the students what to do every step of the process eliminates the need for them to think.

✗ **STOP lecturing too much.** Enough said.

Administrators

✗ **STOP thinking that a quiet classroom of students working busily on textbook problems is an example of student engagement.** Teachers need to know that a robust discussion between students should generate a little noise and that's okay.

✗ **STOP equating good teaching with teachers giving clear explanations and students giving the right answers.** Good explanations and right answers are not enough. Teachers also need to promote explorations and reasoning in solving complex problems that don't have easy answers. Good teaching should be determined by what a student learns (and that should include strong reasoning skills, good work habits, and an appreciation for learning).

✗ **STOP focusing on test scores.** As the old saying goes, you don't make a cow fatter by weighing it more often. Assessments are important for guiding improvement. However, higher scores, in themselves, should not be the purpose for learning. When students understand the math, they *will* be able to solve unfamiliar problems. So even if some specific problem types are not taught, a solid foundation of conceptual understanding will equip students in solving many problems.

✗ **STOP treating teachers like factory workers who just carry out orders.** Teachers have knowledge and expertise that can be used to promote learning. Teachers need time and resources to apply their knowledge and expertise. Teachers need to be trusted to do their jobs. (See the "Do This" section below for more on this.)

GO   NEW STRATEGIES FOR SUCCESS

Teachers, DO This

- ✓ **BUILD on familiar contexts to make the abstract concrete.** For example, in illustrating the concept of rate of change, use situations that students can relate to (such as downloading so many songs from iTunes per day). This is much more powerful than just having them compute the slope using the slope formula. Find out what students are interested in; don't just talk about things you used to be interested in when *you* were in school.

- ✓ **USE patterns and explorations to help students develop their own understanding.** Students can be asked to notice a pattern and test their conjectures. This promotes critical thinking. For example, Dan Meyer has a library of such interesting "hooks" on his blog (check out the Plugged In box) that can help engage students in doing the math.

Plugged In

blog.mrmeyer.com

- ✓ **DESIGN lesson activities that require students to use multiple representations.** The more ways that a problem situation can be represented, the more likely the student can develop a relational understanding. Encourage students to use tables and graphs as often as possible. Diagrams, pictures, or any other representation are also useful.

- ✓ **ALLOW students to work together.** Often, one student may have part of a good idea while another student has the other part. As Steven Johnson (2010) puts it in his book *Where Good Ideas Come From*, breakthroughs occur when people's ideas collide. Plus, this aligns with Fortune 500's desire to hire individuals who are able to collaborate, communicate, and problem solve.

Making Connections

Check out Chapter 10 on Cooperative Learning

- ✓ **GIVE students the "answer" and have them create the "problem" that would generate the given answer.** For example, if you want them to develop both an instrumental and relational understanding of integer operations, give them an "answer" and have them come up with different ways to get that answer based on your parameters (e.g., using only subtraction or using at least one negative number in the "problem").

- ✓ **ASK questions to find out what students are thinking rather than for the "correct answer."** Ask questions like "How did you get that?" or "Is there another way?" instead of "What is the answer?" At the same time, encourage students to ask questions, especially those that help make connections. ("Where does this point appear on the graph and in the table?")

✓ **HAVE students take notes near the *end* of the period.** Taking notes at the beginning is usually an exercise in copying; the notes usually mean very little to the students. Instead, have students take notes *after* they've engaged in the learning activity as a summary of what they've just learned.

Administrators, DO This

✓ **PROVIDE₁as many opportunities as possible for teachers to work together.** Dedicate and protect regular chunks of time for teachers to collaborate. This is not time to plan field trips or to discuss ordering supplies. This time needs to focus on the math that students are learning and for brainstorming the best ways to get through to the students.

✓ **TRUST the teachers to want what's best for their students and empower teachers to be their best.** Teachers need to be supported in doing what they're trained to do. If some are a little rusty in their skills, provide *positive* learning experiences. The type of learning experiences that adults need must honor their knowledge and expertise. Focus on those.

✓ **ENCOURAGE teachers to step outside their traditional boxes** (but do it gently and in a nonthreatening way). It is often easy to settle into a routine, and change can be very uncomfortable. Provide incentives and opportunities for teachers to grow.

✓ **PROVIDE opportunities for special education, English language learner, and other teachers and specialists to collaborate with math teachers.** All of these groups are bound to learn new content and strategies from one another.

✓ **PARTICIPATE in the learning process with the teachers.** It is a team effort because "together everyone achieves more."

JUST FOR FUN

Name: _____

Use what you have learned to solve the following problems.

1. Laura and Miguel are trying to solve the following problem: *Jose can make 20 baskets in 2 minutes. At this rate, how many baskets can he make in 1 hour?* Explain how Laura and Miguel can solve this problem.	2. Laura thinks the correct answer is 10 baskets and Miguel thinks the correct answer should be 600 baskets. Who is correct? Explain.

3. Show how Laura and Miguel can use a table to find their answer.

Time	# of Baskets
0	0

4. Show how Laura and Miguel can use a graph to solve their problem.

TRIANGLE EXPLORATIONS (PART 1)

Name: ———————————————— Date: ————— Per. —————

DIRECTIONS: Cut the triangles out from the cut out page. Measure the length of each side using the grid paper, and record the lengths in the table below.

Record the length of each side of the right triangle, and compute their squares.

Triangle Reference Angle	Length of Adjacent Side A	Length Squared A^2	Length of Opposite Side B	Length Squared B^2	Length of Hypotenuse C	Length Squared C^2
H	Length of Side A		Length of Side B		Length of Side C	
J	Length of Side A		Length of Side B		Length of Side C	
K	Length of Side A		Length of Side B		Length of Side C	
M	Length of Side A		Length of Side B		Length of Side C	
N	Length of Side A		Length of Side B		Length of Side C	

What do you notice about the relationship between the numbers in the squares for each angle?

Can you make a rule for finding the length of side C when you know the length of sides A and B?

TRIANGLE EXPLORATIONS (PART 2)

Name: ————————————————— Date: ———— Per. ————

Pythagorean Theorem

What is the rule that shows the relationship between sides A, B, and C for each right triangle?

Use the rule to help you complete the table below.

Triangle Reference Angle	Length of Adjacent Side A	Length Squared A^2	Length of Opposite Side B	Length Squared B^2	Length of Hypotenuse C	Length Squared C^2
P	Length of Side A 7		Length of Side B 24		Length of Side C	
Q	Length of Side A	81	Length of Side B	1600	Length of Side C	
R	Length of Side A		Length of Side B	225	Length of Side C	289
T	Length of Side A 11		Length of Side B		Length of Side C 61	
V	Length of Side A 12		Length of Side B		Length of Side C	1,369

Can you make a rule for finding the length of side A when you know the length of sides B and C?

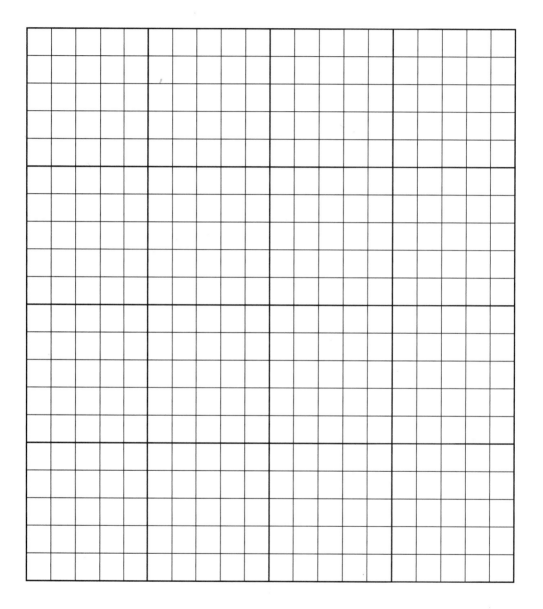

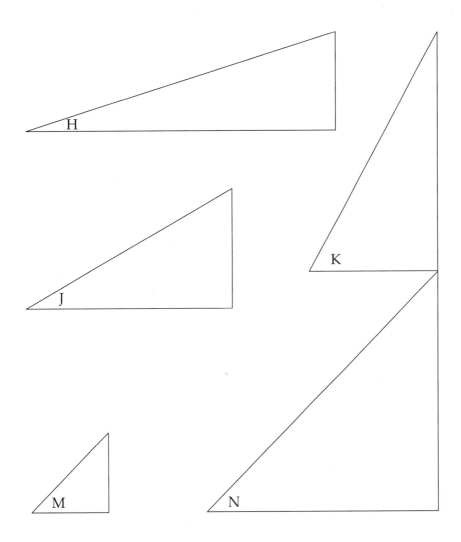

LATTICE POINTS (PART 1)

Name: _____

Step 1: Choose any *two* lattice points from the graph, and enter their coordinates in the table.

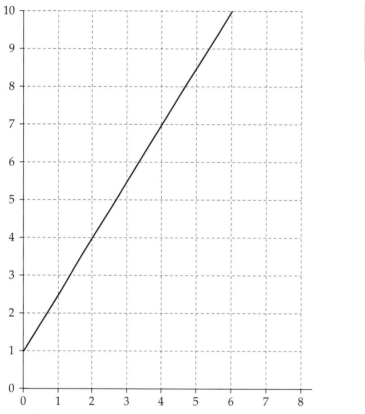

x	y

Step 2: Locate *all* of the lattice points on the graph. Look at the graph. What is the "change in *y*" from one lattice point to the next? What is the "change in *x*" from one lattice point to the next?

Step 3: Look at the table. Find the difference between the *y*-values and between the *x*-values. How do these compare with the "change in *y*" and "change in *x*" values in the graph?

Step 4: Can you make a rule that finds the "change in *y*" and "change in *x*" *without* using a graph?

LATTICE POINTS (PART 2)

Name: —————————————————————————————————

Step 1: Choose any *two* lattice points from the graph, and enter their coordinates in the table.

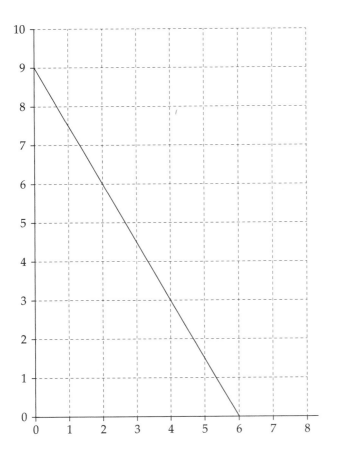

x	y

Step 2: Locate *all* of the lattice points on the graph. Look at the graph. What is the "change in y" from one lattice point to the next? What is the "change in x" from one lattice point to the next?

Step 3: Look at the table. Find the difference between the y-values and between the x-values. How do these compare with the "change in y" and "change in x" values in the graph?

Step 4: Can you make a rule that finds the "change in y" and "change in x" *without* using a graph?

WHAT DOESN'T BELONG?

Name: _____

Which graph does not match the others?

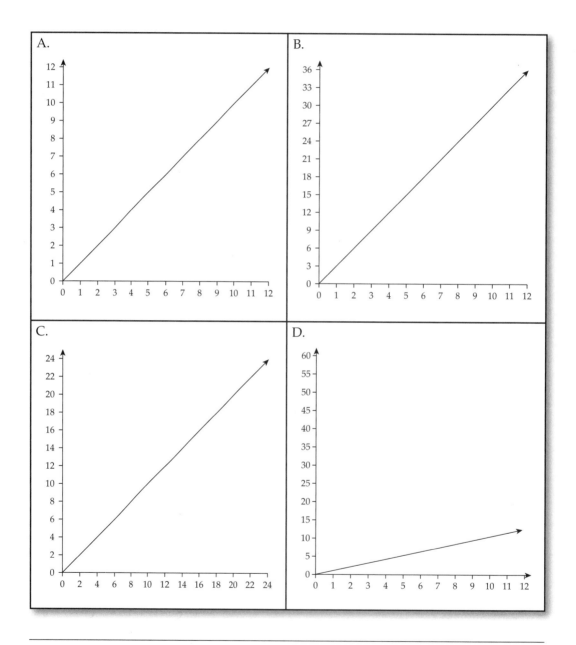

REFERENCES

Bransford, J. D., Brown, A. L., & Cocking, R. R. (Eds.). (2000). *How people learn: Brain, mind, experience, and school*. Washington, DC: National Academy Press.

California Department of Education. (2014). *California Common Core State Standards: Mathematics* [Electronic edition]. Retrieved from http://wwwcde.ca.gov/re/cc/

Harris, P. W. (2011). *Building powerful numeracy for middle and high school students*. Portsmouth, NH: Heinemann.

Johnson, S. (2010). *Where good ideas come from: The natural history of innovation*. New York, NY: Riverhead Books.

National Council of Teachers of Mathematics. (2014). *Principles to actions: Ensuring mathematical success for all*. Reston, VA: Author.

National Governors Association Center for Best Practices & Council of Chief State School Officers. (2010). *Common Core State Standards for Mathematics*. Washington, DC: Authors.

Skemp, R. (1976/2006). Relational understanding and instrumental understanding. *Mathematics Teaching in the Middle School, 12*(2), 88–95.

Stein, M. K., Smith, M. S., Henningsen, M. A., & Silvers, E. A. (2000). *Implementing standards-based mathematics instruction: A casebook for professional development*. New York, NY: Teachers College Press.

RECOMMENDED READINGS

* Murdoch, J., Kamischke, E., & Kamischke, E. (2013). *Discovering algebra: An investigative approach* (3rd ed.). Dubuque, IA: Kendall/Hunt.

* Serra, M. (2007). *Discovering geometry: An investigative approach* (4th ed.). Dubuque, IA: Kendall/Hunt.

GO EVEN FURTHER WITH
THIS TOPIC ON THE WORLD WIDE WEB

- www.nctm.org/
- map.mathshell.org/materials/
- www.illustrativemathematics.org/
- secondarymathcommoncore.wikispaces.hcpss.org/
- blog.mrmeyer.com/

THE Apps WE LOVE

- Desmos
- ExploreLearning
- Quick Graph
- Wolfram Alpha
- Geogebra

2

Rewarding Reading
Practices

Mira Pak
California State University, Northridge

WHAT REALLY WORKS IN
READING IN THE SECONDARY CLASSROOM

Before, During, After: The Challenge

Few would dispute the importance of reading skills in the academic success of students, but what is often surprising for educators is why students who appear successful in high school are underprepared for college success. According to a 2002 report published by the Intersegmental Committee of the Academic Senates, two reasons that may contribute to students' underpreparation are (a) reading not being "formally taught after a certain point in students' education" and (b) expecting the teaching of reading to be completed by the English teacher "while other content area teachers focus on the transfer of information rather than teaching the strategies of reading, thinking, and writing in a particular discipline" (p. 20). Therefore, students who qualify to enter college and whose reading skills were adequate for high school often find themselves at a loss in college. The level of reading and the sheer amount often overwhelm students.

My first year teaching English, I taught four sections of 9th grade regular English language arts and one section of 12th grade creative writing. I was stumped because even though I was a credentialed English teacher, I had no idea how to teach reading. (After all, didn't students learn how to do that in elementary school?) Years later, when I served as a literacy coach in urban schools, I often met hardworking, dedicated teachers who also did not know how to teach reading. Not surprisingly, the problem was not limited to just English teachers. I met plenty of science, social science, mathematics, and psychology teachers, to name a few, who were also baffled and lamenting the same thing: "My students won't/can't read!"

I came to the realization that while I had been well schooled in the pedagogy of teaching writing as a process, I had not been taught that I needed to teach reading as a process. After that, things became easier. As an English language arts teacher, I trusted the process of writing; brainstorming, outlining, drafting, rewriting, conferencing with someone a couple of

Making Connections

Check out Chapter 3 on Writing

times in there somewhere, and then publishing guaranteed that, while I might not have a Pulitzer Prize winner, I certainly would have a better piece than if I jotted down one draft. Reading is much the same. If I go through the process of warming up and helping my brain to anticipate the contents of the text to be read, then help my brain comprehend during reading, and finally assist my mind to process and reflect on what I read, I have a far superior understanding of the text than if I quickly skimmed it once (which is often what students do and then claim "But I did read!").

The ability to read does not just affect academic success; it affects pretty much all learning. A friend decided at the age of 40 years to return to school to become an aesthetician. When she started her program at a local beauty school, the entering class was 41 students, most of them in their late teens or early 20s. After 6 weeks, the number of students had dropped to 19. When I expressed my surprise, my friend responded, "The book was too hard. We're reading about acids and bases, and it's hard science." Not going to college is certainly a viable option after high school, but not having college-ready reading skills might still mean failure.

While students do learn to read in elementary school, they learn to read at an elementary level. Students in secondary schools need to read secondary-level texts, and sometimes that means they need to learn new strategies and activities to help them do that successfully. This chapter uses the "before, during, and after" reading process to assist students to tackle more complex texts.

WHAT DOES THE BRAIN DO DURING READING?

Marilyn Jager Adams (1990) explains that in order for comprehension to occur during reading, the mind takes in the text through the Orthographic Processor, sends the words up to the Meaning Processor, then to the top to the Context Processor, and sometimes back down again. (Don't worry. . . this next part is a step-by-step explanation.) So if I were to read, "Don't go see the movie. The plot is so pedestrian that you'll fall asleep," my mind would see the sentence using the Orthographic Processor (eyes), send the words to my Meaning Processor where my knowledge of vocabulary would kick in, and I might think "Do not go see the movie. The plot is so person walking that you will fall asleep." When that meaning gets sent to my Context Processor, it will not make sense because of the second sentence: "The plot is so person walking that you will fall asleep." My brain would then toss the second sentence back to the Vocabulary Processor and double-check the meaning of "pedestrian" ("yes, a person walking down the street"), then back further to the Orthographic Processor ("hmm, the word is 'pedestrian.' I didn't misread it"). My brain would then send the second sentence back up to the Meaning Processor where I might wonder about the word "pedestrian" before I realized that it has a secondary definition of "banal" or "boring." Sliding that meaning into the second sentence would then satisfy my Context Processor: "Don't go see the movie. The plot is so boring that you'll fall asleep."

The challenge is that this process happens so fast for an expert reader that she or he does not even realize that much more happened than "I just ran my eyes over the words and understood." With such little self-awareness of how we read, it is no surprise that we struggle to teach the skill to students. Like teachers, my expert readers in class were often the worst advisors on reading because they had no awareness of what their process was because it seemed so "natural." (That is, until they hit Advanced Placement classes and then suddenly started struggling for the first time in their academic memory.) Going through "Before, During, and After" activities and strategies with all students assists them to become stronger readers. For readers who skim and then claim to have read but not understood, the process can slow them down enough to read more carefully. For readers who are reading slowly and do not know to do much more than just look at the words over and over in hopes that some magic will happen, these activities and strategies can provide scaffolding.

A "Before" activity can be described as an activity done before reading a text in order to do one or more of the following: create a context, anticipate the content of the text, remind the reader of any prior knowledge he has related to the content of the text, make predictions about the content of the text, and/or assist with difficult vocabulary to be encountered in the text. Like a warm-up assists an athlete or a singer, a "Before" activity warm-up helps the reader before the main event of reading. Athletes stretch or do calisthenics before a game to warm up their muscles, and singers sing through scales before a concert to warm up their voices. So for students, warming up the brain to be prepared to read does not seem so odd a concept when they realize that many other activities also require a person to do something beforehand. In some cases, depending on your student population and the difficulty of the text, you may need to do more than one "Before" activity, or you may need to differentiate by student need.

A "During" activity should have one main purpose: increase comprehension during the reading of a text. Many expert readers, when reading a challenging text, actively do something while they are reading. Some people annotate in the margins, others look up vocabulary, still others jot down summaries on sticky notes. Even the act of rereading is a "During" activity. As a teacher, the key to a "During" activity is to find a task that will assist students to better comprehend the text. Some activities encourage students to read slower (e.g., annotating); others may prompt students back to the text to reread a section or two (e.g., summarizing).

An "After" activity assists students to reflect on and process the text after they read. Many teachers initially confuse an "After" activity with homework or an assessment. An "After" activity has one main purpose: to assist the students in thinking about what they read. Sometimes the "After" activity can also serve as homework or an assessment, but teachers should not assume the reverse, that any postreading homework or test is a true "After" activity. Also, it seems unfair to assess the student before she has had an opportunity to truly digest the reading. In most cases, allowing the student to read and process, then assess, makes more sense.

This chapter is designed to provide the DOs and DON'Ts for teaching reading by identifying actions that are frequently observed that actually act as obstacles for reading success, as well as those actions that maximize students' chances of learning how to read at the secondary level. In recent years, the subject of teaching reading across the content areas in secondary schools has become a hot topic, thank goodness. We now have research-proven and classroom-tried activities and resources. I provide some activities to get you started, and at the end of the chapter, resources and additional reading on teaching reading in cross-content secondary classrooms are provided if you would like to read the research for yourself or go deeper into the topic.

 ## ERRORS TO AVOID

✗ **STOP simply assigning reading.** Many teachers tell their students, "Read Chapter 3 tonight," and then bemoan the fact that students do not read. There are many reasons why students do not read for homework. In my experience, the most common reason is that students feel the reading is too hard, and they do not know what to do to make it any easier. As teachers, we need to provide more tools, and "Before, During, and After" is a way to start students on the road to reading tough text. (See the DO section for "Before, During, and After" strategies.)

✖ **STOP using only the questions at the end as the assessment.**
Teachers often assign reading and then have students answer the
comprehension questions at the end of the
chapter. While there is nothing wrong with
comprehension questions, they should not
be the only method by which students are
assessed or interact with the reading.
Students who know that questions are the
only way they will have to show account-
ability for reading often do not read for comprehension but skim
the text for words that appear to match the questions and use
phrases from the text to answer the questions. Or they copy
answers from a friend. In addition to questions, if you are so
inclined to use them, investigate other ways to have students discuss
and write about the concepts and information in the reading. It is
much harder for students to "fake" understanding when they need
to interact over the reading.

**Making
Connections**

Check out Chapter 14
on Assessment

✖ **STOP being the book for the students.** I observed some incredibly
hardworking teachers who basically did all the work for the students. Explaining to me that their students could not read the text
because it was too difficult, these teachers boiled all of the information down into incredibly beautiful and detailed PowerPoint
presentations. With this kind of support, unfortunately, the students never needed to read the text, and never struggling with the
text ensured that they never *would* learn to read in that content
area. Having taught students whose reading ability is way below
grade level, I understand the frustration teachers feel. However,
by presenting the PowerPoint as a "Before" activity to provide
context, teachers can then use "During" activities for scaffolding as
students grapple with parts of the text in class, even perhaps just
the sections that explain the most important concept(s) for that
chapter. That way, students still receive the information, but they
have to read as well.

✖ **STOP telling students what the reading was about.** Even teachers
who are savvy about student tactics can find themselves summarizing, highlighting, and interpreting a text to the point where the
students no longer have to read; they simply come to class and ask
a couple of well-appointed questions to get the teacher to tell them
about the reading. A better method is to create activities that
require the students to use what was read to summarize, highlight,
or interpret on their own individually, in small groups, or as a class.

✖ **STOP thinking "There's no time for this. I need to teach physics
[or music, or geometry]."** I have heard this sentiment from all content area secondary teachers, even English language arts teachers
who want to teach symbolism or theme, not how to highlight or look
up vocabulary. The problem with this viewpoint is that texts in

different content areas require knowledge about specific genres, jargon, context, organization, and so forth. Few people are better qualified to teach how to read content area texts than the content area teacher. Often, how texts are organized is determined by the schema of the author. Assuming the author was a psychology major, she would organize the reading in a way that would make sense to psychologists but possibly little sense to other content area teachers. Therefore, other teachers could not necessarily teach the reading of the psychology text to students. Teaching the students how to read in a content area *is*, in actuality, teaching that very content area. All content area teachers need to be content area reading teachers.

GO STRATEGIES FOR SUCCESS

Teachers, DO This

- ✓ **TEACH reading as a process.** Make explicit to students that expert readers do not just roll their eyes over the words and have complete understanding—it only looks that way. Then, explain the "Before, During, and After" steps to the reading process. As you do activities in each stage, remind students why they are doing them; metacognitive understanding helps ensure that students will remember that they can do these steps on their own even after they graduate from your class.

- ✓ **WARN your students that reading complex texts is hard and slow— but that it gets better as they become more proficient.** The really disappointing aspect about learning to read is that it is so slow, even when the reader is making progress. When I returned to graduate school after teaching high school English for years, I had to read a research study for a class. It took me 1 hour to get through the first 10 pages (and even then I was not sure I totally understood the thing)! Quitting was not an option, so I kept at it, fearful that someone would find out my slow reading speed and ask me to drop out. It was not until the next year when I was explaining the reading to a first-year student that I realized I had indeed improved both my reading speed and comprehension—but only because I had kept at it.

- ✓ **EXAMINE the text beforehand, and anticipate what will cause students to struggle** (e.g., the overall concept, the author's intent, the different points of view, vocabulary, organization). (See sample chart in the next section.) Use that information to determine what "Before, During, and After" exercises students need. If you have a tough time anticipating students' struggles, consult a special education teacher or a teacher of English learners; they will definitely be able to pinpoint areas with which students may struggle; they may even have some great strategies to assist you.

✓ **When examining a text beforehand, the first few times you do it, WRITE OUT your answers.** If you use the chart in the next section, write all the answers out, then go back and circle the fields on the left of the chart that you would absolutely need to teach to ensure that the students get as much out of the reading as possible. I understand that you cannot teach all of the categories on the chart because of time constraints, so I recommend that you limit the categories to the most important three or so. With those categories and the students' needs in mind, I then decide what activities we need to do before, during, and after the reading.

✓ **USE the "Before, During, and After" model of teaching reading.** None of the activities need to be a complex, complicated exercise, but each should serve the purpose for its stage in the reading process.

✓ **PROVIDE classroom activities for each segment of the reading process.** Even if you have a class of high performers, your students still need some kind of activity for each stage of reading. Sometimes the activity will be short (e.g., a 5-minute whole class discussion on the topic of the chapter), and sometimes it will be longer (e.g., previewing vocabulary, watching a short film on the topic of the reading, and looking at the title, headers, and subheaders to anticipate what the chapter and each section will be about). (See next section.)

✓ **USE the same few "Before, During, and After" activities.** In order to avoid confusing students and creating situations where they spend more time learning how to do the activity than they do about the actual content, have no more than two or three activities in each of the "Before, During, and After" stages, and use them throughout the semester/year. When a student says to me, "Aw, are we doing SQUEEZE again?" I silently rejoice. That comment means that the student is familiar enough with the activity that he is "tired" of it. I know that only after repeatedly doing the same activities does the student have any chance of possibly internalizing them and automatically doing them once he leaves my classroom.

✓ **ASSESS comprehension of the reading in multiple ways.** Much like students not doing homework if they think the teacher will never check, students will not read if they do not believe the next day's activities will include the need to have read. Thinking about the receptive and productive modes of learning helps to ensure that a teacher does not just use one method of assessment.

✓ **ALLOW directed "talk time" about the reading, even if it is only for a few minutes each class.** One activity that my students like to do, and teachers (including myself) often do not spend enough time on, is structured, directed talk about the reading. Even if for only 5 minutes, have students discuss specific topics (the difference between mitosis and meiosis) or general ones (what they did . . . or didn't . . . understand about the reading).

✓ **CREATE a classroom library of books pertaining to your content area.** Surprisingly, students who didn't like to read literature from the canon (usually what was available in the bookroom), often read nonfiction texts on topics that piqued their curiosity. Keeping interesting readings—both nonfiction and fiction—on hand encourages your students to read. A science teacher colleague of mine gives extra credit if students read select chapters from the novel *Outbreak*, by Robin Cook, when the class studies viruses. Because of the lurid, disgusting, and quite scary descriptions of the virus in the book, students love it.

For so many of us, the idea of having to teach reading at the secondary level is odd, but it is a necessity. The problem was even after I became convinced it was necessary, I was not sure I could do it, and I was an English teacher! Once I realized that all I was doing was making the internal, almost secret, processes of reading explicit and then using activities to assist students to practice what so many expert readers do "naturally," I relaxed and realized I could do it. The second insight that calmed me down was the one where I remembered it had taken me pretty much my whole life for me to get to my current level of reading ability. I needed to be realistic and not expect that just because I was explicitly teaching reading that my students would automatically, effortlessly, and dramatically become reading geniuses in one semester. The good news is that if you can structure reading activities (you can, by using the tips in this chapter) and have patience and realistic goals (yes, this is harder), you CAN effectively teach reading in your content area.

EXAMINE YOUR TEXT

Genre	What type of text is this? What do your students need to know about this genre (structure, norms, purpose) before they read or as they read?
Title, Headers, Subheaders	What can you point out to students so they might predict content? What might they learn about the chapter/text organization? What can you ask them about font size, style, color and what they indicate?
Organization	If the title, headers, and subheaders do not assist with knowledge of organization, what do your students need to know about the overall organization of the text before/during reading?
Author's Purpose/ Intent	What about the author's purpose or intent will give students a context for the text? For whom was it written? When was it written? What was the author trying to do?
Vocabulary	With what words and phrases will students struggle? Differentiate between: 1) words they might not know but do not need to know to comprehend the main points of the text and 2) words they absolutely must know to comprehend the main points of the text.
Grammatical/ Mechanical Features	What about the syntax might make this reading difficult? What about the punctuation might you need to review, reteach, or teach?

SAMPLE BEFORE, DURING, AND AFTER READING ACTIVITIES

Name (and Type) of Activity	Purpose	Description
Freewrite (Before) (Elbow, 1973)	• Assist students to access prior knowledge • Assist students to anticipate	Create a question about the text or simply put the topic on the board and give students a set time (e.g., 2–5 min.) to write as much as they know, without stopping, about the prompt. Afterward, have students share with each other or the whole class.
KWL Chart (Before) (Ogle, 1986)	• Assist students to access prior knowledge • Assist students to anticipate • Create a class context • Make known any misconceptions	On chart paper, create three columns. The first should have the title "What We **K**now," the second should be titled "What We **W**ant to Know," and the third should be titled "What We **L**earned." Ask the class what they know about the topic for the reading, and list their responses. Then ask what questions they have about the topic, and list those responses. Be sure to explain that no answer at this stage is wrong, and you will list them all, but that as they learn about the topic, they may find what they thought was true is not. You may get erroneous responses, and while you list those, during the course of your reading/lesson, as the new information comes to light, address the misconceptions you wrote on the KWL Chart. After the lesson, return to the chart and fill in the last column "What We Learned."
Film Clip (Before)	• Assist students to access prior knowledge • Assist students to anticipate • Create a class context • Assist visual learners to create a context	Instead of using the whole length of a film at the end of a unit as a "reward," using clips from a film as a scaffolding tool was far better for the students and teacher. Choosing a film, TV show, or YouTube clip on the topic before discussing it as a whole class and then reading provides an excellent starting point, even for students who know nothing about the topic.
Metacognitve Markers (During)	• Assist students to read more carefully	Introduce symbols students will use to mark in the margins while they read (examples: ✔ means "good point," ? means "I don't know ____," and ☹ means "I disagree"). The number

(Continued)

(Continued)

Name (and Type) of Activity	Purpose	Description
(based on Baker & Brown, 1984)	• Assist students to pay attention to their own thoughts during reading • Assist students to identify content while reading	of symbols will depend on the reading level of your students. I also recommend requiring advanced readers to add written notations to the symbol markers.
Squeeze (During) (Klemp, 1997)	• Assist students to pay attention to each sentence • Assist students to collaboratively create meaning from the text • Assist students to start to learn how to summarize	After prechunking the text, have students in groups of four read aloud (or silently) each chunk, then complete the following roles: Paraphraser, who paraphrases the most important points of the chunk read; Verifier, who verifies that no information was left out and adds it in if needed; Squeezer, who squeezes the important information down to one sentence; Writer, who writes out the squeezed sentence.
KWL Chart (After) (Ogle, 1986)	• Assist students to reflect on the text • Assist student to revisit what they thought about a topic before they read/learned about it	This is a continuation of the "K" and "W" parts of the KWL chart used as a "Before" reading activity. After the reading and lesson/unit, the students fill in the last column with what they learned.
Exit Slip (After) (Gere, 1985)	• Assist students to reflect on the text • Assist students to process the information in the text	Leaving 15 minutes or so at the end of the class, have students fill out the Exit Slip (usually anonymously). Ideally, the Exit Slip asks no more than three questions; they can be general questions (e.g., What did you learn from the reading?) or specific (e.g., What do you think about the author's second claim about the Civil War?). Before students leave the class, they hand you the Exit Slip.

The above chart is just a sampling of activities to illustrate "Before," "During," and "After" activities. It is obviously not an exhaustive listing of activities. A search on the Internet will yield you far more activities than you could do in a year, so choose activities by taking into consideration what your student population needs in relation to your reading goal(s) after you examine the text.

REFERENCES

Adams, M. J. (1990). *Beginning to read: Thinking and learning about print.* Cambridge, MA: MIT Press.

Baker, L., & Brown, A. (1984). Cognitive monitoring in reading. In J. Flood (Ed.), *Understanding reading comprehension* (pp. 21–44). Newark, DE: International Reading Association.

Elbow, P. (1973). *Writing without teachers* (pp. 1–7). New York, NY: Oxford University Press.

Gere, A. R. (Ed.). (1985). *Roots in the sawdust: Writing to learn across the disciplines.* Urbana, IL: National Council of Teachers of English.

Intersegmental Committee of the Academic Senates. (2002). *Academic literacy: A statement of competencies expected of students entering California's public colleges and universities.* Sacramento, CA: Author.

Klemp, R. (1997). Using the directed reading sequence as an interactive strategy in content area reading. *Middle School Journal, 28*(5), 46–49.

Ogle, D. M. (1986). K-W-L: A teaching model that develops active reading of expository text. *Reading Teacher, 39*, 564–570.

RECOMMENDED READING

* Bean, J. C., Chappell, V. A., & Gillam, A. M. (2011). *Reading rhetorically* (3rd ed.). Boston, MA: Pearson.

* Carnegie Corporation of New York. (2004). *Reading next: A vision for action and research in middle and high school literacy* (2nd ed.). New York, NY: Author.

* Lenski, S. D., Wham, M. A., & Johns, J. L. (1999). *Reading and learning strategies for middle and high school students.* Dubuque, IA: Kendall/Hunt.

* Readence, J. E., Bean, T. W., & Baldwin, R. S. (2004). *Content area literacy: An integrated approach* (8th ed.). Dubuque, IA: Kendall/Hunt.

* Schumm, J. S., & Mangrum, C. T. (1991). FLIP: A framework for content area reading. *Journal of Reading, 35*, 120–124.

* Tovani, C. (2004). *Do I really have to teach reading? Content comprehension, grades 6–12.* Portland, ME: Stenhouse.

GO EVEN FURTHER WITH
THIS TOPIC ON THE WORLD WIDE WEB

- www.sccresa.org/toolsforschools/commoncore/contentliteracy strategies/
- www.literacyinlearningexchange.org/resources
- www.edutopia.org/blog/ccia-10-visual-literacy-strategies-todd-finley
- orh.sweetwaterschools.org/files/2012/06/EL-SDAIE-Strategies.pdf

THE Apps WE LOVE

- iTooch Language Arts
- Reading Trainer
- Free Books
- InferCabulary
- The Right Word

3

Teaching Writing Right

Kathleen Dudden Rowlands

California State University, Northridge

WHAT REALLY WORKS IN
WRITING IN THE SECONDARY CLASSROOM

Three Views of Writing and Writing Instruction

School writing can be thought about in three ways. The first is *assigning* writing. A teacher gives students a writing task. They complete it. The teacher collects the work and spends a number of evenings or weekends reading and correcting 20, 30, or 40 papers on the same topic that say pretty much the same thing in pretty much the same way. Sadly, all this expended effort on the part of both students and the teacher accomplishes little learning. Students can dutifully complete such writing tasks for an entire school year with little growth as writers.

Using writing is the second way to think about it. Here is some surprising news. Writing is an effective tool for thinking and learning, not just for expression. As such, exploratory writing can be a highly effective pedagogy. Janet Emig (1977) claimed, "Writing represents a unique mode of learning—not merely valuable, not merely special, but unique" (p. 122).

Emig noted that, "What is striking about writing as a process is that, by its very nature, all three ways of dealing with actuality [by doing, by graphic depiction, and by restating in words] are simultaneously or almost simultaneously deployed" (p. 124).

Effective learning occurs as the result of repetition or reinforcement. Because, as Emig observed, writing simultaneously involves "hand, eye, and brain [it] marks a uniquely powerful multi-representational mode for learning" (pp. 124-125); the repetition and reinforcement are embedded in the act of writing itself. Emig's work quickly inspired the development of the Writing Across the Curriculum (WAC) movement in universities.

Although efforts to infuse writing instruction throughout university disciplines have been common since the early 20th century, the current shape of writing across the curriculum practices began with the work of Toby Fulwiler in 1977. For Fulwiler, a key principle of WAC is "that writing can be used to promote learning as well as to measure it" (1984, p. 114). Professors were encouraged to assign informal journal writing to help students grapple with course content. In *The Journal Book*, Fulwiler (1987) provides readers with a rich collection of essays written for teachers and professors at all grade levels that provide examples of practice for using writing-to-learn strategies in courses as disparate as music appreciation, physics, and beginning French. Because the audience for journal writing was the student writer herself as a learner, and because the writing was produced spontaneously without opportunities for revision or editing, instructors were advised to focus on content and ignore mechanics when using writing as a tool for thinking and learning.

Historically, the WAC movement (and the more recent WID—Writing in the Disciplines) has been more widely accepted and adopted at the university level. However, the Common Core State Standards for literacy (reading and writing) in history and social studies, and in science and technical subjects, encourage K–12 teachers to recognize writing as a way of helping students of all ages master course content. Using writing to help students think and learn is an immensely valuable pedagogical tool and is a topic unto itself. So how do we do that?

That leads us to the third way of thinking about writing—*teaching* it. This will be the focus of the remainder of this chapter. Don't worry. You will become the writing teacher you always wanted to be.

KEY RESEARCH ON WRITING INSTRUCTION

Here is the good news. Writing can be taught (and you can be the one to teach it . . . even if you are a math, science, or PE teacher!). The field of composition studies (how to teach writing) emerged in the late 1960s and early 1970s, and many of its key understandings remain grounded in the work of practitioners who observed themselves and their students as writers, sought to extract general principles about writing from those observations, and then used those principles to guide writing instruction. Want to teach writing effectively? Then consider these principles.

Writing generates thinking. The human mind is never quiet. One thought leads to the next thought, which leads to the next thought, and so on. Peter Elbow's (1973) *freewriting*, a process for generating ideas where a writer begins writing on a topic and continues to write steadily for an established period of time, uses the generative power of the human mind, making the writer's thinking concrete and available for discussion, revision, and extension. This same generative principle underlies Janet Emig's discovery of writing as a tool for thinking and learning, the entire WAC movement's use of journals, and the current practice of asking students to produce "quick writes" as entrance or exit tickets, or as preparation for discussion.

Developing writers need rehearsal writing. A common mantra among writing teachers is "fluency, form, correctness." That is, writers need to develop fluency—the ability to get language into print smoothly and quickly. Second, writers need ways to organize content effectively, considering both their audience and their purpose for writing. Finally, writers need to edit writing so that it uses language that is appropriate and conventionally correct. Development in each of these areas requires safe, repeated practice. Notice, however, that correctness is the last of the three considerations.

Writers need time for prewriting—lots of time. Donald Murray (2003) understood that teaching composition means teaching a process. As a Pulitzer Prize winning journalist and an observer of his own processes, Murray advocated that 85% of a writer's time should be spent in prewriting. Prewriting activities might include gathering and organizing ideas, activating prior knowledge, and even daydreaming.

Effective writing depends upon revision. The act of writing not only generates but shapes thinking. Putting thought into language defines the thought. Murray (1981) saw revision as a central (although under researched and under taught) part of the writing process. He wrote, "All writers write badly—at first. . . . Then they rewrite. Revision is not the end of the writing process, but the beginning" (1998, p. 1). Linda Flower (1979) labeled early draft writing as "writer-based prose" and saw it as an essential part of the writing process. Writer-based prose is inconsiderate of readers. Ideas are not fully developed, logically arranged, or clearly presented. Flower noted that "Effective writers do not simply express thought but transform it in certain complex but describable ways for the needs of a reader" (p. 19). That is, they transform writer-based prose into "reader-based prose." Transforming writing from egocentric writer-based prose to reader-based prose is the focus of revision.

Reflective practice—both for writing teachers and for writers—is central to writing improvement. George Hillocks (1995) argues that writing teachers must constantly test theoretical knowledge against practical applications. They must assess their pedagogies against their success with students. Many writing teachers use their own experiences as writers to guide their instruction. As effective "kid watchers" (Short, Harste, & Burke, 1996), writing teachers view student performances as instructional starting points. Writers, as well as writing teachers, need to be mindful of their processes. They need strategies for gathering and organizing content, and they need to be purposeful in the choices they make. Developing writers are often unaware that there are options available. Learning to reflect on both their products and their processes accelerates student development as writers.

Connecting reading and writing instruction improves both. Graham and Hebert (2010) tell us that writing can potentially enhance reading in three ways. First, as Emig and Fulwiler believed, writing about reading empowers learning from the reading. Second, writing and reading are both meaning making processes by which the reader/writer creates understandings. Finally, "writers . . . gain insight about reading by creating their own texts" (p. 4).

Making Connections

Check out Chapter 2 on Reading

Understanding texts as writers—from inside particular forms—empowers students when they become readers of similar forms.

Effective teachers of writing write. The practitioner tradition in writing instruction is strong. Thousands of National Writing Project teachers share a belief that writing teachers should write. Although teacher-writers share what they have learned from students in articles and books, writing teachers need not publish to understand the craft of writing from the inside.

🛑 INSTRUCTIONAL PRACTICES TO AVOID

Here is the bad news. In spite of what some textbooks might suggest, there are no formulas for either writing or writing instruction. That said, there is a great deal of solid research-based information about effective practices for teaching writing. In a meta-analysis of writing studies, Steve Graham and Dolores Perin (2007) identified 11 key elements of effective adolescent writing instruction (see page 43). While much has been published summarizing effective practices, little available advice suggests practices to avoid. The list that follows is grounded in more than 30 years of personal experience as both a writer and a writing instructor from middle school through doctoral programs, and enumerates common practices of many well-intentioned (but ineffective) teachers.

- ✖ **STOP making all the decisions and doing all the thinking about the writing.** Don't choose all the writing topics. Don't tell students how many words or paragraphs or pages their writing needs to be. Don't tell them how to make their writing better without asking what they think will make it better.

- ✖ **STOP confusing form with genre or content.** This means not requiring a certain number pages in an essay, a set number of paragraphs (often five), or a certain number of sentences in a paragraph (sometimes 11). It means not telling students that the thesis sentence should always be the first (or last) sentence in the introductory paragraph. Training students to jam complex material into artificial formats guarantees the production of obedient, linear, obvious, and boring work that nobody would read—by choice.

- ✖ **STOP asking students to write before they have something to say.** Writers need to develop a rich bank of material upon which they can draw while composing. One reason the personal essays often assigned in English classes at the beginning of the year reflect stronger abilities than later writing is simply because they *are* personal. When writing about areas of expertise—their own lives— students have much to say and the confidence to say it well.

- ✖ **DO NOT ask students to write in forms they have no experience with as readers.** If the only reading students have experienced is in textbooks, they won't know how to write a news article, a speech, or a public service announcement. They certainly won't know how to produce decent literary analyses. They may not even know how to write a thank-you note!

- ✖ **STOP accepting first drafts as finished work unless students are practicing on-demand (timed) writing.** Few—if any—experienced writers produce decent work on the first try. Why should students expect to produce quality writing in a first draft? Why should teachers encourage those expectations?

- ✖ **STOP acting as the only reader of your students' writing.** If you are the only audience for students' writing, they waste precious time trying to determine what will please you instead of focusing how to present content in a clear and interesting manner to an authentic audience.

- ✖ **STOP collecting and grading everything students write.** For students to develop necessary fluency, they need to produce two or three times more writing every week than even the most dedicated writing teacher possibly has time to read. The football coach doesn't grade practices. Don't grade rehearsals. Save your scoring for game day.

✗ **STOP teaching grammar out of context and expect student writing to improve.** More than 150 years of research demonstrates little or no transfer between isolated grammar instruction and writing improvement (Weaver, 1996). Some studies even suggest that such instruction makes writing worse (Durst, 1984).

✗ **STOP marking or correcting every mechanical error.** Correcting is not teaching, and you are not every writer's editor. Marking errors after a piece is "finished" does nothing to improve students' conventional English. Respond selectively to drafts. Use errors instructionally. Are there patterns that students can identify and learn to edit for? (Andrasick, 1993). If students don't identify and correct their conventional errors, they make no improvement (Bardine, Bardine, & Deegan, 2000). Further, students who receive praise on their work develop positive attitudes toward writing and increase their efforts to improve.

✗ **STOP just assigning writing.** Use writing as a tool for learning and thinking to develop fluency. Use every writing task as an instructional opportunity to help students develop the writer's craft. Save yourself the effort of reading and marking poor writing.

GO INSTRUCTIONAL STRATEGIES TO EMBRACE

Helping students develop into fluent writers, capable of producing clear and interesting purposeful texts that are respectful of the needs and interests of many different audiences, is possible. . . if you slow down. Think about the semester or the year as a whole. What do these students need to know and know how to do at the end of the course? Writing development is a slow process, requiring many opportunities for safe practice. Plan sequences of writing experiences (Moffett, 1965, 1968) and conversations around those experiences that will help students grow. Although progress is rarely linear and the experience is rarely tidy, comparing work produced at the beginning of the course with work produced at the end should be gratifying for both you and your students. The suggestions below echo the findings of Graham and Perrin's (2007) meta-analysis of effective practices that help adolescents learn to write well.

✓ **LET students write.** Make writing an integral part of every class. Use writing as a tool for learning. Response writing (e.g., "write for 10 minutes in response to your reading and the questions you have about it") can generate thinking prior to class discussion. Such writing can be collected as a credit/no credit pop quiz intended to check that students completed reading assignments (Andrasick, 1990). Use writing for formative assessment (Graham, Harris, & Hebert, 2011).

✓ **TEACH writing.** Teach students to consider purpose and audience as they develop and organize content. Remind them that form follows function. The way writers shape content depends upon purpose and audience. ("What if you are writing to friends? Your parents? A judge?") Find many ways to teach and reteach these principles throughout the course.

✓ **TEACH writing as a process, and teach writing processes.** Teach students that writing well is a messy, recursive process, and that multiple drafts have value. Writers cannot get to a final draft without producing—and rejecting—much early garbage.

✓ **TEACH invention.** Part of the writing process is generating content. Writers must have something to say. Students asked to write about literary texts, for example, must develop a full and nuanced understanding of the text before they can write meaningfully. Without developing a strong reading for themselves, they retreat to plot summary, Spark Notes, or the Internet. Students asked to analyze historical events or scientific experiments need to have a thorough understanding of the material before they can shape a written response. Provide students with a toolbox of invention heuristics beyond brainstorming such as focused freewriting, Aristotle's topoi for systematic exploration (definition, comparison and contrast, cause and effect, support from evidence or expert testimony), cubing (see page 44), the journalist's questions ("who, where, why, what, when, and how"), Berke's (1990) 20 questions for the writer, and mindmapping, causal chains, or idea webs. Teach students to research, gather, and vet information from multiple sources.

✓ **TEACH revision.** The real work of writing for most practiced writers comes with revision. Teach four basic revision strategies: addition, substitution, subtraction, and reordering. Have students apply these strategies to every draft moving toward publication.

✓ **TEACH students to fit text structures to content.** Effective writers shape material in response to considerations of content, audience, and purpose. Beginning with form instead of content is analogous to trying to fit a "crab into a square box" (Williams, 1986, p. 365). The only way to accomplish the task is "to cut his legs off to make him fit." The problem is that "when you get through you don't have a crab any more" (p. 365). Withhold the use of graphic organizers until after writers have generated content and choose (or create) the organizer to fit the content.

✓ **CONNECT reading to writing.** For far too long, reading and writing have been thought about—and taught—as separate skills. No longer. Current research suggests they are learned (and should be taught) in a holistic, integrated way. Reading and writing are both processes of developing understanding and making meaning. Having students write about the texts they read is one of three writing practices that enhance students' reading. The other two are teaching students writing processes and skills and simply having students write more (Graham & Hebert, 2010). When writing about their reading, students can write notes, personal responses, and textual analyses and interpretations (Andrasick, 1990). Students can use summary writing using ReadWriteThink's (n.d.) "Get the GIST" strategy to increase comprehension. They can use the rhetorical précis, an easy-to-teach form of academic summary. Reading selections can serve as mentor texts to teach writing strategies, text structures, genres, and language use. Have students imitate passages to explore stylistic choices.

✓ **USE the power of word processing.** Word processing encourages expansion and revision and is a particularly powerful tool for English language learners (because of spell check and grammar check) and for many students with special needs.

✓ **DO have students read and write in many forms and many genres.** The Common Core State Standards expect students to develop proficiency in three text types: opinion/argument, informative/exploratory texts, and narrative. These three types are broadly categorized by rhetorical purposes and in no way limit the genres or text structures that writers might use. A poem (in the broadest sense of the genre) might present an opinion or argument, might inform or explain, or might present a story. Use reading selections as mentor texts to teach students about genres and the multiple possibilities they offer writers.

✓ **USE mini-lessons to develop writer's craft.** Use short (10–15 minute) targeted direct instruction as needed for the whole class or a small group of students. Teach "show, don't tell." Teach style. Teach students to craft titles and opening paragraphs. Introduce them to Nodan's (1999) "image grammar." Use every writing task purposefully to teach writer's knowledge and writer's skills. See page 46 for a list of possible mini-lessons.

✓ **TEACH students to reflect on their own progress.** Help students participate in their learning. Ask what they were trying to accomplish with a piece, why they chose a particular title, and what other titles they considered. If you have a large class, put reflection questions on the board and have student pairs ask and answer the questions. Trust students (and teach them to trust themselves) to choose topics and set goals. Ask for a weekly reflection: "What did you learn as a writer this week? What will you work on next week?" Help students see their progress. Have them date everything they write. Save their writing for them. Several times during the year, ask them to review past work and choose pieces that demonstrate an aspect of their writer's craft: use of dialogue; show, don't tell; or powerful titles, for example.

✓ **GIVE students ownership over their writing.** Writers need choices about content and form. Offer some possibilities within a broad subject range and let them choose. If you are studying a particular novel, provide a list of writing choices, or invite them to determine a topic for your approval. Use RAFT prompts to provide choices (ReadWriteThink, n.d.). Instead of telling students what they need to do to make their writing better, invite them to set goals. Include student goals on your assessment rubric (Gallagher, 2006). Teach students editing responsibilities (Anderson, 2008; Andrasick, 1993).

✓ **READ student work as a coach.** Identify what the writer is doing well (specifically) in a particular piece; suggest one or two things to work on. Effective writing classrooms provide safe opportunities for rehearsal—practice bits designed for low-stakes experimentation with style or form. Offer feedback, not assessment, at these developmental stages.

✓ **PROVIDE authentic writing tasks and authentic audiences.** Arthur Applebee's work (1981, 1984) provides solid evidence for the value of providing students with authentic audiences beyond the teacher. Writers need feedback from a number of readers. A single teacher, however well intentioned, simply cannot meet that need. Furthermore, if students are dependent only on the teacher for approval or disapproval of their writing, they become dependent on what Donald Graves (1984) called "welfare." Such dependency is crippling; students never learn how to make the independent choices all writers must make for themselves as they identify content, determine a purpose, and craft their content and language to communicate to an audience. Use peer response. Have students read their work aloud (or parts of it) to peers or parents. They will often hear (for themselves or for others) parts that bother their ears. Reading aloud develops voice.

✓ **TEACH conventional language use in context** (Weaver, 1996). Have students fix their mechanical errors and identify patterns of spelling and conventional misuse in order to edit for several patterns. Create spelling sticky notes with frequently misspelled words. On each note, write the word correctly emphasizing the trouble spot by size or color. Students keep these reminders where they will be seen often (on binders or a bathroom mirror) until they have mastered the spelling (Andrasick, 1993). Ask students which mechanical conventions they would like you to read for and identify when grading finished work (Gallagher, 2006).

✓ **DO demystify on-demand, timed writing.** Because students encounter high-stakes on-demand timed writing such as the SAT, the ACT, and Advanced Placement exams, it is important to include timed writing experiences in writing instruction. This is not "teaching to the test." As Gere, Christenbury, and Sassi (2005) point out, "Test preparation and good writing instruction are not incompatible" (p. 30). Students need to understand their audience (impersonal and formal) and purpose (to demonstrate an ability to respond to a specific task accurately in clear, conventional prose, in a limited period of time). They need to transfer what they have learned as writers to the testing context. Teach them the importance and value of planning time. If they are writing practice essays, forbid them from beginning for the first 10 minutes or so. During that time, allow them to annotate the prompt, sketch notes, chart their organizational structure, and perhaps craft a title. When finished, use the scored essays to point out how their planning time helped them focus. Teach them the importance of a strong opening. Teach them to double space and leave wide margins, so they can revise and edit if they have time. Provide practice analyzing prompts and using scoring rubrics on their own or a classmate's efforts. Use the student-scored papers for instructional conversations without grading them. Offer them sample strong responses to prompts they have written to, and ask them to discuss "what works" in the samples. Invite them to revise their responses with an eye to improvement. Again, use this work for instruction without grading it.

Overall, effective writing instruction is designed to help students become fluent, flexible writers, capable of producing writing in a broad range of genres for a wide variety of authentic purposes and audiences. A holistic approach that seeks to teach the many disparate aspects of writing in an integrated, connected fashion is most likely to give students the instruction they need to develop into skilled writers.

ELEVEN INSTRUCTIONAL RECOMMENDATIONS FROM GRAHAM AND PERIN'S (2007) *WRITING NEXT*

The following is a list of effective practices that help adolescents learn to write well. Each of these strategies is addressed in the list of recommended practices previously outlined in this chapter. Graham and Perin (2007) warn that the list does "not constitute a full writing curriculum" (p. 4). The practices presented earlier provide additional suggestions not covered by this research.

1. **Writing Strategies**, which involves teaching students strategies for planning, revising, and editing their compositions.

2. **Summarization**, which involves explicitly and systematically teaching students how to summarize texts.

3. **Collaborative Writing**, which uses instructional arrangements in which adolescents work together to plan, draft, revise, and edit their compositions.

4. **Specific Product Goals**, which assigns students specific, reachable goals for the writing they are to complete.

5. **Word Processing**, which uses computers and word processors as instructional supports for writing assignments.

6. **Sentence Combining**, which involves teaching students to construct more complex, sophisticated sentences.

7. **Prewriting**, which engages students in activities designed to help them generate or organize ideas for their composition.

8. **Inquiry Activities**, which engages students in analyzing immediate, concrete data to help them develop ideas and content for a particular writing task.

9. **Process Writing Approach**, which interweaves a number of writing instructional activities in a workshop environment that stresses extended writing opportunities, writing for authentic audiences, personalized instruction, and cycles of writing.

10. **Study of Models**, which provides students with opportunities to read, analyze, and emulate models of good writing.

11. **Writing for Content Learning**, which uses writing as a tool for learning content material.

CUBING TECHNIQUE FROM ELIZABETH AND GREGORY COWAN'S (1980) *WRITING*

Cubing is an invention technique for swiftly considering a subject from six points of view. Copy the form on the next page (students often like the cubes on colored paper). Have students cut out the form, fold and tape it to create the cube. They write their topics on clean sheets of paper, choose one side of the cube, and write down its title:

Describe it.

Compare it.

Associate it.

Analyze it.

Apply it.

Argue for or against it.

Set a timer for 3–5 minutes, and have students use focused freewriting or brainstorming to write everything they can about their topic as the chosen side of the cube instructs. When the timer sounds, they repeat the process with a different side of the cube. The process is repeated until all six sides of the cube have been addressed. When they have completed cubing, they read over what they have written and use that material to begin a draft. Of course, this process could be completed without a physical cube, but the cube adds a tactile element that students enjoy. The cubes can be stored in an accessible container in the classroom to be used whenever students wish.

Describe it.
What is it like?
What are its characteristics?

Compare it.
How is it similar to, or different from, other similar things?

Apply it.
What do people do with it? How is it used?

Associate it. What connections between this and other events, persons, concepts, times, places come to mind?

Analyze it.
What are its parts? How do they work?

Argue for or against it (seriously or humorously).

SELECTED MINI-LESSONS

Mini-lessons take between 10–15 minutes and should be targeted to specific students' needs. An Internet search for "mini-lessons" leads to many useful examples crafted for classroom use.

Choosing a topic

Invention heuristics

Four ways to revise (addition, substitution, subtraction, reordering)

Text structures

Effective leads

Effective closings (beyond summary)

Effective titles

Parallel structure and zeugma

Show, don't tell in narrative

Show, don't tell in nonfiction writing

Empty words (e.g., *very, really, nice, fun, good, I think*)

Effective diction

Verbal clutter: prepositional phrases

Effective verbs

Long and short sentences

Loose and periodic sentences

Transitions

Paragraphing

REFERENCES

Anderson, J. (2008). The express lane edit: Making editing useful for young adolescents. *Voices from the Middle, 15*(4), 40–44.

Andrasick, K. D. (1990). *Opening texts: Using writing to teach literature*. Portsmouth, NH: Heinemann.

Andrasick, K. D. (1993). Independent repatterning: Developing self-editing confidence. *English Journal, 82*(2), 28–31.

Applebee, A. N. (1981). *Writing in the secondary school: English and the content areas* (Research Monograph 21). Urbana, IL: National Council of Teachers of English.

Applebee, A. N. (1984). *Contexts for learning to write: Studies of secondary school instruction*. Norwood, NJ: Ablex.

Bardine, B. A., Bardine, M. S., & Deegan, E. F. (2000). Beyond the red pen: Clarifying our role in the response process. *English Journal, 90*(1), 94–101.

Berke, J. (1990). *Twenty questions for the writer* (5th ed.). San Diego, CA: Harcourt Brace Jovanovich.

Cowan, E., & Cowan G. (1980). *Writing*. New York, NY: Wiley.

Durst, R. K. (1984). The development of analytic writing. In A. N. Applebee (Ed.), *Contexts for learning to write* (pp. 79–102). Norwood, NJ: Ablex.

Elbow, P. (1973). *Writing without teachers*. New York, NY: Oxford University Press.

Emig, J. (1977). Writing as a mode of learning. *College Composition and Communication, 28*(2), 122–128.

Flower, L. (1979). Writer-based prose: A cognitive basis for problems in writing. *College English, 41*(1), 19–37.

Fulwiler, T. (1984). How well does writing across the curriculum work? *College English, 46*(2), 113–125.

Fulwiler, T. (Ed.). (1987). *The journal book*. Portsmouth, NH: Boynton/Cook & Heinemann.

Gallagher, K. (2006). *Teaching adolescent writers*. Portsmouth, ME: Stenhouse.

Gere, A. R., Christenbury, L., & Sassi, K. (2005). *Writing on demand: Best practices and strategies for success*. Portsmouth, NH: Heinemann.

Graham, S., Harris, K., & Hebert, M. A. (2011). *Informing writing: The benefits of formative assessment. A Carnegie Corporation Time to Act report*. Washington, DC: Alliance for Excellent Education.

Graham, S., & Hebert, M. A. (2010). *Writing to read: Evidence for how writing can improve reading. A Carnegie Corporation Time to Act report*. Washington, DC: Alliance for Excellent Education.

Graham, S., & Perin, D. (2007). *Writing next: Effective strategies to improve writing of adolescents in middle and high schools. A Carnegie Corporation Time to Act report*. Washington, DC: Alliance for Excellent Education.

Graves, D. H. (1984). *A researcher learns to write: Selected articles and monographs*. Exeter, NH: Heinemann.

Hillocks, G., Jr. (1995). *Teaching writing as reflective practice*. New York, NY: Teachers College Press.

Moffett, J. (1965). I, you, and it. *College Composition and Communication, 16*(5), 243–248.

Moffett, J. (1968). *A student-centered language arts curriculum K–13: A handbook for teachers*. Boston, MA: Houghton Mifflin.

Murray, D. M. (1981). Making meaning clear: The logic of revision. *Journal of Basic Writing, 3*(3), 33–40.

Murray, D. M. (1998). *The craft of revision* (3rd ed.). Fort Worth, TX: Harcourt Brace College.

Murray, D. M. (2003). Teach writing as a process, not product. In V. Villanueva (Ed.), *Cross-talk in comp theory: A reader* (2nd ed.) (pp. 3–6). Urbana, IL: National Council of Teachers of English.

Nodan, H. (1999). *Image grammar: Using grammatical structures to teach writing.* Portsmouth, NH: Heinemann.

ReadWriteThink. (n.d.). Get the GIST: A summarizing strategy for any content area. Retrieved from http://www.readwritethink.org/classroom-resources/lesson-plans/gist-summarizing-strategy-content-290.html

ReadWriteThink. (n.d.). Using the RAFT writing strategy. IRA and NCTE. Retrieved from http://www.readwritethink.org/professional-development/strategy-guides/using-raft-writing-strategy-30625.html

Short, K. G., Harste, J. C., & Burke, C. (1996). *Creating classrooms for authors and inquirers* (2nd ed.). Portsmouth, NH: Heinemann.

Weaver, C. (1996). *Teaching grammar in context.* Portsmouth, NH: Boynton/Cook.

Williams, W. C. (1986). The crab and the box. In X. J. Kennedy (Ed.), *An introduction to poetry* (6th ed.) (p. 365). Boston, MA: Little, Brown.

RECOMMENDED READINGS

* Fletcher, R. (2011). *Mentor author, mentor text: Short texts, craft notes, and practical classroom uses.* Portsmouth, NH: Heinemann.
* Gallagher, K. (2011). *Write like this: Teaching real-world writing through modeling and mentor texts.* Portsmouth, ME: Stenhouse.
* Kittle, P. (2008). *Write beside them: Risk, voice, and clarity in high school writing.* Portsmouth, NH: Heinemann.
* Newkirk, T. (2007). *Teaching the neglected "r": Rethinking writing instruction in secondary classrooms.* Portsmouth, NH: Heinemann.
* Rief, L. (2014). *Read write teach: Choice and challenge in the reading-writing workshop.* Portsmouth, NH: Heinemann.

GO EVEN FURTHER WITH THIS TOPIC ON THE WORLD WIDE WEB

* www.nwp.org
* wac.colostate.edu/intro/
* www.ncte.org
* www.ttms.org
* writingfix.com/index.htm

THE Apps WE LOVE

- Apps Gone Free
- Inspiration Maps
- TopNotes
- Werdsmith
- Write 2 Lite

4

Successful Social Studies

Greg Knotts and Joyce H. Burstein
California State University, Northridge

WHAT REALLY WORKS IN SOCIAL STUDIES IN THE SECONDARY CLASSROOM

Do Secondary Schools Even Do Social Studies?

Yes. And no. Both middle and high school students do learn social studies but almost always as individual social sciences in individual silos: history, geography, economics, political science. Whereas elementary students learn these disciplines in an integrated way as the social *studies*, the system of Western (liberal arts) education has separated these disciplines out into their unique subjects, providing a more concentrated and dedicated focus on a topic, but often shortchanging the notion of integration and looking at any topic in a more holistic way. However, these social sciences are the building blocks of social studies, the study of human beings. Secondary social studies is often focused on themes or periods, like ancient, world, or U.S. history, or political systems like communism, democracy, or totalitarian governments. No matter how we study human beings, three principles drive our engagement. One is the widening horizons concept that presents content and curriculum to students in progressively larger (wider) environments and requires secondary students to connect content in various contexts: first, concentric to self, then family and community, progressing to the larger environment of the nation-state and then the world. This helps answer the proverbial "What does this have to do with me?" question by helping students connect content to themselves and their own worlds, as well as the "world" in which the event/topic actually happened.

A second organizing principle is the spiral curriculum, through which content and curriculum are presented in age-appropriate and developmentally appropriate ways, but themes, concepts, and ideas repeat throughout the progression of the curriculum. While the widening or expanding horizons concept drives the content (smaller to wider environments), the spiral curriculum visits themes and ideas that repeat in that content and those varied contexts. For instance, a kindergarten student who takes a colored pencil or crayon from another student because she "wants it" or "likes green" is just demonstrating the concept of supply and demand in the middle grades, which evolves to more sophisticated issues in the Industrial Revolution, global trading, and finance in high school. The spiral curriculum suggests that all concepts get taught over and over again through different content, with differing and varied levels of complexity, but that major concepts are introduced as early as kindergarten and just reappear in various guises throughout the curriculum. This emphasis on conceptual thinking should drive both your and your students' understanding of the discipline and its content.

The third component of the content is the content itself: What is actually being taught to students? The very nature of the discipline's name, social studies, suggests the plurality of this content area. There are many ways to socially study human beings: historically, culturally, geographically, economically, and politically, for instance. The point of this study is to better understand yourself and others in context. The point of all study of the social sciences in secondary school is to ensure students have been introduced to the complex world around them, to help them make sense of that world, and to aid them in discovering ways of making the world a better place in which to live. High school is set up so that all the social studies are covered—but typically in silos of economics, history, or geography. This does not prevent integration, but it does not encourage it either. The secondary student must see "the world" from a variety of perspectives, and here the silos can be helpful in isolating a particular lens or focus. Ultimately, though, our job is to bring "the world" to students and help them make sense of it, a little bit at a time.

HOW SHOULD I TEACH SOCIAL STUDIES?

The National Council for the Social Studies (2010) states that the primary goal of social studies education is "to help young people develop the ability to make informed and reasoned decisions for the public good as citizens of a culturally diverse, democratic society in an interdependent world" (p. 9). The goal is an informed citizenry; to reach the goal, we study human beings. Beyond knowing the dates of events and the names of important historical figures, secondary students and teachers need to consider if those events and those persons are even the ones that merit study in the first place. If social studies is the study of human beings, the question of how society should study those human beings is fraught with political, ideological, and conceptual debate. A leading voice in this debate is Ronald Evans (2004, 2006), who offers a widely accepted lens of the various "camps" or schools of thought on the teaching of social studies. As teachers, we typically fall into one of these camps (perhaps without knowing it!) and then teach from that perspective, which influences how we communicate content to students. As you read about the different camps, reflect on which camp sounds most like you.

The first camp is one of the traditional historians. This ideology emphasizes basic content acquisition, the idea of chronology, and textbooks as the major source of information. The second camp is the social sciences approach. Supporters believe in a "structure-of-the-disciplines" approach as advocated by Jerome Bruner. This approach is based in the different social sciences—a more integrated approach. The third camp is one of social efficiency educators. Supporters believe in borrowing from business, and instruction is designed to prepare students for specific roles and to become efficient contributors to the larger society. The fourth camp is one of the social meliorists. Supporters believe in the development of students' reflective thinking and the development of higher order critical thought and awareness, believing that reflection will lead to social improvement. Advocates like John Dewey and John Goodlad call for schools to be places of social action and change. The fifth camp is the social reconstructionists. Supporters agree that education is about transforming society but emphasize critical pedagogy, questioning social structures and power relationships, and equality of opportunity and parity within the larger societal whole. Critical thought is a hallmark of this camp and draws from theorists like Paolo Freire and Antonio Gramsci who call for social movements, political and social consciousness, and a restructuring of norms and power relationships. So you have five choices. Which are you? Have you ever thought about it? It is very likely that one of these "camps" makes better sense to you!

We agree with Evans (2004, 2006) that teachers should make choices about how they believe social studies might or should be structured in their classrooms. You cannot simply pick up a teacher's manual and begin teaching without first considering what you want as an end goal; after 180 days of instruction, do you want a traditional historian or someone who questions social norms and advocates for social change? Both are valid, of course; but your teaching should be driven by focus and intention. In addition, we advocate that you be aware of how curriculum guides and textbooks are written and adopted and to make conscious decisions about how you want to deliver instruction balanced with the practical realities that your job dictates. You should also consider four even larger options for framing social studies:

Multicultural Education. Nieto (2004) provides a widely accepted definition of a multicultural education that accepts and affirms the notions of cultural pluralism, knowledge, reflection, and action, implemented as comprehensive school reform. Nieto demands that teachers ask critical questions leading to raised consciousness of students regarding social justice issues. While there are many competing definitions of a multicultural education, they typically involve examining the plurality of issues "within the context of the nation in which students live" (Lucas, 2010, p. 212).

Global Education. The second framing option steps outside the nation-state and into a global world. Global education advocates (DiPardo & Fehn, 2000; Ukpokodu, 1999) suggest looking outside the nation of residence and focusing on people across political and politicized boundaries. A gendered norm in Kansas, for instance, may not be a gendered norm in Estonia, Cambodia, or Sierra Leone (and is comparing a state to a country even appropriate?). Ultimately, a global educator supports the examination of global issues across contexts, making the human experience more important than the political boundaries of a particular nation's experience.

Transnational Education. The third option is the recent trend of transnational education (Camicia & Saavedra, 2009), which asks educators and students to both embrace and step beyond political borders, nation-states, and affiliations to acknowledge the multiplicity of affiliations that many people feel in this multinational, transnational world. One's place of birth, affiliation with a geographic or politically bounded national culture, and simply how one looks often begs the question of (dual) citizenship, affiliation, and identity. Just think of President Barack Obama! Ultimately, a transnational educator supports expanding the notion of identity to embrace the duality and "otherness" that historically marginalized communities have felt by centering a discussion on the changing communities that make up a national landscape. Transnational educators help students grapple with questions like, "Can I be proud of my Slovakian culture and still consider myself a proud American as well?" or "If my father is Asian American and my mother is African American, what am I?" Dual and multihyphenate identities are becoming normalized, but does everyone know how to navigate complex identities?

Democratic Education. Perhaps the oldest trend in social studies education is citizenship or democratic education (Dewey, 1916, 1933; Martorella,

1998), which can be traced to Thomas Jefferson, the European Enlightenment, and even the ancient Greeks. Advocates of a democratic education argue for school as a place to produce effective and productive citizens. Voting, active participation, and civic duty are all hallmarks of a democratic or citizenship education. Ultimately, a democratic educator supports advocating for students to find their individual "voice" in the larger social/ cultural whole.

All of these trends in social studies education beg the question, "Which is the best or right way to teach social studies to secondary students as they prepare to enter the world of adults?" And the answer is, "Yes." We advocate for components of all these trends. More importantly, we advocate that teachers be aware of all these trends so that as they gain experience, practice, and knowledge from the field, they can be better informed to have a foundational framework from which to operate inside the classroom. "Good teaching" is not enough, neither is a love of social studies. Good practice must be informed by a solid theoretical understanding of how the trends of the discipline have operated, how the discipline is presently working, and how it might function in the future so that students can be intentionally taught. If high school is preparing secondary students to live "in the world," then what "kind" of student is being prepared? A student who has a vast knowledge and fact-based account of history or one who wants to advocate for social change? Or both? What kind of world are teachers preparing them to live within? A world focused on issues close to home (or abroad) or a world focused on individual responsibility as a democratic citizen? Or both? How does one do that exactly, you might ask yourself! You stop doing some traditional actions, and you embrace some new ones—or just get a bit braver in trying the strategies you KNOW to be best.

STOP TEACHING HOW YOU WERE TAUGHT!

Teachers

- ✖ **STOP teaching in a silo.** Even if you are a single-subject disciplinary teacher, you must teach your discipline in an integrated way. Link to the other social sciences, and keep the social *studies* in mind, rather than only the social science you are tasked with teaching. You can be a history teacher studying the Han Dynasty of Ancient China with a focus on dynastic rulers, impacts, and events but still explore economic concepts created by the Silk Road.
- ✖ **STOP teaching chronologically.** Look again at all the principles, trends, and arguments in social studies discussed above. If you stop your curriculum and instruction at chronological thinking,

your teaching will be mired in fill-in-the-blank dates and names rather than conceptual thinking, framing, and helping students form relevant connections to themselves and their own adult lives. Afraid kids will forget the dates? Not to worry—those dates are only a thumb-click away!

✘ **STOP teaching from textbooks (only).** A state-adopted textbook is typically aligned with content standards, and presumably with the Common Core in the near future, and is a good place to *start*; but teaching any of the social science disciplines to secondary students has to be about relevance, personal meaning and utility, and contextualization in the world in which those students live—you cannot stop at the textbook.

✘ **STOP teaching through lecture (only).** Social science education is meant to be *social*. If content is being presented as direct instruction from teachers only, and never being constructed collaboratively through inquiry-based, student-directed activities, you will quickly become the disembodied voice from Charlie Brown cartoons, "mwah, mwah ma mwah ma ma mwah."

✘ **STOP teaching with worksheets.** Fill-in-the-blank, multiple choice, matching, and true/false responses all have their place in terms of front-loading content, perhaps, but an overreliance on worksheets steeped in the most base level of Bloom's Taxonomy keeps social studies boring, limited to fact regurgitation, and inspires disengagement. In many cases, worksheets also limit students with disabilities by playing to their disability instead of their strengths.

✘ **STOP relying on text(book)s.** The social sciences are perceived to be fact and content driven, and many teachers use text-based and heavily loaded reading(s) to deliver content. There are many other resources, beyond literal text, that could bring content to students—all students—since the use of realia is a major tool in addressing differentiation needs.

Administrators

✘ **STOP deemphasizing the discipline.** Although the recent accountability-driven assessments have prioritized language arts and mathematics, social studies (all the social sciences) must not be seen as a secondary citizen—by teachers or students.

✘ **STOP being driven by the system.** If the goal of all schooling is an informed citizenry, then secondary schools must be holistic places that encourage the development of the whole person, and the social sciences must be developed to allow students to find personal meaning and relevance as they are about to embark into the adult world.

START TEACHING THE WAY YOU KNOW TO BE RIGHT

Teachers, DO This

✓ **START teaching concepts over content.** When you privilege concepts (i.e., freedom, movement, discovery), secondary students can move beyond the content of a particular year's curriculum (i.e., European history, Ancient China) and begin making connections that will help them in the larger world (Bruner, 1977; Burstein & Knotts, 2011). This does not diminish the need for solid instruction regarding content; but once one knows the location and dates of a particular battle, it is more important to know *why* the battle was fought and the *results* of the outcome than it is to simply stop the discussion at the general's name who was in charge of the winning or losing side. This move toward conceptual thinking is the focus of the Common Core Standards and should be the focus of instruction.

✓ **START making the social sciences relevant.** Too many students find little or no use for social studies (Hutton & Burstein, 2008; Zhao & Hoge, 2005) because teachers have them read Chapter Blah Blah and answer questions on Page Blah Blah and call it a day. Students must find personal meaning and relevance, so teachers must reposition themselves; your focus must shift away from the content for content's sake and move toward finding ways to get kids to *connect* to the content. Assessment must move from answering fact-based questions toward answering questions about what they *think* about the facts. Do not have students answer the dates and locations of the Trail of Tears—have them defend the policy from the position of the U.S. government, or create an alternate policy that would have made sense at the time but better honored the traditions and lives of the first peoples.

✓ **START integrating.** It is important to integrate content so that facts/topics/periods are not disconnected and seen in isolation. Build on the elementary world of social *studies* and ensure you are always looking at content from multiple angles and perspectives. It is particularly important to integrate the arts (Burstein & Knotts, 2010, 2011; Eisner, 2000) so that students see human beings in their cultural contexts and make connections across place and time. Although a separate "arts program" is often not available at the secondary level, and many secondary teachers find the arts to be "fluff," use of music, dance, visual arts, and drama is extremely engaging for students. Have

> **Making Connections**
>
> Check out Chapters 6 and 11 on Arts Instruction and Universal Design for Learning

students make a music video about the effects of World War I on urban communities instead of a five-page written report. Learn more about Universal Design for Learning so this isn't overwhelming to you.

✓ **START using primary sources and start moving beyond text (book)s.** While texts and textbooks are important, it is imperative that secondary students use primary sources (as other kinds of text!) so they are exposed to a variety of ways and places to get information. Photographs; documents like journals, letters, and bills of sale; or newspapers, advertisements, recordings, and physical realia (farm implements, flags, tools) help students engage, inquire, and discover content in visceral and memorable ways. A weekend trip to a garage sale or thrift store could potentially gain you a myriad of (affordable!) resources that students have never encountered.

✓ **START teaching through inquiry by starting with the students as opposed to the content.** If I am a 16-year-old sophomore from a rural environment in the Midwest, why would I care about the Industrial Revolution in 19th century New England? Begin with connection, concept, and relevance, as opposed to beginning with the curriculum and content. Let students ask questions (begin with a Carousel Walk, for instance, of various photographs of kids working on factory assembly lines, as coal miners, or steel workers; students are more likely to see versions of themselves in history and find relevance to their own lives today).

✓ **START teaching social sciences SOCIALLY.** Secondary students must be given the opportunity to collaborate on performance-based projects and authentic assessments (Belgrad, Burke, & Fogarty, 2008; Popham, 2008). Students must be given real-world problems to solve (do not ask what the tenets of Jacksonian Democracy are on a worksheet; have students describe/design how they would like to make their classroom an *example* of Jacksonian Democracy). Students must be given opportunities to work in small groups, creating outcomes with positive interdependence, in order to gain insight and perspective from others, as well as develop and share their own voice (Gallavan & Kottler, 2009; Meyer, 2010; Slavin, 1995).

Making Connections

Check out Chapters 10, 14, and 19 on Cooperative Learning, Assessment, and Social Skills

✓ **START teaching multiple perspectives.** It is important for students to be prepared to live "in the world" on their own. So it is important to move students beyond their possibly ethnocentric, geographic, parametized realities. Introduce them to many realities—the voices of the victor *and* the voices of the marginalized and conquered must be presented.

✓ **START teaching discernment.** This will be a natural progression if you are teaching multiple perspectives. Students have to be taught how to compare and analyze resources, their validity and value, and their appropriateness. Students must learn how to question a source's context, its creation, and the actual content being communicated. In a world of ever-increasing sound bites and if-it's-on-the-Internet-it-must-be-real mentality, students must be walked through processes of discerning how to utilize resources and which ones to utilize in the first place.

✓ **START doing your homework.** Search websites for teachers so you are not doing all the work on your own. Find lesson plans that have worked for others. Search Google Images. Go to a garage sale, antique, or thrift shop. Bring in resources. Collaborate and co-teach across disciplines. Never walk out of your classroom unless you have tomorrow's resources ready.

Administrators, DO This

✓ **START scheduling Professional Development sessions for social science instruction.** If language arts and mathematics, assessment, and compliance processes are the only areas of focus of professional development, teachers in the social sciences (and other disciplines!) simply feel diminished. The Common Core State Standards (CCSS), project-based assessment, Universal Design for Learning, differentiation, and the use of technology in instruction might be easy places to begin this process.

✓ **START being an instructional leader at your site.** It is important to meet your accountability, assessment, and performance goals, but it is also important to create a school culture that privileges a clear and shared ideology and teacher voice and has a focus on quality instruction. Discussing what kinds of citizens you want at your site (and living next door to you when they graduate!) is a great way to privilege how social science could shape a conversation around developing professionally and shaping/creating a school culture. Many secondary sites are adopting Professional Learning Communities (PLCs) or Small Learning Communities (SLCs). With an SLC or PLC, it might be possible to create clusters of teachers instead of just content-based departments. Could department chairs ask social studies teachers to come up with common themes or have these themes be a part of the PLC?

LESSON PLAN IDEAS

- Have students view videos on YouTube from SoomoPublishing or Historyteachers (American Revolution, Suffrage, French Revolution, Catherine the Great, and more). They could deconstruct and analyze for content, as well as create new music videos of their own following a template.
- Have students use Google Earth to investigate a historical site of some significance. Design a pamphlet advertising it in its historical context (two panels), present context (two panels), and predicted future context (two panels).
- Have students create rap songs describing various art forms (literature, music, poetry) of artists in the Harlem Renaissance.
- Have students create a modern-day American classroom and history curriculum based on the idea that the Axis powers had won World War II.
- Have students create a U.S. Foreign Policy for 2050, based on 2000 and 1950.
- Have students create a mock Supreme Court based on their predictions of appointments in the next 14 years. Have students write case briefs and summary outcomes for the landmark cases during that time.
- Have students create a company for a product or service that does not yet exist and describe the company's effect on the U.S. and global economies.

INQUIRY-BASED
SOCIAL STUDIES ACTIVITIES

Some prompting questions that consider a variety of access strategies to help with inquiry are listed below. Consider this list of questions as a starting point for planning your instruction. The list of questions is not exhaustive or finite but provides a variety of techniques for you to consider as you begin the instructional planning process in inquiry.

A) What can students VIEW to gain access?

1) _____

2) _____

*Consider: primary sources, artifacts, DVDs

B) What can students LISTEN TO in order to gain access?

1) _____

2) _____

*Consider: primary sources, CDs, read-alouds

C) What can students WRITE to gain access?

1) _____

2) _____

*Consider: creative responses, reflective or predictive writing

D) What can students READ to gain access?

1) _____

2) _____

* Consider: primary source materials, texts, Internet sites, children's literature

E) What can students DISCUSS to gain access?

1) _____

2) _____

* Consider: Think-Pair-Share topics, debate

F) What can students CONSTRUCT/INVESTIGATE to gain access?

1) _____

2) _____

*Consider: primary sources, engagement with art

G) What can students RESEARCH to gain access?

1) _____

2) _____

*Consider: primary sources, teacher-chosen Internet sites

H) What can students COMPLETE to gain access?

1) _____

2) _____

*Consider: teacher- or text-made worksheets, brainstorms

INTEGRATED SOCIAL STUDIES UNIT: INSTRUCTION PLANNING GUIDE

Use this planning guide to integrate concepts across a common theme.

I.   ORGANIZING PRINCIPLES

Title/Topic/Central Theme: _____

Social Studies Standards: _____

Arts Standard(s): _____

Rationale: What is the value or significance of selecting this unit? Why do students need to learn about this unit? How does this unit relate to real life experiences? Explain how social studies and arts are integrated. What is the importance in combining this subject matter and concepts? Are there critical issues that arise from the content in this unit?

- •   _____
- •   _____
- •   _____
- •   _____
- •   _____

Essential Questions/Big Ideas: What are the three to five enduring questions you want students to understand as a result of this unit? (These are usually broad and conceptual.)

- •   _____
- •   _____
- •   _____
- •   _____

Unit Goals: What do you want students to learn as a result of this unit of study? What are the concepts that students will have that help concretize the big ideas and essential questions?

- •   _____
- •   _____
- •   _____

II.   LESSON PLANS

Initiation: How will students be introduced to and interested in the unit? Create a concrete introduction to your unit that previews concepts or skills that will be taught in the unit.

_____

_____

Lesson Content Outline:

Did I include: ___ Technology ___ Literature ___ Primary Sources ___ Arts

CONCEPT 1: _(_____)_____

CONCEPT 2: _(_____)_____

CONCEPT 3: _(_____)_____

CONCEPT 4: _(_____)_____

CONCEPT 5: _(_____)_____

CONCEPT 6: _(_____)_____

CONCEPT 7: _(_____)_____

Culminating Activities: How will students synthesize and put together the various learning they encountered during this unit of study?

- _____
- _____
- _____

III.   LEARNING CENTER(S): to be used autonomously by students to supplement their learning of the objectives and content of the unit; what are the main concepts being delivered in the Learning Centers?

- _____
- _____
- _____

IV.   INSTRUCTIONAL MATERIALS: a bibliography of children and teacher books and resources for this unit with other visual and hands-on resources you will use.

**This might include charts, maps, art prints, interdisciplinary materials, artifacts, posters, photographs, government documents, music CDs, films, etc.

- _____
- _____
- _____
- _____

REFERENCES

Belgrad, S., Burke, K., & Fogarty, R. (2008). *The portfolio connection*. Thousand Oaks, CA: Corwin.

Bruner, J. S. (1977). *The process of education*. Cambridge, MA: Harvard University Press.

Burstein, J. H., & Knotts, G. (2010). Creating connections: Integrating the visual arts with social studies. *Social Studies and the Young Learner, 23*(1), 20–23.

Burstein, J. H., & Knotts, G. (2011). *Reclaiming social studies for the elementary classroom: Integrating the arts through culture*. Dubuque, IA: Kendall/Hunt.

Camicia, S. P., & Saavedra, C. M. (2009). A new childhood social studies curriculum for a new generation of citizenship. *International Journal of Children's Rights, 17*, 501–517.

Dewey, J. (1916). *Democracy and education*. New York, NY: Free Press.

Dewey, J. (1933). *How we think*. Boston, MA: D.C. Health.

DiPardo, A., & Fehn, B. (2000). Depoliticizing multicultural education: The return to normalcy in a predominantly white high school. *Theory and Research in Social Education, 2*(28), 170–192.

Eisner, E. (2000). Arts education policy? *Arts Education Policy Review, 101*(3), 4–6.

Evans, R. (2004). *The social studies wars: What should we teach the children?* New York, NY: Teachers College.

Evans, R. (2006). The social studies wars, now and then. *Social Education, 70*(5), 317–321.

Gallavan, N. P., & Kottler, E. (2009). Constructing rubrics and assessing progress collaboratively with social studies students. *Social Studies, 100*(4), 154–159.

Hutton, L., & Burstein, J. H. (2008). The teaching of history-social science: Left behind or behind closed doors? *Social Studies Research and Practice, 3*(1), 96–108.

Lucas, A. (2010). Distinguishing between multicultural and global education: The challenge of conceptualizing and addressing the two fields. *The Clearing House, 83*, 211–216.

Martorella, P. H. (1998). *Social studies for elementary school children: Developing young citizens*. Upper Saddle River, NJ: Prentice Hall.

Meyer, N. (2010). Collaboration success for student achievement in social studies: The Washington state story. *Teacher Librarian, 37*(4), 40–43.

National Council for the Social Studies. (2010). *National curriculum standards for social studies: A framework for teaching, learning, and assessment*. Washington, DC: Author.

Nieto, S. (2004). *Affirming diversity: The sociopolitical context of multicultural education* (3rd ed.). New York, NY: Longman Press.

Popham, J. (2008). *Transformative assessment*. Alexandria, VA: Association of Supervision and Curriculum Development.

Slavin, R. E. (1995). *Cooperative learning* (2nd ed.). Needham Heights, MA: Allyn & Bacon.

Ukpokodu, N. (1999). Multiculturalism vs globalism. *Social Education, 63*(5), 298–300.

Zhao, Y., & Hoge, J. (2005). What elementary students and teachers say about social studies. *Social Studies, 96*(5), 216–221.

RECOMMENDED READINGS

* Dewey, J. (1966). *Democracy and education: An introduction to the philosophy of education*. New York, NY: Free Press.

* Endacott, J. L., & Sturtz, J. (2014). Historical empathy and pedagogical reasoning. *Journal of Social Science Research, 39*(1), 1–16.

* Freire, P. (1990). *Pedagogy of the oppressed*. New York, NY: Continuum.

* Goodlad, J. (1992). The moral dimensions of schooling and teacher education. *Journal of Moral Education*, 21(2), 87–97.

* Goodman, J. F., & Lesnick, H. (2004). *Moral education: A teacher-centered approach*. Boston, MA: Pearson.

* Jacobs, B. M. (2013). Social studies teacher education in the early twentieth century: A historical inquiry into the relationship between teacher preparation and curriculum reform. *Teachers College Record, 115*(12), 1–33.

* Library of Congress. (2010). The learning page: Using primary sources in the Classroom. Retrieved from http://memory.loc.gov/learn/lessons/primary.html

GO EVEN FURTHER WITH
THIS TOPIC ON THE WORLD WIDE WEB

- www.teacherspayteachers.com/Browse/Grade-Level/9-12
- www.archives.gov/education/
- www.loc.gov/teachers/classroommaterials/lessons/
- www.educationworld.com/a_tech/tech/tech071.shtml
- www.lessonplanspage.com/history-social-studies/high-school/

THE Apps WE LOVE

- MyCongress
- HistoryTools
- Constitution and Federalist Papers
- Worldbook: This day in history (for iPad)
- History Maps

5

Sensible Science Strategies

Stacey E. Hardin

Illinois State University

Nanci Hanover

Los Angeles Unified School District

WHAT REALLY WORKS IN SCIENCE IN THE SECONDARY CLASSROOM

Full STEM Ahead With the New Science Standards

> *One of the things that I've been focused on as President is how we create an all-hands-on-deck approach to science, technology, engineering, and math.... We need to make this is a priority to train an army of new teachers in these subject areas and to make sure that all of us as a country are lifting up these subjects for the respect that they deserve.* (President Barack Obama, 2013)

That's right. The President of the United States himself has identified science, technology, engineering, and math (aka STEM) as major topics that deserve his focus. He wants an "army of new teachers in these subject areas." Why? What's the big deal? We've had teachers in these areas for years, so why the call for action now? Unfortunately, the United States has fallen behind other countries in the STEM areas (Machi, 2008). As we seek to regain a higher status in STEM areas and careers, the push to educate our students in STEM, especially science, has become a primary and hot topic around the country. The STEM fields are growing and becoming even more critical to our progress as a nation. So much so that even the U.S. president chose to focus on and push forward a STEM agenda to ensure that students become more marketable and are capable to address the STEM demands we as a country face nationally and internationally. The field of science education has undergone major changes to address the challenges students face when learning science concepts. In this chapter, we will let you know what has happened in the STEM areas in the past but, more importantly, how we are using that knowledge to create the path we are taking as a country through the Next Generation Science Standards (NGSS).

KEY RESEARCH YOU NEED TO KNOW ABOUT TEACHING SCIENCE

Science concepts can be quite complex for students to grasp if the concepts are not taught clearly and in a creative way. The strategies discussed within this chapter will make it easier for you to teach difficult concepts and align your instruction with the fast paced field of science education. Three areas that really work in secondary science classrooms are (a) explicitly teaching the Nature of Science (NoS), (b) Scientific Inquiry, and (c) Project-Based Learning (PBL).

Explicitly teach Nature of Science. Nature of Science (NoS) refers to the understanding of science and how it works, as well as the origins of science concepts (Lederman, 1992). The strategy that really works here is explicitly teaching NoS to your students. Not quite sure what this means or how you'll actually go about doing this with kids? No worries. We're going to help you out with that.

Let's say you were going to teach about the states of matter. For years, students have studied them, memorized them, and maybe even have done a lab on them. Certainly, knowing that there are different states of matter, and what they are, is important. However, even more important is truly understanding the NoS (remember, that's Nature of Science). Stick with us here. A few of the main ideas, concepts, or categories for NoS as acknowledged by the NGSS are (a) scientific investigations use a variety of methods, (b) scientific knowledge is based on empirical evidence, and (c) science is a human endeavor. So you are ready to teach your lesson about the states of matter, and you bring in real life activities and ideas in to the classroom—such as an ice cube to represent a solid. Using a hair dryer, you explain solids versus liquids to help your students gain a better understanding of this concept. You have your students conduct the science project to see what happens, allowing them a chance to be involved in their own learning. You then engage your students in a class discussion about other ways you could have explained the states of matter, as well as what happened during the process of their personal science experiments. This is where explicitly teaching the NoS concepts come in. You let the kids know explicitly that the NoS concept that you are achieving by completing this activity is "scientific investigations use a variety of methods." What do we mean by explicit? We mean you flat out tell them "I could have taught this concept in all the many ways you just came up with. The reason we are talking about this is that it is important that you know that scientific investigations use a variety of methods. If you investigate an idea one way, but your friend does it another way, that's okay. We are all still investigating, and that's what makes science so amazing!" Note that in the past, students have been programmed to use the "scientific method"; however, just like there is more than one way to skin a cat, there are definitely multiple ways to arrive at a scientific solution! You have just taught them that. And hey! They learned the states of matter while you were at it.

Are you surprised we are taking the time to mention this? Are you thinking to yourself that, of course you would explicitly teach the NoS? Well, actually, a study conducted by Capps and Crawford (2013) found that teachers do not explicitly teach aspects of NoS. They teach content over concepts, and though they may even include a few instances of implicit instruction in their lessons, the absence of explicit instruction of NoS aspects leaves a void in students' science education. Students know basic science facts for the tests but not the overarching concepts that hold them all together. Implicit instruction is mostly used in classrooms around the country. However, during implicit instruction, the teacher does not confirm or ensure students' understanding of the process of science and the NoS concepts. On the other hand, explicit instruction allows for the check and balance that students need by explicitly teaching concepts while involving students in hands-on and interactive activities. Explicit instruction also offers a reflective component to help students delve deeper into science concepts. When a science teacher explicitly teaches NoS aspects, students gain a richer understanding of the ideas of science and their relevance to everyday life. This is what we know really works for improving science education!

NoS should be explicitly taught throughout the school year and intertwined within your lesson plans. Sure, many of the categories of NoS can be quite difficult to teach to students as straight up information. Lucky for us, researchers suggest taking an explicit approach to teaching NoS as they are uncovered during classroom instruction (Lederman, 2007; Schwartz, Lederman, & Crawford, 2004). This means that as teaching moments arise in the science classroom, teachers should explicitly discuss the aspects of NoS. Link them to what you are doing in the class. Make them real. Bring them to life. The concepts of the NoS have been around for years; however, they have not been explicitly infused and taught in science classrooms around our country, leaving our students ill-prepared to compete in such a scientifically competitive society (Capps & Crawford, 2013). You're ready to fix that now though, aren't you? Bring on the teaching moment!

Scientific Inquiry. Another area that is closely aligned to NoS is Scientific Inquiry. Scientific Inquiry and NoS are two distinct teaching strategies in science education; however, they align nicely together. We've established that NoS involves making explicit to students what the concepts are behind certain actions, reactions, and outcomes. Let's focus on Scientific Inquiry now. Scientific Inquiry is more than asking questions, and it isn't just about the processes of science. It is taking those processes and then encouraging students to inquire and critically think about them. As students analyze and question and reflect, they can use their newfound science knowledge (NoS, anyone?) to arrive at creative solutions and answers (Lederman, Lederman, & Antink, 2013). For example, if you wanted your students to learn more about beach erosion, you would act as the facilitator to help them come to their own conclusions about beach erosion. You don't just give them the facts and have them regurgitate them. If teachers are intertwining explicit instruction of NoS concepts and science inquiry, an interactive activity would take place; however, instead of teachers leading the activity, teachers would act as the facilitators, and students would collaborate and ask questions of each other until a solution was found. The teacher would then explicitly discuss NoS concepts and how the concepts align with the activity conducted, as well as other real life experiences. Thus, the Scientific Inquiry by the students actually helps them understand and really "get" the NoS concepts. Cool, huh?

By the way, Scientific Inquiry can be teacher initiated or student initiated. Yep, student initiated! In fact, when lessons are student initiated, students have more ownership of their own instruction and take more responsibility for their own learning (Capps & Crawford, 2013). Don't be afraid to let your students start the questioning. As long as you are a strong facilitator, you'll guide them in the right direction and then be able to ensure that they learned the critical content and concepts.

Making Connections

Check out Chapter 10 on Cooperative Learning

Project-Based Learning. One of the best ways to incorporate student-initiated Scientific Inquiry is to incorporate Project-Based Learning. Project-Based Learning involves students collaborating with their peers to examine and explore scientific questions through activities and other works

(Filippatou & Kaldi, 2010). Project-Based Learning gets students up and talking about science concepts. During this time, teachers are really able to see and hear the rich conversation and learning that can take place in the science classroom.

Now, stop! Imagine a classroom run by students, facilitated by the teacher. How do you think that would look? Do you imagine a room of chaos? One in which students are texting, doodling, and chatting, rather than working on their STEM-related work? Interestingly enough, when students take responsibility of their own education and instruction, they often take ownership of their learning and begin to use higher level critical thinking skills (Capps & Crawford, 2013). How is this different from the labs we've done for years, you ask? Good question.

Typical secondary science instruction has involved a teacher lecturing on content while expecting students to take copious notes. After three or four days of note taking, students are expected to spend one or two days completing a lab. The lab often involves following concrete steps laid out by the teacher. Students are expected to answer specific questions, given by the teacher, into their lab notebook. Though some labs are "fun" (especially those that explode), many students get more out of the social aspect of the lab than any true academic learning. On the other hand, with PBL, students are exploring from the beginning. Teachers can give a question and have students attack it from various angles, or the students can even generate the questions themselves. Thus, PBL is a strategy for enabling students to really engage in that Scientific Inquiry we just emphasized. Pulling it all together then, (a) you use PBL strategies to get students to (b) use methods of Scientific Inquiry, which (c) lead to a discovery of NoS, which you explicitly identify for them before they move on to the next lesson. Basic lecture and regurgitation of facts is "out," and real critical thinking and application is "in." Yay for us!

By the way, we are not the only ones who are encouraging this type of instruction as "what really works" in science education. Turns out there are experts all over the country who have come together to create what they call the Next Generation Science Standards (NGSS) in order to create an environment for just that type of critical thinking. This next section tells you a bit more about the standards and how they can also help with ensuring you are doing what really works in your classroom.

THE NEXT GENERATION SCIENCE STANDARDS

For the past umpteen years, science classes have had students pushing pencils along a page, with an occasional laboratory experiment thrown in for good measure. If the students were paying attention, they might understand the connection between the notes and the lab. For the most part, students were just happy to be out of their seats and doing something that was interactive. For many, science class was just plain boring, unless you had a mind for science. That said, according to the 2012 ACT College Readiness Benchmark Report, 54% of American high school graduates did not meet college readiness benchmark levels in math, but even more staggeringly, 69% failed to meet the college readiness benchmark levels in science (ACT, 2012). So what does that tell us? Students just weren't getting it, nor did they care to. Simply put, those methods were not working. We had to find ways to engage them. A recent Stanford study shows that students learn better when first exploring an unfamiliar idea or concept on their own, rather than reading a text or watching a video first (Schneider, Wallace, Blikstein, & Pea, 2013). Researchers showed that when the order was reversed, the students' performance improved substantially (Schneider et al., 2013). Students became more interested, and that is exactly the intent of the new Next Generation Science Standards (NGSS; Achieve, 2013). Oh, hey. Notice how that also connects to what we just discussed related to Project-Based Learning and Scientific Inquiry? We're just that good.

Back to NGSS. In July of 2011, The National Research Council (2012) produced *A Framework for K–12 Science Education: Practices, Crosscutting Concepts, and Core Ideas*. At that time, science standards had not been reviewed for over 10 years, and it was time to revisit them, especially since major advances in scientific fields and changing industries now increasingly require a scientifically minded workforce. With this, the field of science education rose to the challenge and created the NGSS, a guide for teachers to use and adhere to as they develop their lesson plans and consider pushing the future, our students, into a more scientifically competitive position. The final version of the new standards were released in Spring of 2013. Nervous about getting new standards? Don't be. These are very well explained and broken down into specific parts, to help you as you use them. Look at the diagram on page 72 depicting what each part of the standard reflects. That's not that bad, is it?

When teaching is aligned to the NGSS, students become more engaged, learn ownership, and develop a deeper understanding that will develop the skills and knowledge necessary for success. In addition to using methods to increase student engagement is a new focus on topics that are relevant, interesting, timely, and controversial, such as global warming, evolution, and genetically modified foods. They bring reality into the classroom. We need all students to be able to speak "science-ese" and be able to participate in discussions that will affect them.

With these standards so new, how do we know they really work? Great question. We know because these standards are based on substantive research regarding how students learn science most effectively. In fact, the National Research Council has published their results in multiple formats, to include *How Students Learn, Taking Science to School*, and *A Framework for*

K–12 Science Education (see Recommended Readings). In addition to the National Research Council, many states have had input in creating these standards, as have the National Science Teachers Association and the American Association for the Advancement of Science among others (www.nexgenscience.org).

Though these individuals and groups have done most of our work for us by analyzing what is, and what isn't, working in science education, just giving you a bunch of standards and saying, "These are good. Use these" may not be all that helpful for you. Instead we offer suggestions for what to do and to stop doing, based on our personal knowledge of the research, the NGSS, and of common teacher practices when it comes to secondary science instruction. Enjoy!

STOP DON'T OVERTHINK THIS! IT'S TIME TO MAKE SOME CHANGES

- ✗ **STOP being the "Sage on the Stage" or the "Talking Head," and let students *do* science.** No more spending an entire class period lecturing. Look at every other chapter on secondary content instruction, and you'll see essentially the same suggestion: get off the stage. The NGSS, explicit teaching of the NoS, Scientific Inquiry, and Project-Based Learning are all more about facilitation than about direct instruction through lecturing. That doesn't mean you should give up your day job! Quite the contrary. This is your opportunity to help the students think for themselves. If we begin a topic with an introduction that catches them, reels them in, and interests them, we have them hooked, and we can start the real instruction at that point.

- ✗ **STOP asking them to sit still, taking note after note as they daydream about being miles away.** Get your students up and involved and engaged! Give them the idea and let them run with it. When taught correctly, Scientific Inquiry and Project-Based Learning allow them the freedom to critically think and engage each other as they learn science concepts. Don't worry that students will be disruptive during the activities. They won't be disruptive if they are engaged and involved. Well, okay. They may actually be seriously disruptive, but they would be learning! Isn't this what it's about? Getting them excited about science?

- ✗ **STOP doing it all yourself.** Volunteer to co-teach with a special educator, an English language learner coach, or another science teacher. In addition

Making Connections

Learn more about co-teaching in Chapter 13

to having two brains to engage in the science instruction, having a co-teacher also helps with classroom management (Murawski, 2009). If you have a class of 40 students and there are two of you in a classroom, the ratio of students to teachers has just been cut in half. Whew!

✗ **STOP talking to students about science in boring ways.** You have extensive credentials, and you are creative people! Discussing cells doesn't have to be boring. Quit making scientific topics sound dry. Instead, talk to students about a disease that is in today's newspaper and let them explore the how's and why's of it.

✗ **STOP making science one-dimensional.** Look for cause and effect, patterns, or models that show how science interacts with life. Science is way more than one-dimensional! Why not teach it that way?

✗ **STOP being stressed out about NGSS.** It's fun and much easier than you think. Reach out to your local museums and conservation groups. They have been doing NGSS lessons for a long time. They don't have pencils and desks. They have nature and other incredible resources to share with you. Many of them will want to come and meet with you—to co-teach in your classroom or even out in nature. Anyone else thinking field trip?

✗ **STOP feeling like you always have to front-load** *all* **of your vocabulary.** Let's take a quiz. Which are you more likely to remember: (a) a list of words on a board you've been asked to sit and copy and then look up in a dictionary or (b) words that you come across in context and actually talk, or ask, about? Hope you picked (b). We did. This doesn't mean you shouldn't be prepared to teach vocabulary; just think about *how* you are doing that.

✗ **DON'T go into your classroom and close the door.** Welcome your colleagues, whether other teachers or administrators, who can offer feedback. We cannot always *see* how the lessons go when we are alone; we are too "in the moment." Constructive criticism is a good thing! Besides, the teacher next door might have some great ideas to share with you.

GO IT'S EASIER THAN YOU THINK!

Teachers, DO This

✓ **START each lesson or unit by looking in the newspaper or on the Internet for breaking stories.** Every day includes something relevant about science. It might be something from NASA, the controversy surrounding the drought in California, mountain lions living in an urban area, how a new drug works, or even a cool video on parkour that leads you to talk about physics. They may act like secondary students who are above it all, but you have the power to grab their attention. This provides the real life connections that NGSS is all about, and it offers you something timely that you can use in your lessons that day. Hook your students into the world around them!

✓ **MAKE lists of what your students know about the topic, and work from there.** Ogle's (1986) K-W-L activity, where the teacher finds out what the students *Know, Want* to know, and *Learned*, is a popular instructional strategy that will work very well with science, especially with the NGSS. Find out about your students' preconceived notions and then, once you've listed them, let them go to work to find out whether they are correct or not. This type of investigation is exactly what NGSS is about.

✓ **DIFFERENTIATE!** We all know that students learn differently—and even show what they've learned differently—so the NGSS enables teachers to be more flexible with instruction and assessment. You may have a Performance Expectation that needs to be addressed, but there are many ways your students can reach that goal. Embed more choice into your lessons and activities, and watch them meet those expectations time and again. Embedding more choices could include creating the lesson with video, a hands-on activity, and written information. This would benefit each type of learner you may have in your classroom.

Making Connections

Check out Chapter 11 on Universal Design for Learning

✓ **USE the 7Es—Elicit, Engage, Explore, Explain, Elaborate, Evaluate, and Extend (Bybee et al., 1989)—to help guide what students are doing.** Check out page 83. We've given you a description of each of the Es as well as some examples of how to make them explicit in your classroom. To engage your students in Scientific Inquiry, why don't you make up a worksheet that lists these Es on the side or even have the students put this on the left side of a science notebook? Then using prompts from you, students can extend their own work. This is particularly appropriate for your gifted learners, but don't discount any of your students. You may be surprised who is able to come up with a more complex or in-depth application of your challenge.

✓ **SHARE with your colleagues what you are doing.** That may be another teacher who also teaches science with you, or you may want to talk with your English or math counterparts in your same grade. Elicit their assistance in using your topic at the same time you are teaching a particular part of the NGSS lesson, and see if they can give a complementary assignment and/or work from something you've begun in science. In one school, we saw a unit on stars in science lead to a complementary unit on graphing stars' luminosity in math, a frame of reference lesson in English wherein students were asked to write an essay looking back on their life as a star from a white dwarf back to a nebula, and a robust discussion in social studies regarding space exploration. Each lesson made sense to students because it was so integrally linked with the other content areas. Check out page 80 to see how the NGSS might overlap with the Common Core Standards in other content areas.

✓ **BE the teacher with the lessons that excite learners.** Remember back to when you were young and in school. What do you remember? We would venture to guess that you don't remember the endless days of copying off the board. But you might remember the volcano you built that actually boiled over, or the funny skit you were in when you played the cell membrane, or even making a diorama to explain a science concept. Think about how your science teacher could have used those "fun" lessons to explicitly teach the NoS concepts. You have so many options as you redesign your science instruction; go crazy!

✓ **USE technology where you can.** There are many wonderful tools out there that can easily be applied to the science classroom. They include: Moodle, Edmodo, Google forums, Evernote, Flashcard Machine, Mindmeister, Blendspace, Prezi, Wix, ThingLink, Jing, Skitch, Google Earth, Voki, PicFont, Teadable, and Remind 101. As an example, you can start a lesson with a quickwrite on Google documents. Students can have 30 seconds to type in what they might know on a topic and the screen in front of you will be filled with information!

Making Connections

Check out Chapter 7 on Engagement and Technology

✓ **DO explicitly teach the Nature of Science.** Incorporate hands-on and interactive activities that address the various concepts of NoS. But you can't stop there! Explicitly make the connections from the hands-on and/or interactive activities to the NoS concept. You can do this in multiple ways! For example, while teaching a lesson on photosynthesis, teachers can provide reflection questions or activities to help students gain a better understanding of the NoS by explicitly connecting the activity to NoS concepts. For example, you could allow students to compare and contrast a leaf that used sunlight as it changed and a leaf that was given another source of light to understand the multiple ways to arrive at a scientific solution.

✓ **INCORPORATE Project-Based Learning.** What about asking your students to build an app or use another multimedia platform to show their mastery of knowledge in various science concepts? Let's illustrate: When teaching about living organisms, students could create an app to show what living organisms are and how they work together to achieve a certain purpose or goal. The same idea could be used in a Prezi, Voki, or VoiceThread! Of course Project-Based Learning does not have to be entirely technological. Students could create poster boards about living organisms or picture collages and so on. Project-Based Learning allows students to be creative while learning.

✓ **USE Scientific Inquiry to help students take ownership of their learning.** Student facilitated activities, discussions, and lessons will allow students to take the initiative and become in charge of their own learning. Scientific Inquiry can be implemented in group activities or individual activities, depending on the needs and culture of your classroom. One example is to give student groups a topic and instruct them to come up with their own questions. Then guide them in the creation of a science experiment, in which you facilitate them talking and inquiring about each phase of their science project. Although Scientific Inquiry can be teacher led, remember that if it is student led, students can collaborate with peers, thereby creating positive peer interactions!

Administrators, DO This

✓ **BUILD into your schedule time for teachers to collaborate and plan, so they can work together.** The NGSS lessons really need to be developed as a group. Many minds working together will make for richer and more rigorous lessons. Ensure that this time for new curricular design doesn't result in slapped together lessons because stressed teachers simply do not have the time to be creative.

✓ **WORK with your teachers to offer practical, active feedback.** Move away from your desk. Come into the classroom and have a discussion with the science teacher. Make your feedback specific to what you observed and offer suggestions for improvement, rather than just identifying errors or issues. Remember, constructive feedback is much more effective than criticism.

✓ **PLAY Santa Claus!** Your teachers will need resources to develop their new, creative, more hands-on and real-world science lessons. Many can be brought in from the outside. Museums, conservatories, universities, and private or nonprofit organizations all have great things to offer. Please help support your teachers' needs by forwarding information you receive from district-approved groups in a timely fashion. Encourage teachers to get on www.DonorsChoose.org, which connects donors with worthwhile classrooms in need.

Plugged In

www.DonorsChoose.org

✓ **HELP make cross-curricular connections.** You're the big picture person. Help your teachers see where they might collaborate across disciplines. There is a wonderful opportunity here to connect math and language arts to science. Take the time to become familiar with the overlap. To do so, you'll need to familiarize yourself with the NGSS. They are very user friendly . . . once you can follow the pattern of them. Don't be intimidated. You can do it. And as one of the instructional leaders of the school, you really should.

✓ **BE supportive.** As teachers begin to infuse the aforementioned strategies into their science classrooms, they will need your support. Whether it is moral support, support with getting necessary resources, or just plain emotional support, your teachers will need you! The field of science education is progressing in a way to ensure our students are competitive in today's scientific society.

EARTH'S PLACE IN THE UNIVERSE—AN EXAMPLE STANDARD

5-ESS1 Earth's Place in the Universe

5-ESS1 Earth's Place in the Universe

Students who demonstrate understanding can:

5-ESS1-1. Support an argu[ment] [Names of each performance expectation] ...ces in the apparent brightness of the su... [Assessment Boundary: Assessment is limited to relative distan... ...ellar masses, age, stage).]

5-ESS1-2. Represent data [Names of each performance expectation] ...ys to reveal patterns of daily changes in ... and night, and the seasonal appearance of some stars in the night sky. [Cla... ...does not include other the position and motion of Earth with respect to the sun and selected stars that are visible only in particular... include causes of seasons.]

> If an asterisk is in the assessment component, it indicates an engineering connection in the practice, core idea or crosscutting concept

The performance expectations above were developed using the following elements from the NRC document...

Science and Engineering Practices	Disciplinary Core Ideas	Crosscutting Concepts
Analyzing and Interpreting Data Analyzing data in 3–5 builds on K–2 experiences and progresses to introducing quantitative approaches to collection data and conducting multiple trials of qualitative obs... possible and feasible, digital tools should b... • Represent data in graphical displays (b... and/or pie charts) to reveal patterns... relationships. (5-ESS1-2) **Engaging in Argument from Evidence** Engaging in argument from evidence in 3–... experiences and progresses to critiquing th... explanations or solutions proposed by peers by citing relevant evidence about the natural and designed world(s). • Support an argument with evidence, data, or a model. (5-ESS1-1)	**ESS1.A: The U...** • The sun is a... ...stars becau... ...m Earth. **B: Earth** ...e orbits d... ...rth, toge... ...North an... ...lude day and night; daily change... in the length and direction ...shadows; and different positions o... ...different times of the day, month, and ye... (5-ESS1-2)	**Patterns** • Similarities and differences in patterns can be used to sort, classify, communicate and analyze simple rates of change for natural phenomena. (5-ESS1-2) **Scale, Proportion, and Quantity** • Natural objects exist from the... small to the immensely larg... (5-ESS1-1)

Connections to other DCIs in fifth grade: N/A

...iculation of DCIs across grade levels: **2.ESS1.A** (5-ESS1-2); **1.ESS1.B** (5-ESS1-2); **3.PS2.A** (5-ESS1-2); **MS.ESS1.A** (5-ESS1-1),(5-...

Common Core State Standards Connections:

ELA/Literacy –

RI.5.1	Quote accurately from... when explaining ...inferences from the text. *(5-ESS1-1)*
RI.5.7	Draw on information from multiple print or di... ...an answer to a question quickly or to solve a problem efficiently. *(5-ESS1-1)*
RI.5.8	Explain how an author uses reasons and evi... ...fying which reasons and evidence support which point(s). *(5-ESS1-1)*
RI.5.9	Integrate information from several texts on th... ...e subject knowledgeably. *(5-ESS1-1)*
W.5.1	Write opinion pieces on topics or texts, suppo... ...on. *(5-ESS1-1)*
SL.5.5	Include multimedia components (e.g., graphics, sound) and visual displays in presentations when appropriate to enhance the development of main ideas or themes. *(5-...*

Mathematics –

MP.2	Reason abstractly and quantitatively. *(5-ESS1-1),(5-ESS1-2)*
MP.4	Model with mathematics. *(5-ESS1-1),(5-ESS1-2)*
5.NBT.A.2	Explain patterns in the number of zeros of the product wh... decimal is multiplied or divided by a power of 10. Use wh... ...nd explain patterns in the placement of the decimal point when a ...0. *(5-ESS1-1)*
5.G.A.2	Represent real world and mathematical problems by grap... ...inate plane, and interpret coordinate values of points in the context of the situation. (5-ESS1-2)

Annotation callouts:
- Names of each performance expectation
- Names designate which of the performance expectations use this practice
- Names designate which of the performance expectations incorporate this disciplinary core idea
- Names designate which of the performance expectations incorporate this crosscutting concept
- Connections to the Common Core State Standards for ELA/Literacy and Math
- Italics indicate a potential connection, rather than required prerequisite knowledge

*The performance expectations marked with an asterisk... ...gineering through a Practice or Disciplinary Core Idea.
The section entitled "Disciplinary Core Ideas" is reproduced verbatim from A Framework for K–12 Science Education: Practices, Cross-Cutting Concepts, and Core Ideas. Integrated and reprinted with permission from the National Academy of Sciences.

May 2013   ©2013 Achieve, Inc. All rights reserved.   1 of 1

Source: NGSS Lead States (2013). Achieve, Inc. on behalf of the twenty-six states and partners that collaborated on the NGSS.

THE OVERLAP OF ENGLISH LANGUAGE ARTS STANDARDS, MATH STANDARDS, AND SCIENCE STANDARDS

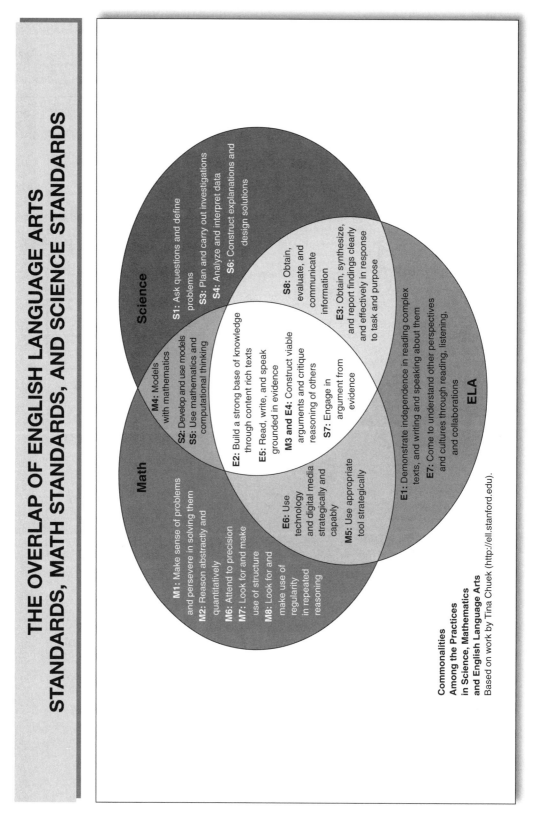

Science

S1: Ask questions and define problems

S3: Plan and carry out investigations

S4: Analyze and interpret data

S6: Construct explanations and design solutions

S8: Obtain, evaluate, and communicate information

Math

M1: Make sense of problems and persevere in solving them

M2: Reason abstractly and quantitatively

M6: Attend to precision

M7: Look for and make use of structure

M8: Look for and make use of regularity in repeated reasoning

M4: Models with mathematics

S2: Develop and use models

S5: Use mathematics and computational thinking

E6: Use technology and digital media strategically and capably

M5: Use appropriate tool strategically

E2: Build a strong base of knowledge through content rich texts

E5: Read, write, and speak grounded in evidence

M3 and E4: Construct viable arguments and critique reasoning of others

S7: Engage in argument from evidence

E3: Obtain, synthesize, and report findings clearly and effectively in response to task and purpose

ELA

E1: Demonstrate independence in reading complex texts, and writing and speaking about them

E7: Come to understand other perspectives and cultures through reading, listening, and collaborations

Commonalities Among the Practices in Science, Mathematics and English Language Arts
Based on work by Tina Chuek (http://ell.stanford.edu).

TEMPLATES AND IDEAS

Below is a template for designing lessons, which was created by the Los Angeles Unified School District (LAUSD) Common Core Science Fellows, Cohort 1, 2013-14, along with some other ideas teachers can use to help them create lessons. Please feel free to use them for designing your lessons!

Name of Lesson/Unit:

Topic: Grade Level:

Section 1: Lesson Summary

NGSS Performance Expectation: **Identify the most applicable Crosscutting Concept(s):**   **Identify the most applicable Engineering Practice(s):**   **CCSS ELA Standards:**   **CCSS Reading Standards:**   **CCSS Math Standards:**   **Current State Science Standard:**
Objective of the Lesson or Unit: **How is this objective relevant to students?**
Culminating Assessment

What has been taught in my class to prepare students for this topic?

Description of the Lesson/Unit		
7E	*Short Description of Activity*	*Purpose/Intention for the Activity or Key Learning*
Elicit		
Engage		
Explore		
Explain		Use C-E-R Claim: Evidence: Reasoning:
Elaborate		
Evaluate		
Extend		

IDEAS FOR THE 7 Es

7 Es	What Are They?	Ideas for Use
Elicit	Help students identify preconceptions about the topic.	K-W-L chart Foldables Graphic organizer Concept map Lesson demo Word wall/vocabulary
Engage	Motivate students; can be done through creative activities, by using different methods of delivery, by providing choice, by identifying students' strengths and interests, and so forth.	Video clips Newspapers Magazines Internet Foldables Create question cards
Explore	Activate students' thinking by using newspaper clips, video clips, Internet resources, etc.	Use C-E-R C—Claim E—Evidence R—Reasoning Internet research Local source info Data collection Graphing Charts Tables
Explain	Provide stimuli for science discussions; can use Internet resources, multimedia, and personal knowledge or expertise; clarify and provide direct instruction as needed.	Using the above for reference, class presentations, discussion, Socratic seminars, debate; Internet resources
Elaborate	Initiate Scientific Inquiry and idea exploration; allow students to delve deeper.	Mapping results Actual field data collection Co-teach with field expert Guest speakers
Evaluate	Improve questioning and quality of student responses. Provide teacher to student feedback, as well as peer and self-assessment.	Storyboard creation Games—Pictionary, matching vocabulary to definitions, Jeopardy, Red Light/Green Light, Inside Out, game boards, Scavenger Hunt

(Continued)

(Continued)

7 Es	What Are They?	Ideas for Use
Extend	Extend student learning through challenging them through higher level questioning and critical thinking. This oftentimes leads to student reflection.	PowerPoint/Prezi presentation; personal research; blogging

Source: Adapted from Eisenkfraft (2003).

REFERENCES

Achieve. (2013). Next Generation Science Standards. Retrieved from http://www
.nextgenscience.org

ACT. (2012). The condition of college and career readiness, 2012. Retrieved from
http://media.act.org/documents/CCCR12-NationalReadinessRpt.pdf

Bybee, R. W. et al. (1989). *Science and technology education for the elementary years:
Frameworks for curriculum and instruction.* Washington, DC: The National
Center for Improving Instruction.

Capps, D. K., & Crawford, B. A. (2013). Inquiry-based instruction and teaching
about nature of science: Are they happening? *Journal of Science Teacher
Education, 24,* 497–526.

Eisenkraft, A. (2003). *Expanding the 5E Model.* Arlington, VA: The Science Teacher,
National Science Teacher Association.

Filippatou, D., & Kaldi, S. (2010). The effectiveness of project-based learning on
pupils with learning difficulties regarding academic performance, group
work and motivation. *International Journal of Special Education, 25*(1), 17–26.

Lederman, N. G. (1992) Students' and teachers' conceptions of the nature of science: A review of the research. *Journal of Research in Science Teaching, 29*(4),
331–359.

Lederman, N. (2007). Nature of science: Past, present, and future. In S. Abell & N.
Lederman (Eds.), *Handbook of research on science* education (pp. 831–879).
Mahwah, NJ: Lawrence Erlbaum.

Lederman, N. G., Lederman, J. S., & Antink, A. (2013). Nature of science and scientific inquiry as contexts for the learning of science and achievement of scientific literacy. *International Journal of Education in Mathematics, Science and
Technology, 1*(3), 138–147.

Machi, E. (2008). *Improving the U.S. Competitiveness with K–12 Education and
Training* (SR 57). A Report on the STEM Education and National Security
Conference October 21–23, 2008. Retrieved from http://www.heritage.org/
Research/Education/sr0057.cfm

Murawski, W. W. (2009). *Collaborative teaching in secondary schools: Making the co-
teaching marriage work!* Thousand Oaks, CA: Corwin.

National Research Council. (2012). *A framework for K–12 science education: Practices,
crosscutting concepts, and core ideas.* Washington, DC: National Academies
Press.

Office of the Press Secretary. The White House. (2013, April 22). Remarks by the
President at the 2013 White House Science Fair. Retrieved from http://www
.whitehouse.gov/the-press-office/2013/04/22/remarks-president-
2013-white-house-science-fair

Ogle, D. M. (1986). K-W-L: A teaching model that develops active reading of
expository text. *Reading Teacher, 39,* 564–570.

Schneider, B., Wallace, J., Blikstein, P., & Pea, R. (2013). Preparing for future learning with a tangible user interface: The case of neuroscience. *IEEE Transactions
on Learning Technologies, 6*(2), 117–129.

Schwartz, R. S., Lederman, N. G., & Crawford, B. A. (2004). Developing views of
nature of science in an authentic context: An explicit approach to bridging the
gap between nature of science and scientific inquiry. *Science Education, 88*(4),
610–645.

RECOMMENDED READINGS

* National Research Council. (2012). *A framework for K–12 science education: Practices, crosscutting concepts, and core ideas.* Washington, DC: National Academies Press.

* Bybee, R. (2013) *Translating the NGSS for classroom instruction.* Arlington, VA: NSTA Book Press.

* Harland, D. (2011) *STEM student research handbook.* Arlington, VA: NSTA Book Press.

* Brunsell, E., Kneser, D. M., & Niemi, J. J. (2014). *Introducing teachers and administrators to the NGSS: A professional development facilitator's guide.* Arlington, VA: NSTA Book Press.

* Pratt, H. (2013) *The NSTA reader's guide to* A Framework for K–12 Science Education, Second Edition: Practices, crosscutting concepts, and core ideas. Arlington, VA: NSTA Press.

GO EVEN FURTHER WITH THIS TOPIC ON THE WORLD WIDE WEB

- www.nextgenscience.org
- www.acceleratelearning.com
- www.nasonline.org
- www.nsta.org
- www.lewiscenter.org/AAE/Departments/Science/Teaching-the-Next-Generations-Science/index.html
- tinyurl.com/MarineCSI-HS
- tinyurl.com/MarineCSIK–8
- www.facebook.com/TeachMarineCSI

THE Apps WE LOVE

- Next Generation Science Standards
- Pocket Universe
- Video Science
- Frog Dissection
- Science360

6

Awe-Inspiring Arts Instruction

Mary Wolf

Daemen College

Rachel Lyons

Buffalo Academy for Visual & Performing Arts

WHAT REALLY WORKS IN ARTS INSTRUCTION IN THE SECONDARY CLASSROOM

It's as Easy as ABC

Have you ever stopped and peered into an art class and wondered, "What is going on in there?" To the untrained eye, it may seem like chaos that somehow leads to creative expression. That perception is understandable since some students may be getting supplies, others may be cleaning supplies, some may be working quietly, while still others may be discussing their work with a peer. You may think that it's easy to be an art teacher—all you have to do is let kids draw all day, right? You may look at the front of the room and ask yourself, "Where is the art teacher?" She's not up front; instead, she is often weaving throughout the room to be sure everyone is doing what they are supposed to be doing, how they are supposed to be doing it, where they are supposed to be doing it, and taking away what they are supposed to take away from it. To the trained eye of an art teacher, this is not chaos. It is the process of learning *in*, *about*, and *through* art. All students do not learn in the same way, at the same time, or at the same rate. Furthermore, not all students are interested in or "good" at art, which is why you so often hear them say, "But I can't draw...." So how do art teachers help initially uninterested and often artistically untalented students engage and find success? It's as easy as ABC. Art teachers who create artistic learning communities by supporting students' **A**utonomy, **B**elonging, and **C**ompetence know that this leads to students' personal, social, and artistic development.

In this chapter, we will explain the ABCs of arts instruction and highlight a collaborative art project completed with high school art students and college art education majors. After reading this chapter, we hope the art teachers reading this will recognize and enhance their ABCs and that the next time you stop by an art class, you will see the ABCs (rather than chaos) and better understand what really works in arts instruction. By the way, those of you who are not art teachers will find quite a few tips to integrate in your content classes as well—so read on!

AUTONOMY, BELONGING, AND COMPETENCE: THE ABCs OF ARTS INSTRUCTION

A: Autonomy. No, we are not referring to the myth about "those" oddly creative people who work in isolation to create masterpieces. We are referring to the need for independence and self-actualization (Maslow, 1968). Artistic autonomy (voice and choice) is vital to art making, and therefore, it is important in the teaching of art. However, autonomy is not an isolated goal for the art room; it is vital for learning in all disciplines. See! We told you everyone could find something in this chapter. Ryan and Powelson (1991) note the importance of students' ability to self-rule and self-regulate and the importance of autonomy on student motivation and learning. Art teachers, specifically, support students' autonomy by providing them with choices in subject matter, content, materials, and composition, which motivates them to create their own meaning, both cognitively and artistically. This is why "good art education" leads to a variety of individual works of art, not "cookie cutter" art projects that all look alike.

A traditional school art style focuses solely on step-by-step techniques that lead to stale, similar art projects. Back in 1976, Efland argued that a school art style that is regulated by the teacher differs significantly from child art, which is done outside of the school and is self-regulated. Efland might argue that there is true creativity in the latter and only suggested creativity in the prior. The ABCs of arts instruction encourage students to make their artwork personal, creative, social, and meaningful. By providing students with choices, they are forced to use their minds to make decisions and they begin to develop an individual, artistic voice. Alfie Kohn (1998) supports the need to have students make decisions by stating that students need to feel a sense of control, responsibility, and self-determination. When students are offered choices, they can take responsibility for their art making, which contributes to developing responsibility, self-determination, and their overall sense of well-being. That's step one. We're not done yet.

B: Belonging. Artists often surround themselves with other artists and work in artistic communities that provide a sense of belonging, care, and support. This can be seen in arts organizations such as The Art Students League. You are likely aware of similar organizations where you live and, if not, we encourage you to take a look and see what's out there. In our case, the Buffalo Arts Studio is a good example of a communal arts environment that encourages collaborative and individual artistic growth. This type of artistic community can be emulated in the classroom. We all know that secondary students need peer groups for socialization. Why wouldn't you want your students hanging around creative thinkers?

Wolf (2010) describes a sixth-grade art classroom community in which students' sense of belonging improved. Nel Noddings (1992) explains that care is reciprocal in nature and although the students in Wolf's study did not initially accept or reciprocate the teacher's caring, care did develop over time. The art room is an ideal setting for developing such rapport among teachers and students, but it is not the only place it should happen. Ryan and Powelson (1991) argue the importance of relatedness throughout education, describing it as the emotional and personal bonds in which everyone looks out for the well-being of each other. All teachers can support students' sense of belonging by encouraging peer-to-peer collegial collaboration. Art teachers can model and encourage caring support during collaborative activities such as group brainstorming, in-process peer feedback, and whole class critiques. Through such activities, students' artistic choices and voices are seen, heard, and valued by their art teacher and their peers. As that caring support is reinforced, given, received, and reciprocated, a sense of trust can develop among students and with their art teacher. In education, there needs to be an "ethic of care" (Noddings, 1992); commitment, respect, trust (hooks, 2003); and sense of belonging (Osterman, 2000). These are natural aspects of human life that can and should be addressed in all classrooms. However, this cannot happen if students do not feel competent enough to participate, thus bringing us to <u>C</u>.

C: Competence. There are skills, concepts, information, and dispositions related to art, art history, and art making that need to be learned and developed in order to become knowledgeable about and skillful in art. As much as thinking skills are required in all subject areas, they are also vital in the art room. Marshall (2008) reinforces this concept stating, "While metacognition is critical to learning in all disciplines, understanding what you are doing in working with techniques, materials, design principles, and with ideas is an especially important goal of art education" (p. 39). These thinking and art making skills lead to student competence in art.

Competence is successfully stretching beyond one's capability when challenged to achieve a goal, which leads to a sense of accomplishment (Ryan & Powelson, 1991). The notion of offering students art challenges contradicts the poorly implemented school arts style of teaching that requires all students to make the same thing and requires little thinking and even less choice. The arts are a perfect way to challenge students to think critically and creatively as they use their art making skills to bring their thoughts to life. Quality art teachers challenge their students to (a) remember important information about artists, art movements, and artworks; (b) discuss, analyze, and interpret artwork and art concepts; and (c) use proper materials and techniques to create works of art that express ideas, emotions, and visions of the world and beyond. Efland (1990) argued that the arts contribute to cognitive development because making sense of art requires contextual understanding and making meaning in one's own art requires imagination. Therefore, he posits that the arts enhance both critical and creative thinking. If this is sounding overwhelming, worry not. We are simply using big words to say that art helps kids think and be imaginative. That's a good thing. When students know key information, understand vital concepts, and apply appropriate artistic materials, techniques, and dispositions, they become more competent in art. Competence leads students to more confidently participate in all aspects of the artistic process from initial brainstorming to planning, revising, creating, and critiquing. This participation demonstrates both cognitive and artistic competence. In a nutshell, we are saying that when students develop confidence and competence in art, they are likely to be more engaged; doesn't this apply to other disciplines as well?

CONTINUING TO MAKE SENSE OF CHAOS

So what do the ABCs of arts instruction look like? The following is the story of collaboration among the art students of the Buffalo Academy for Visual and Performing Arts and Daemen College's Art Education program that took place in Buffalo, New York. As you read, see if you can identify the ABCs of Art Instruction. The learning experience focused on contemporary artist Ryan McGinness's (2013) work *Something About the Collapse of Art and Language*, which was on display at the nearby Albright-Knox Art

Gallery. Art students in seventh and eleventh grades were able to see the work in person at the gallery and learn about the artist and work. The students' positive reaction to the work inspired their art teacher to learn more about the artist and to develop a project that would eventually grow to include the participation of five art teachers, 144 students in Grades 5 through 12, and five undergraduate art education college students. All of the students learned valuable information about McGinness's life and vital concepts contained in his work. McGinness used iconography and symbols inspired by pop and street culture and layered them extensively in ways that abstracted the representational symbols, thus leaving the viewer to make meaning of the visual chaos. Students at the various grade levels discussed, analyzed, and interpreted his work, noting the significance of the title and the importance of *reading* his *visual* work and the numerous ways that it could be read. They shared their thoughts and interpretations through writing and class discussions.

Then students took the information and concepts they learned and transformed them into their own collaborative artwork. The art teacher demonstrated the skills required to design and create a stencil that had appropriate bridges so that the negative spaces of the images would not fall out. She also modeled how to effectively print the image ensuring clean edges, smooth paint, and interesting layering effects. Each high school student was challenged to choose and/or design a symbol inspired by his or her cultural context. One student who had recently overcome some personal adversity designed a Phoenix. Another student created a lotus flower to symbolize the personal growth she has achieved as a young artist. Each personal symbol was transformed into a stencil to be printed. College students facilitated the printing on one large canvas by helping students think about and choose where to print their stencil in the composition by asking them what it would mean if they placed their symbol next to or on top of someone else's symbol. In essence, because of these choices, each student had a voice—both visually and verbally—in the larger artwork as a way to support their _autonomy_. Students took ownership of the artwork, and classroom leaders began to help other students think critically about the ways they were applying their stencils. The project fostered a sense of community, with many students stopping by during other classes to show their friends where their stencils were. Even non-art students stopped to ask how the artwork was progressing. This contributed to the students' sense of _belonging_, as each student was recognized and included as a vital part of the learning and art making process. Student _competence_ was demonstrated throughout the project as students shared knowledge and demonstrated skills with their classroom peers, other students in the school, the college students and their professor, their art teachers, and other teachers and administrators in the school.

The approach of ABCs in arts instruction resulted in personal growth as students reflected on their cultural context and made stencils that were personally meaningful, which contributed to a collaborative artwork that was equally important to them. They were able to share parts of themselves with peers, college students and their professor, teachers, and administrators. It also resulted in social growth as students learned more about others through discussions about all of the artwork from the unit. Additionally, students grew cognitively and artistically by expanding their knowledge of art and their skills in designing, drawing, and printmaking. This learning experience drew to a close when the artwork was chosen by the Albright-Knox Art Gallery to receive an award. The internal and external validation gleaned from this experience helped students develop personally, socially, cognitively, and artistically, thus demonstrating how the ABCs can *really* work in arts instruction.

However, as you can see it is not *really* as *easy* as ABC. The work of an art teacher is quite complicated, which is why it may appear chaotic at first; however, with this information, you should be able to see through the chaos and find the ABCs. When art teachers seek to develop students' autonomy, belonging, and competence in an artistic learning community, arts instruction works. We are sure all teachers can do the same in their classrooms to develop strong learning communities. Although, as we all realize, it takes planning, patience, consistency, time, and support from students and administration to make it *really* work.

THE ABCs OF ARTS INSTRUCTION REALLY WORK, BUT YOU HAVE TO STOP DOING THE FOLLOWING

Teachers

- ✘ **STOP focusing on and promoting technique alone.** Even top art colleges such as Maryland Institute College of Art and Rhode Island School of Design seek students who can think creatively and critically as well as make good art. Artistic <u>C</u>ompetence is more than rendering an image realistically.
- ✘ **STOP using an outdated approach to teaching art.** Many art teachers and school districts still take a Discipline Based Art Education (DBAE) approach to teaching art. In the past, it was a valid effort to make art education more comprehensive by supplementing art making with criticism, aesthetics, and art history. However, it is outdated and on its own is ineffective in contemporary times.
- ✘ **STOP providing cookie cutter projects with little differentiation.** Heather Fountain (2014) clarified, "Differentiated Instruction . . . helped me create an art room where all individuals are a part of a community of learners . . . my students not only learn about art, but also about themselves and each other" (p. 4). In an ABC approach to

art instruction, teachers do not see all students as the same but understand and highlight their similarities and differences in a community that celebrates diversity.

Making Connections

Check out Chapter 12 on Inclusion

- ✖ **STOP limiting your students to traditional art elements and principles of design.** Though they are important aspects of art, they are not the only ones of importance to art making today.

- ✖ **STOP trying to control everything.** We know that principals look for classes to be managed properly and that one way to make the art class look manageable is to control everything. However, when teachers seek total control, they run into resistance as students also seek control and Autonomy.

- ✖ **STOP expecting students to know how to collegially collaborate in the art classroom.** Creating a sense of Belonging among adolescents is not easy. Many students come to school with walls of self-protection up and have the urge to strike negatively first rather than be on the receiving side of negative comments. These attitudes and behaviors often clash with teachers' expectations for students' positive participation. This is why art teachers must model and facilitate positive collaboration.

- ✖ **STOP expecting *your* expectations of success to be the same as *your students'* expectations for success.** Students often come to art class with a lack of confidence and fear of failure. They worry they can't draw realistically and therefore will embarrass themselves if they even bother. They have low expectations for their abilities to succeed. Knowing this will help you meet students where they are rather than where you want them to be in regard to expectations for success.

- ✖ **STOP thinking about art as an isolated experience.** Many artists work in collaborative artistic communities. Collaboration between students, projects, or even disciplines and classes should be encouraged.

Administrators

- ✖ **STOP thinking about art as an isolated experience too.** Allow time for teachers to plan and collaborate with other art teachers and teachers of other subject areas. If there is only one art teacher in your building, she likely feels isolated. You can help her feel a sense of Belonging by offering professional development opportunities where she may interact with art teachers from other schools.

- ✖ **STOP thinking about art class as a break for the other teachers.** The thinking skills learned in the art room can strengthen students' ability in other classes. However, throwing 60 or more children in one room at the same time can create a situation wherein very little thinking, or listening, or art making can truly happen. When this happens, the art teacher may need to focus on *managing* the class rather than *teaching* the class.

✗ **STOP expecting a successful art room to look like other classrooms.** The process of being an artist can be messy and appear chaotic. Any art room that is truly functioning will have similar characteristics. But don't worry, look closer, they are learning!

GO SO THAT'S WHAT TO STOP DOING, BUT WHAT SHOULD YOU START DOING?

Teachers, DO This

✓ **BALANCE artistic thinking and artistic making.** Artists don't simply make things; they think, too. So art students must do the same. By creating lessons that balance concepts, skills, information, and dispositions, students receive a more thorough art education.

✓ **USE a contemporary approach to teaching art.** Anderson and Milbrandt (2004) expand on traditional DBAE to include creativity, technology, and visual culture which are inclusive of the needs of a 21st century art education. They also discuss the importance of a sense of community in education stating, "The idea that knowledge is constructed rather than given from on high suggests that teaching and learning are centered on community" (p. 28).

✓ **USE terms and concepts used by contemporary artists.** Olivia Gude argues for a new school art style (2013) and offers a great start toward using more contemporary terms such as juxtaposition and interaction of text and image in her "postmodern principles" (Gude, 2004). She also offers new, more contemporary concepts such as "playing, forming self, and investigating community themes" in her "principles of possibility" (Gude, 2007).

✓ **NEGOTIATE control by providing opportunities for students to take responsibility through decision-making.** Herbert Kohl (1991) differentiates between choosing not to learn and not being able to learn stating that students who feel controlled are more likely to choose "not learning." Therefore, negotiate control by allowing students to have some.

✓ **MODEL caring interaction in the art classroom.** When teachers initially model care and support, it is often ill-received by students. However, it is in the consistent demonstration of care over time that leads to a sense of trust between teacher and students. Additionally, the teacher needs to have high expectations for students to interact positively in order to build similar respect among students.

✓ **ADJUST your expectations and meet students where they are.** Help bridge the gap between their low expectations and your high expectations by scaffolding your expectations and teaching in their zone of proximal development (Vygotsky, 1978). In other words, if they are at 1 and you want them to get to 3, be sure to meet them at 1, help them to 2, and then move on to 3. Don't think that they will be willing to just meet you at 2 as a compromise. It doesn't work that way.

✓ **GET TO KNOW your students' strengths, needs, and interests in order to provide them what they need to succeed.** Provide authentic learning experiences that are meaningful for your students *and* relate to the real world (Anderson & Milbrandt, 2004). So often, art teachers create a still life of objects that are irrelevant to students but challenging to draw. The art teacher designs the still life, and students are simply expected to replicate it on paper using pencils or other drawing materials. Instead of a teacher-centered still life, why not ask students which objects are important to them? Even better, why not ask them to bring the objects in and arrange them in a way that is meaningful to them? The art teacher can certainly make suggestions or additions that might ensure the students are challenged, but a more student-centered still life is a better enticement for students to participate.

✓ **INCLUDE more collaborative experiences into your lesson to promote an artistic learning community.** "Collaboration may be one of the most effective tools in this difficult process of understanding, constructing, and restructuring community" (Anderson & Milbrandt, 2004, p. 27). The ABCs of arts instruction acknowledge the importance of collaboration as part of constructing knowledge and constructing community. Work with other content teachers to bring their content into the art room and to bring art into their content classes. This type of collaboration helps to truly support communication and differentiation for student success (Murawski & Spencer, 2011).

Making Connections

Check out Chapter 4 on Social Studies Instruction

Administrators

✓ **PRACTICE the ABCs yourself!** Supporting teachers' autonomy, belonging, and competence leads to teacher development. Allow teachers to feel they are experts at what they do, thank them for doing it, and offer them chances to have quality, relevant professional development in order to continue developing their own competence in art and teaching.

✓ **PARTICIPATE in art making and dialogue about art.** If you want to help students foster a sense of community and **b**elonging, drop by the art room and make something with them, or talk to them about what they are making. Ask them why they are making it and how their ideas developed. Let them teach you!

✓ **BE a resource for collaboration.** Collaborating with other teachers during the traditional school day can be tricky and sometimes prevents good ideas from getting off the ground. If art teachers want to collaborate with others, offer time and resources whenever possible to support them in doing just that. Then, watch as students who love art, but who have been failing their content classes, start to succeed when their content teachers learn ways to incorporate art in those disciplines.

We hope this chapter has provided art teachers, principals, and all teachers with valuable information about the ways autonomy, belonging, and competence are relevant in a variety of educational settings. The ABCs transcend the walls of the art room and are applicable to all students. They transcend the walls of the classrooms and are applicable to teachers and staff, as well. Finally, they transcend the walls of the school as everyone wants to feel like an independent, accepted, contributing, and valuable member of their community. So now that you know your ABCs, next time won't you use them with me—and your students, and your colleagues, and your teachers? Trust us, it *really* works!

THE ABCs CHECKLIST FOR PLANNING ARTS INSTRUCTION

A.   Does this unit support students' sense of **Autonomy**?

_____ Does this unit encourage student choice? Are there opportunities for students to make choices related to . . .

      _____ ideas, content, or subject matter?

      _____ composition and the use of modern/postmodern art elements and principles of design?

      _____ materials, media, and techniques?

_____ Does this unit encourage student voice? Are there opportunities for students to . . .

      _____ develop an artistic voice?

      _____ express their voices verbally?

      _____ express their voices visually?

_____ Is the development of an independent artistic sense of self a probable outcome of this unit?

B.   Does this unit support students' sense of **Belonging**?

_____ Does this unit encourage positive collaboration? Are there opportunities for collaboration during . . .

      _____ the planning phase of the art making process?

      _____ the art making phase?

      _____ the sharing/critique at the end?

_____ Does the teacher model and facilitate . . .

      _____ positive interaction?

      _____ caring?

      _____ support?

_____ Is the development of a respectful and trusting artistic community a probable outcome of the collaboration?

C.   Does this unit support students' sense of **Competence**?

_____ Does this unit support the acquisition of knowledge? Are there opportunities for students to . . .

_____ think critically?

_____ think creatively?

_____ gain factual information about artists, artworks, and art movements?

_____ gain understanding about meaningful concepts related to art, themselves, others, and the world?

_____ Does this unit support the acquisition of skills? Are there opportunities for students to . . .

_____ play with materials to gain a hands-on understanding of those materials?

_____ investigate a particular media for an extended period of time?

_____ practice specific techniques before using them in the final artwork?

_____ Is the development of artistic confidence a probable outcome of the unit?

THE ABCs OF ARTS INSTRUCTION: BRAINSTORM HOW YOU CAN INCORPORATE THE ABCs INTO YOUR CLASSROOM/INSTRUCTION

Autonomy

Student Choice + Student Voice + Personal Engagement = Independent Students

What are some ways you can support students' sense of autonomy in your classroom/instruction?

> ➢
> ➢
> ➢

Belonging

Positive Collaboration + Care + Support = Valuable Members of a Learning Community

What are some ways you can support students' sense of belonging in your classroom/instruction?

> ➢
> ➢
> ➢

Competence

Critical/Creative Thinking Skills + Discipline Specific Skills/Knowledge = Confident Contributors

What are some ways you can support students' sense of belonging in your classroom/instruction?

> ➢
> ➢
> ➢

REFERENCES

Anderson, T., & Milbrandt, M. (2004). *Art for life: Authentic instruction in art.* New York, NY: McGraw-Hill.

Efland, A. (1976). The school art style: A functional analysis. *Studies in Art Education, 17*(2), 37–44.

Efland, A. (1990). *A history of art education: Intellectual and social currents in teaching the visual arts.* New York, NY: Teachers College Press.

Fountain, H. (2014). *Differentiation in art.* Worcester, MA: Davis.

Gude, O. (2004). Postmodern principles: In search of a 21st-century art education. *Art Education, 57*(1), 6–14.

Gude, O. (2007). Principles of possibility: Considerations for a 21st century art and culture curriculum. *Art Education, 60*(1), 6–17.

Gude, O. (2013). New school art styles: The project of art education. *Art Education, 66*(1), 6–15.

hooks, b. (2003). *Teaching community: A pedagogy of hope.* New York, NY: Routledge.

Kohl, H. R. (1991). *I won't learn from you: The role of assent in learning.* Minneapolis, MN: Milkweed Editions.

Kohn, A. (1998). *What to look for in a classroom and other essays.* San Francisco, CA: Jossey-Bass.

Marshall, J. (2008). Visible thinking: Using contemporary art to teach conceptual skills. *Art Education, 61*(2), 38–45.

Maslow, A. H. (1968). *Toward a psychology of being* (2nd ed.). New York, NY: Van Nostrand Reinhold.

McGinness, R. J. (2013). *Something about the collapse of art and language* [Artwork, acrylic on canvas]. Retrieved from http://www.albrightknox.org/collection/recent-acquisitions/piece:something-about-the-collapse-of-art-language/

Murawski, W. W., & Spencer, S. (2011). *Collaborate, communicate, and differentiate! How to increase student learning in today's diverse schools.* Thousand Oaks, CA: Corwin.

Noddings, N. (1992). *The challenge to care in schools: An alternative approach to education.* New York, NY: Teachers College Press.

Osterman, K. F. (2000). Students' need for belonging in the school community. *Review of Educational Research, 70*(3), 323–367.

Ryan, R. M., & Powelson, C. L. (1991). Autonomy and relatedness as fundamental to motivation and education. *Journal of Experimental Education, 60*(1), 49–66.

Vygotsky, L. S. (1978). *Mind in society: The development of higher psychological processes.* Cambridge, MA: Harvard University Press.

Wolf, M. M. (2010). *A narrative inquiry into the construction of community in a sixth grade art class.* Pennsylvania State University, University Park. Retrieved from https://etda.libraries.psu.edu/paper/10537/6268

RECOMMENDED READINGS (JOURNALS FOR TEACHING ART)

* Scholastic Art art.scholastic.com/
* Arts & Activities www.artsandactivities.com/
* School Arts Magazine www.davisart.com/Promotions/SchoolArts/Default .aspx
* Art Education Journal www.arteducators.org/research/art-education
* Studies in Art Education Journal arteducators.org/research/studies
* International Journal of Education & the Arts www.ijea.org/
* The Journal of Social Theory in Art Education www.jstae.org/index.php/jstae

GO EVEN FURTHER WITH THIS TOPIC ON THE WORLD WIDE WEB

* www.arteducators.org/
* www.pbs.org/art21/
* www.uic.edu/classes/ad/ad382/
* www.artiseducation.org/
* www.aep-arts.org/
* www.americansforthearts.org/
* www.davisart.com/Products/1045/art-education-in-practice-series-digital.aspx

THE Apps WE LOVE

* Morpholio
* Procreate
* Sketchbook Pro
* Art Discovery
* Art History Interactive

SECTION II

What Really Works in Instruction

7

Tuning in With Technology

Lisa A. Dieker, Lauren Delisio, and Caitlyn A. Bukaty

University of Central Florida

WHAT REALLY WORKS IN ENGAGEMENT IN THE SECONDARY CLASSROOM

Enhancing Engagement via Technology

Another day, another confiscated cell phone. Seriously, you are starting to think that you spend 30% of your day teaching your content and the other 70% rounding up iPads, smart phones, not-as-smart-but-still-able-to-text phones, and other types of technology. You see your students tweeting, updating their Facebook status ("Bored in Math"), snapchatting, playing Plants vs. Zombies or Candy Crush, texting friends, and ordering things on Amazon. Does it bother you? A little. More than that though, you are jealous. You'd rather play PvZ instead of trying to yell over a bunch of teenagers! The ironic thing is, you ask every year for more computers in your classroom, and here are all these students with more advanced technology in their hands than you'll ever have in your class—and yet, the school policy is "No personal technology." The result? Disengaged students, a lack of useful technology, and an exasperated teacher who needs strategies. This chapter is for you.

Technology use has exploded across every facet of society and education. However, the increased use of technology in classrooms has boiled down to a basic question: Does technology simply increase student engagement because of its entertainment value, or are students actually learning content and social skills? The answer is yes. And no. Despite this tension, teachers need to be aware of emerging trends in technology, as well as the most recent research with regard to strategies for engaging learners through the use of technology. As new technology emerges almost daily, you need to understand the potential as well as the pitfalls in purchasing, adopting, and using a wide array of technologies that are innovative, yet may only hold promise to impact practice and student engagement without producing real results.

In order to stay abreast of the near- and far-term technology that is emerging in our field, as well as the potential impact of these tools on students in the present day and in their future employment opportunities, we strongly suggest you read the New Media Consortium's (NMC) Horizon Report each February when it is released. We know you have no time to read. We know that a report on technology sounds like it is way outside

Plugged In

www.nmc.org/horizon-project

the realm of your expertise, but trust us! Over the last decade, this report has been right on target in their predictions. More than 8 years ago, they predicted that everyone would be using tablet computers. The authors of the 2014 report remind the field that we have some challenges ahead of us associated with the adoption and rewards of these emerging advances in technology related to education. Page 114 shows information pulled from the Horizon Report that reminds the field that there is still work to be done and hurdles to overcome. There are so many incredible advancements that we can use in the secondary classroom—advancements that our students will love, and we want them to be ready to be employed in these advancing areas. However, they are pointless if they do not help students to master content more deeply or increase their ability to sustain their attention to learn more information. It is this blending of technology and engagement that is the focus for this chapter. We know that using technology as a tool for engagement, with an ultimate goal of increased and improved student learning, is something that can really work. That's a pretty good goal, right? If you agree, keep reading. If you don't . . . well, we're not sure how to help you.

Borrowing terms from the NMC, we know students are currently engaged with technology and we know what is changing in their world technology-wise. This report also helps us realize that we need to consider the far-term horizon as it relates to education and technology as well. For now, page 114 also provides us with what is present and what is approaching. That's just not enough! Let's look at how we used to engage kids using the "old school" methods of paper-pencil and group work; now, let's apply these methods to new innovations in technology, both ones that are sustaining (meaning that they continue or evolve a technology we already know) or are disrupting (meaning that they are changing the field and maybe even displacing an older technology). The purpose of this approach is to help you think about what really works for the future of students who, born today, will be working in our society until approximately the year 2080. 2080! Scary, huh? So with that as our forecast for what really works, let's think about what we already know.

KEY RESEARCH YOU NEED TO KNOW ABOUT TECHNOLOGY AND ENGAGEMENT

The shift in standards is leading teachers to focus not on bell-to-bell teaching, but on bell-to-bell engagement; this shift is at the core of the College and Career Ready Standards. With this in mind, think about the impact and intertwining that technology can have. We encourage you to first think about who is disengaged in your class: Is it the student who loves technology, or the males, or the females, or the gifted, or the struggling learners? To do what really works, you must first have in mind which students to target in order to tackle the issue of engagement. The definition for disengagement, according to the Merriam-Webster Dictionary (2014), is "to stop being involved with a person or group." So as we think about integrating practices that increase engagement, we need to look first at the populations we most often disengage. There are some known populations in the literature that we are failing as a nation (minority males, students who are struggling with schoolwork; Jackson & Hilliard, 2013). However, to really do what works, each individual teacher needs to examine his or her own practices and classes of students (Smyth, McInerney, & Fish, 2013). What are we doing, or not doing, on a daily basis that might be causing these particular groups of students to disengage? Data-driven instruction is an effective way to address factors of disengagement (Datnow, Park, & Kennedy-Lewis, 2012). By spending time each day examining the data, a teacher can determine which group or individual student did not meet the standard for learning or behavior and can then redirect the course of the next day's lesson to ensure engagement with those students; naturally, the ultimate goal remains a mastery of content and improved learning outcomes.

Making Connections

Check out Chapter 9 on Classroom Management

Want real engagement? Start with ensuring active learning. When you ask your students a question, do you always pick the few with their hands raised? Do you move on once one or two students have answered? Instead, we suggest that teachers encourage every student to answer every question asked throughout the day. How do you do that without losing all your time? Some simple examples (low- to high-tech) might include: (a) using clickers, (b) asking students to stand or sit depending on the answer, or (c) using bring your own devices (BYOD) with socrative.com. Any of these formative assessment tools can change student behavior, as well as allow teachers to measure who does and who does not understand a concept. Oftentimes, when we discuss classroom management, we talk about managing behavior. In Chapter 9 on classroom management in this book, author Rebecca Mieliwocki clarifies that classroom management involves both behavior and instructional management. We concur and suggest that teachers should be managing not just behavior but also the engagement of all learners. A student can be sitting quietly with absolutely no behavior issues, but she's completely disengaged in the lesson; that's something we don't want to see anymore.

In fact, the shift in toward College and Career Ready Standards and the push in education in general related to more inquiry-based instruction requires an increase in student discourse. (We know, many of us have spent years trying to get our kids to stop talking all the time . . . now we're asked to encourage it! But hang with us. There's a rationale here. And it's a good one.) Many students with or without disabilities may be shy to talk, find they need more time to share their opinion, or might need coach-

Plugged In

www.teachthought
.com/technology/26-
teacher-tools-to-create-
online-assessments

ing or scaffolding to ensure they are successful. Providing safe and ongoing ways to participate ensures they are not disengaged and provides for more robust assessment opportunities. A plethora of online assessment tools exist. Included in this article is a summary of 26 great tools to try that really work. Try a few. You'll love them.

Why worry about engagement at all? Well, researchers involved in looking at student engagement found that disengaged behavior is directly linked to dropping out of school (Reschly & Christenson, 2006). The participation-identification model proposes that if students participate or are engaged in the school setting, regardless of whether it's in an academic or social context, the student will begin to identify with school, thus creating a positive cycle centered on school success (Finn, 1989). That doesn't surprise any of us, does it? To engage students in the academic setting, it is important to consider the individual needs of each student. Classrooms across the country are comprised of diverse learners who need to be catered to academically, socially, and behaviorally. Catering to students? If that idea bothers you, just think about it as differentiation; all you are doing is being a great teacher by figuring out what each student needs and then figuring out how to get it to him so he can be successful. If you are doing this proactively, we call it Universal Design for Learning. No catering apron required.

School engagement and self-advocacy also have the potential to affect long-term academic and social outcomes for all students (Errey & Wood, 2011). Previous researchers have reported that a strong, albeit negative, relationship exists between school engagement and school dropout (Reschly & Christenson, 2006). Students are engaged? They tend not to drop out of school. It is as simple as that. So how do we engage them? We suggest that what really works are (a) Project-Based Learning (PBL), (b) peer support/collaborative structures, and (c) self-management strategies, all of which can involve some form of technology.

Project-Based Learning. Project-Based Learning is an instructional model whereby students learn by investigating and solving authentic problems and projects (Blumenfeld et al., 1991). Although PBL is a student-centered model of education, that does not mean that teachers no longer have a role in the classroom; in fact, their role is highly critical to the overall success of PBL. Successful implementation begins with a classroom climate of openness and inquiry, as well as effective social structures (Barron et al., 1998). Classroom teachers must create this climate of cooperative work by encouraging out-of-the-box thinking, questioning, and student discourse. Great social media tools and various components of the Google platform (e.g., Google Hangouts, Google Helpout, and Google Docs) can all help with PBL activities. Remember, all PBL models are created with problems and projects as the core outcome. Provide more of a Universal Design for Learning (UDL) approach, and let students use an array of technologies within the PBL models (Morra & Reynolds, 2010). The principles of UDL are the following: (a) provide multiple means of representation, (b) provide multiple means of action and expression, and (c) provide multiple means of engagement (Rose & Meyer, 2000). Although UDL has not been as extensively researched as the other components we recommended, allowing students with disabilities multiple ways to express and show their skills will certainly cater to the unique needs of diverse students (Morra & Reynolds, 2010). Obviously, you'll need to add technology to your list of choices for students to engage, express, and represent their knowledge. (Want to learn more about UDL? Read Chapter 11 by Dr. Tamarah M. Ashton!) Additionally, throughout the use of PBL, students must be provided with necessary scaffolds, multiple ways to express their learning, and opportunities to self-reflect, assess, and revise their work (Barron et al., 1998). What better way to help them shape the problem than by allowing students to work in cooperative groups to integrate technological tools in order to address the problem posed. Remember, this might be the perfect time for your students to introduce *you* to a useful technological device or app!

Making Connections

Check out Chapter 11 on Universal Design for Learning

Peer Support. Students can address any lesson using various types of peer structures. The use of peer structures is clearly supported in the literature to increase engagement; it is so clearly supported that it made our top three as something that really works for engaging learners. Peer structures are also natural conduits to integrate an array of technologies. Consider how to use peer tutoring (same age or cross age) via Skype or embrace the highly engaging role that cooperative learning can play in your classroom, with each student being given a different role for learning and using technology. Peer structures allow students to learn and teach each other as a means to better understand the content being covered (Hughes, Carter, Hughes, Bradford, & Copeland, 2002). You already know that secondary students typically like to work together in class. How cool is it that you can validate the use of small groups because you know combining rich evidence-based practice with an array of technological tools to effectively engage students?

Self-Management Strategies. The caveat with both technology and engagement is that synergy is needed in both cases for the learner to have some level of self-discipline. Ever go onto the computer and spend more time on Facebook or checking e-mail than completing the task assigned? Welcome to the temptation students face between writing that paragraph and going off on a random search for the latest and greatest YouTube video. Clearly, with both technology and engagement, you need to have synergy in both cases to attain some level of self-discipline. Self-management techniques do work and typically involve students using self-monitoring, self-evaluation, and self-instruction (Mooney, Ryan, Uhing, Reid, & Epstein, 2005). When using a self-management strategy, students monitor and record their own behavior, academically and socially, to increase academic outcomes (Mooney et al., 2005). Consider today how self-management tools could be electronic. A great discussion about tools, many of which involve technology and self-management, can be found at the Intervention Central website identified on our Plugged In box. We suggest you consider looking at ClassDojo or Goalbook and other personal time management apps, along with numerous other low-tech tools, such as behavioral rating sheets, to ensure time with technology is truly engaged time for learning.

Plugged In

www
.interventioncentral.org

Now, as you begin to think about what really works with technology, be sure to keep your thinking laser focused on engaged learning—not just on buying more stuff. Shiny objects can dazzle learners, but being dazzled may not produce the outcomes we all desire in this high stakes, learning outcome-driven environment. As we noted, technology is not the only answer, but if you want to do what works, stop fighting and start learning from your students about what works for them. . . . What technological tools do they use? What keeps them engaged? Keep in mind, we will always continue to evolve as a society, and the jobs of the future will include higher and higher levels of technology competency, so think about how you might use some of the ideas provided to get kids ready for the year 2080 and beyond.

In the next sections, we funneled down activities we see frequently that do not enhance engagement or technology use and those we wish teachers would do more of. Read on, and take copious notes . . . on your tablet, smart phone, laptop, or even with a pen and paper.

STOP IF YOU WANT AN ENGAGED CLASSROOM IN THE WORLD TODAY . . .

Teachers

✗ **STOP teaching to those who already learn the way you teach.** Look at your daily assessments, observe your students' behavior, and think about who is disengaged and how they learn. Then, change the way you teach to these students.

✗ **STOP using a one-size-fits-all strategy.** Whether it is technology, cooperative learning, or peer tutoring, consider a range of social, technological, and engagement activities daily. Students learn differently but also engage differently, so broaden the menu of options.

✗ **STOP talking.** Students are not engaged when the teacher is doing all of the talking. Make everything about students—let them do the talking, drawing, moving, and/or listening to each other. Make sure they know that these activities help them to learn.

✗ **STOP removing technology from kids as they move from one grade to another.** Let kids state what they need, and give it to them, from birth and on throughout their lives. Too many times, technology is teacher selected, instead of student driven. We have to stop allowing access or engagement in one grade or content area, but not another. We should allow students to learn the way they learn, whether that is with a paper and pencil or with a tablet computer.

✗ **STOP trying to micromanage all technology.** Let kids use what they want to use. Students have their own technologies, but schools and classrooms try to restrict the use of these technologies instead of embracing the billions of dollars of self-purchased tools. The movement to use Bring Your Own Device (BYOD) is an essential tool, but students must be provided with clear directives and class parameters to ensure proper use of their devices.

✗ **STOP making it about *stuff*.** Look at the verb instead of the noun; don't just buy an app—find an app that changes outcomes in math. Let the verb of what you want students to do be the driving force. Instead of thinking, "We need to buy more iPads," you should be thinking about what you want the iPad to *do*.

Administrators

✖ **STOP creating policies that work against the use of creative teachers.** BYOD can be used well and effectively, but many teachers will avoid figuring out its use if the school policy is "no cell phones, no iPads, no . . . no . . . no . . . ."

✖ **STOP thinking old school.** Technology moves more quickly than we can keep up. Try not to hold firm to how teachers used to teach and how curriculum used to be designed. Be open to a curriculum committee that eschews textbooks in favor of online research and virtual field trips.

GO WANT TO UP YOUR ENGAGEMENT? THEN, YOU NEED TO

Teachers, DO This

✓ **ASSESS who is and is not *learning* or *engaged* on a daily basis.** As you reflect each day, do not just think about who learned the class objective, but also ask this question: How engaged were the students? Did your students who were gifted learn immediately and master the content but then quickly become disengaged? Did your student who struggles academically or socially fail to master the lesson due to a lack of engagement? Either way, ask students who are disengaged what you might change in your teaching to make them more active in their own learning. Middle and high schoolers can certainly tell you what they'd like more or less of in their class. Consider using the form in the resources section (on page 115) to help you think about how you are meeting the needs of students. How will you help those students engage? Is technology warranted? Might it help? If so, what, how, and with whom?

✓ **ENSURE teacher talk is less than 50%.** Ever go to a lecture for an hour and make your grocery list? Remember, students are in school for 6 hours a day, and even 3 hours of listening is too much to ask of a student. Remember, students who struggle often "think differently," so pause and ask students to share their thoughts with their peers. You will have increased engagement; you will be able to assess students understanding. Stand back and watch in awe: As your level of teacher talk decreases, student learning increases.

✓ **USE evidence-based practices.** Cooperative learning, peer tutoring, positive behavioral supports: Commit to learning something new and then use technology to accomplish that learning goal. Beyond a Google search, what could you use to increase engagement? Some of our favorites are Edmodo, Puppet Pals, and Socrative, but remember,

Plugged In

www.edutopia.org/
technology-integration-
research-evidence-
based-programs

randomly selected technology may have the same outcome we had before: We like it, but students find what we selected "boring." Want ideas related to evidence-based practices that use technology for each disparate content area? Check out this helpful resource from Edutopia in the Plugged In box.

✔ **KEEP CURRENT with everything.** Find materials to read (like the NMC report), or find information online (on websites like Edutopia), or even just talk with knowledgeable colleagues to make sure that you are on the cutting edge.

✔ **LEARN and UNLEARN.** The most effective leaders today have to be ready to unlearn as much as they are to learn. Sure, we used to use a fax, but now we scan. We used to e-mail, but now we text or IM. Find shortcuts to do things that are critical. If you need help, use technology to help you. That's what your kids would do!

✔ **EMPOWER kids.** A great way to get students engaged is to give them a role in technology adoption. Think of the school district that bought all PCs for their computer lab, though most of the students at the school, when polled, preferred Macs. What a quick way to disengage the learners at the school! Want to know a real way to include kids in technology adoption? A great website for this is Genyes (www.genyes.org). The leaders of this initiative believe that students should be leading school and district technology initiatives.

✔ **TEACH self-advocacy while keeping technology at the core.** Students need to know which tools will help them be engaged— from a timer, to using Dragon Dictate, to turning on the voice to text when reading. When you make sure that students adopt technology that really works for them, you are helping to ensure they know how to advocate for themselves so that they are able to continue to use those tools in the future.

✔ **DO let kids give and receive with technology.** Consider having international pen pals (there are secure websites), or have your students Skype with older adults on a weekly basis about history questions or a variety of other topics. The point is that kids, especially those with disabilities, need to give as much as they receive, and technology provides an easy way to give back. Have you heard of the Free Rice website (www.freerice.com)? The beauty of this particular site is that it lets all students learn vocabulary across content areas, while giving food to kids who are hungry in other countries. Now you are teaching content, while using technology, while also helping out those in need—that sounds pretty engaging to us!

✔ **INVOLVE a range of service delivery providers to ensure students with disabilities have all of the supports they need to use**

technology. For example, you could involve the Occupational Therapist who comes in once a week to help kids with the physical activity of being able to swipe on the glass pane to use an iPad. She may be there for just one particular student, but teaching this action could be helpful to many in your class. We've already mentioned tools such as Edmodo, Goalbook, and Google docs. Now consider using those same tools for sharing materials and resources for a specific student. Often, a quick 5-minute meeting via Skype or Google Hangouts between professionals can change the way you provide services to a student and is typically invaluable for engagement and learning.

✓ **DON'T BE INTIMIDATED to allow students to BYOD (bring your own device).** School policy and budgets often prevent the use of technology. Teachers frequently fear allowing students to use their own tools because they may get lost, stolen, broken, or used inappropriately. However, research has found that the schools that allow these tools result in students who are more engaged, while teachers are able to use those same devices for content creation (Hartnell-Young & Vetere, 2008), student-centered learning, collaboration (Corbeil & Valdes-Corbeil, 2007), and differentiation of instruction (Kukulska-Hulme, 2007).

Administrators, DO This

✓ **ENGAGE your faculty.** If you use technology with your faculty, they will see opportunities for how to do it with their own students? Consider flipping your faculty meetings, using Google Chat for a curriculum meeting, or having a school wiki for instructional ideas.

✓ **ASK the students and their families.** At the secondary level, students can usually articulate their ideas and may have additional motivation to change the way things are done. Ask them for apps, software, and instructional ideas for improving learning at your school.

LEARNING FROM THE HIGHER EDUCATION HORIZON REPORT (NEW MEDIA CONSORTIUM, 2014)

Level of Challenge	Type of Challenge	What Does It Mean?
Solvable Challenges:		Those that we understand and know how to solve
	Low Digital Fluency of Faculty	How do we get teachers to adopt the technology in students' everyday lives?
	Relative Lack of Rewards for Teaching	What incentives will get teachers to adopt new technology?
Difficult Challenges:		Those we understand but for which solutions are elusive
	Competition from New Models of Education	How do educators have time to do one more thing with so many new initiatives (testing, standards, etc.)?
	Scaling Teaching Innovations	How do we take what works that is innovative and get it in the hands of all teachers?
Wicked Challenges:		Those that are complex to even define, much less address
	Expanding Access	How do we ensure everyone has access to the best in the easiest way possible?
	Keeping Education Relevant	How do we make teachers use technology for learning and make it not just about the technology?

Years to Adoption	Technology	What Is It?
One Year or Less	Flipped Classroom	Send home the low-level tasks (watching a video, reading to find facts or Google it) and spend class time applying basic knowledge.
One Year or Less	Learning Analytics	Find ways to use what we already know about students' learning profiles instead of always creating new ones.
2–3 years	3-D Printing	Being able to print with materials and new products.
2–3 years	Games and Gamification	Using games for learning.
4–5 years	Quantified Self	Using data and storing data to have a more comprehensive view of a learner.
4–5 years	Virtual Assistants	OnStar in your car, Siri on your iPhone, and the Mayday button on the Kindle. The future will provide you will immediate assistants for many tasks that are all virtual.

Source: Adapted from New Media Consortium (2014).

ASSESSING ENGAGEMENT AND CHANGING YOUR BEHAVIOR

Assessment of Your Lesson Today

Student Engagement

Teacher Behaviors

☐ What population of students were disengaged?

☐ Did I have all students answer all questions?

☐ Were students engaged through all types of intelligence?

☐ Did students talk with each other on topic the majority of class time?

☐ Were all students equally involved?

☐ Did I focus on very specific target skills and assess the target?

☐ Were boys as equally involved as girls?

☐ Were my examples boy and girl friendly?

Three things I will do differently to increase student engagement that reflects changes in my behavior.

_____

_____

_____

HOW DID YOU ADDRESS EACH TYPE OF MULTIPLE INTELLIGENCE IN YOUR CLASSROOM TODAY?

Use this checklist daily as you plan your instruction. If you co-teach, a great role for your partner would be to use this form throughout the lesson to ensure you both are addressing the range of learners in your classroom.

Multiple Intelligence Checklist	✔	Ideas for Each
Kinesthetic (body smart)		
Musical (musical smart)		
Naturalistic (nature smart)		
Spatial (picture thinker)		
Linguistic (word smart)		
Interpersonal (people smart)		
Intrapersonal (self-smart)		
Existential (deep thinking smart)		
Logical-Mathematical (numbers/reasoning smart)		

SAMPLE LESSON

Essential Question	
What is an adaptation?	
Learning Goal(s):	
Students will be able to state the characteristics of an animal that could not exist without its unique adaptation.	
Formative Assessments	Define "adaptation" orally and in writing. (A change or the process of change by which an organism or species becomes better suited to its environment.) Identify animals with adaptations. Identify animals' specific adaptations and the functions of those adaptations.
Ensuring types of intelligence	Allow students to make a short song about their animals. (Musical) Allow students to create their own adaption to show they understand how adaptations work. (Visual) Encourage students to play charades and act the various adaptations they have read about. (Kinesthetic) Designing a new animal on the computer using 3-D graphics.
Lesson activity	Engage students in a web-enabled scavenger hunt. Students should search for descriptions, characteristics, and examples of various animal adaptations.
Technology integration	Use blabberize.com or oddcast.com to sing their song. Allow students to watch YouTube videos of animal adaptations to reinforce the concept in centers. Allow students to use VoiceThread to make a comic strip about their animal and it's adaptation as their final assignment. Watch a documentary video on animal adaptations. Direct students to an online virtual zoo to explore more animal characteristics.
Academic Vocabulary	
Adaptation **Evolve** **Migration** **Camouflage**	

REFERENCES

Barron, B. S., Schwartz, D. L., Vye, N. J., Moore, A., Petrosino, A., Zech, L., & Bransford, J. D. (1998). Doing with understanding: Lessons from research on problem- and project-based learning. *Journal of the Learning Sciences, 7*(3–4), 271–311.

Blumenfeld, P. C., Soloway, E., Marx, R. W., Krajcik, J. S., Guzdial, M., & Palincsar, A. (1991). Motivating project-based learning: Sustaining the doing, supporting the learning. *Educational Psychologist, 26*(3–4), 369–398.

Corbeil, J. R., & Valdes-Corbeil, M. E. (2007). Are you ready for mobile learning? *EDUCAUSE Quarterly, 30*(2), 51–58.

Datnow, A., Park, V., & Kennedy-Lewis, B. (2012). High school teachers' use of data to inform instruction. *Journal of Education for Students Placed at Risk, 17*(4), 247–265.

Errey, R., & Wood, G. (2011). Lessons from a student engagement pilot study: Benefits for students and academics. *Australian Universities' Review, 53*(1), 21–34.

Finn, C. E. (1989). A nation still at risk. *Commentary, 87*(5), 17–23.

Hartnell-Young, E., & Vetere, F. (2008). A means of personalizing learning: Incorporating old and new literacies in the curriculum with mobile phones. *Curriculum Journal, 19*, 283–292.

Hughes, C., Carter, E. W., Hughes, T., Bradford, E., & Copeland, S. R. (2002). Effects of instructional versus non-instructional roles on the social interactions of high school students. *Education and Training in Mental Retardation and Developmental Disabilities, 37*(2), 146–162.

Jackson, B. T., & Hilliard, A. (2013). Too many boys are failing in American schools: What can we do about it? *Contemporary Issues in Education Research, 6*(3), 311–316.

Kukulska-Hulme, A. (2007). Mobile usability in educational contexts: What have we learnt? *International Review of Research in Open and Distance Learning, 8*(2), 1–16.

Merriam-Webster Dictionary. (2014). Disengagement. Retrieved from http://www.merriam-webster.com/dictionary/disengagement

Mooney, P., Ryan, J. B., Uhing, B. M., Reid, R., & Epstein, M. H. (2005). A review of self-management interventions targeting academic outcomes for students with emotional and behavioral disorders. *Journal of Behavioral Education, 14*(3), 203–221.

Morra, T., & Reynolds, J. (2010). Universal Design for Learning: Application for technology-enhanced learning. *Inquiry, 15*(1), 43–51.

New Media Consortium. (2014). *NMC horizon report: 2014 higher education edition.* Austin, TX: Author.

Reschly, A., & Christenson, S. (2006). Prediction of dropout among students with mild disabilities: A case for the inclusion of student engagement variables. *Remedial and Special Education, 27*(5), 276–292.

Rose, D., & Meyer, A. (2000). Universal Design for Learning. *Journal of Special Education Technology, 15*(1), 67–70.

Smyth, J., McInerney, P., & Fish, T. (2013). Blurring the boundaries: From relational learning towards a critical pedagogy of engagement for disengaged disadvantaged young people. *Pedagogy, Culture, and Society, 21*(2), 299–320.

RECOMMENDED READINGS

* Articles on www.edutopia.org/
* Articles from www.edtechmagazine.com
* 21st Century Learning & Technology tools from Corwin's e-library at www.corwin.com

GO EVEN FURTHER WITH
THIS TOPIC ON THE WORLD WIDE WEB

* www.edmodo.com
* www.classroom20.com
* www.edupln.ning.com
* www.masteryconnect.com
* www.genyes.org
* www.nmc.org/horizon-project
* www.co-operation.org/home/introduction-to-cooperative-learning
* www.interventioncentral.org www.teachthought.com/technology/26-teacher-tools-to-create-online-assessments
* www.interventioncentral.org/

THE Apps WE LOVE

* Flashcards
* Puppet Pals
* Bitsboard
* Educreations Interactive Whiteboard

8

Perfectly Positive Behavior

Brittany L. Hott

Texas A&M University–Commerce

Dodie Limberg

University of South Carolina

WHAT REALLY WORKS IN POSITIVE BEHAVIOR SUPPORT IN THE SECONDARY CLASSROOM

A Rationale for Positive Behavioral Supports

There are multiple factors that may affect adolescents' well-being and ability to succeed academically. For example, in 2011, 20% of students reported being bullied at school, 32% reported being in a physical fight, and 7% reported a suicide attempt (Centers for Disease Control and Prevention, 2011). Additionally, 1 in 4, or approximately 19 million children in the United States under the age of 18 are exposed to alcohol abuse or dependence in their family (Grant, 2000). Further, according to the U.S. Department of Health and Human Services (2000), 1 in 5 children and adolescents experience a mild to moderate mental health issue, while 1 in 20 experience a serious emotional or mental illness. As a result of the mental health and environmental concerns faced by students, school personnel are increasingly expected to provide prevention-oriented interventions to reduce negative student outcomes (Fenning et al., 2012). All while trying to teach students some content and dealing with adolescent hormones!

Positive Behavior Supports (PBS) is an evidence-based approach to address student discipline, academic achievement, and personal/social development (Lewis, Barrett, Sugai, & Horner, 2010). Yes, we threw an acronym at you, but don't worry. We'll explain it. Let's start with why PBS is important.

There is a rich body of research supporting the use of PBS in Grades K–12. In secondary (Grades 6–12) settings, PBS may be challenging to implement due to the different schedules and faculty involved with each student. Therefore, PBS is most effective at the secondary levels when it is adopted schoolwide and supported by all stakeholders (i.e., administrators, teachers, school counselors, staff, related service personnel, and parents).

PBS is implemented at three tiers of increasingly intense interventions. The first tier (primary prevention) is designed to prevent new cases of problem behavior and includes interventions that all students receive. In primary prevention, all students learn about expectations and appropriate behaviors are reinforced. In the second tier (secondary level prevention), practitioners focus on smaller group or simple individualized interventions with students already experiencing concerns in order to reduce the number of current cases of problematic behavior. Within the third tier (tertiary level prevention), the focus is on highly individualized and intensive interventions for students who continue to experience behavioral challenges despite previous intervention attempts. The goal at the tertiary level is to reduce the intensity and severity of the current cases. The three tiers provide a framework for secondary educators to use as resources to implement preventative strategies that increase all students' academic and behavior performance. Overwhelmed? Don't be. We'll walk you through this and give you concrete DOs and DON'Ts related to PBS, even if this is your first go at it. First though, we have to convince you why it is so important! Read on.

POSITIVE BEHAVIOR SUPPORTS: AN OVERVIEW OF THE EVIDENCE

According to Lewis and Sugai (1999), the core components of PBS include (a) a purpose statement, (b) expectations (i.e., positive behaviors) that are shared and understood schoolwide, (c) techniques to support expectations, (d) techniques to discourage negative behavior, and (e) use of data to monitor and evaluate PBS. Coffey and Horner (2012) found that schools who utilize data-based decision-making, in combination with administration support and a clear communication plan of schoolwide expectations, have more sustainable PBS programs.

Nocera, Whitbread, and Nocera (2014) examined the effectiveness of a PBS program implemented in a middle school (Grades 7–8). The program was applied to address all three tiers. Tier 1 included (a) a positive reward system that recognized positive behavior of all students, (b) a revised discipline system that clearly outlined all the expectations and consequences, and (c) increased visibility of faculty during nonclass time. Tier II focused on conflict resolution. Tier III included Functional Behavior Analysis (Miller, Tansy, & Hughes, 1998) for those students who needed it. After 2 years of implementation of the PBS program, office referrals decreased by 36% and suspensions decreased by 39%, suspensions of special education students declined by 51%, and overall problem behaviors decreased by 40%. According to the faculty, the most beneficial components of the program included (a) the reward system, (b) faculty investment to the program, (c) administrative support and leadership, (d) a consistent approach to responding to behavior, and (e) the support of a school data team that guided the program based on data-driven decisions. See? Not overwhelming at all.

Making Connections

Check out Chapter 9 on Classroom Management

Fitzgerald, Geraci, and Swanson (2014) evaluated a PBS program, developed by a district team, and implemented it in both a middle and high school. The team initiated eight components of the program that were based on previous research. Positive incentives included (a) students were recommended to have lunch with the principal, (b) students received coupons for ice cream on their birthday, (c) an antibullying awareness presentation which included students pledging against bullying, (d) student inservice days, (e) after-school activity days, (f) a reward system that recognized students who exemplified PRIDE (participation, respect, integrity, dedication, and excellence), (g) recognizing a star homeroom, and (h) an opportunity for students to recognize teachers. After a year of the program, there was a decrease in verbal warnings (78%), detentions (73%), out-of-school suspensions (50%), in-school suspension (36%), bus discipline (50%), total absences (37%), excused tardiness (77%), and unexcused tardiness (56%). In fact, at the end of the school day, all teachers and students sang "Happy" by Pharrell Williams together. Okay, that last line is a joke, but we needed to make sure you were paying attention.

Flannery, Fenning, Kato, and McIntosh (2014) compared problem behaviors in eight high schools that implemented PBS to four high schools that did not (36,653 students total) for 3 years. During year one, baseline data were collected at each school, and faculty and staff (at the eight PBS schools) were provided training and professional development focused on how to conduct PBS at their schools. During years two and three, PBS was infused into the eight schools. Overall, problem behaviors, specifically office discipline referrals, decreased in the schools that implemented PBS compared to the schools that did not. Flannery and colleagues suggest that PBS at the high school level requires some adjustments to meet the developmental needs of high school students. For example, getting students involved in the communication plan (i.e., sharing it with other students) of PBS is important to support peer influence. Additionally, the reward system should be adjusted to what is important to high school students such as parking spaces, prom tickets, and gift cards, as opposed to recognizing good behavior during announcements. Overall, the results of this study support the effectiveness of PBS at the high school level.

This purpose of this chapter is to provide you with effective strategies for implementing positive behavior support (PBS) programs.

STOP: SUGGESTIONS TO OPTIMIZE PBS

When implemented in conjunction with quality academic instruction, schoolwide PBS translates to improved achievement and social outcomes for secondary students (e.g., Horner, Sugai, & Anderson, 2010). Putting a STOP to these common pitfalls will help to avoid PBS implementation barriers.

- ✘ **STOP creating individual expectations and rules.** PBS involves the application of positive, schoolwide systems that require that all members of the school to operate from the same agreed upon set of expectations. Understand the schoolwide PBS plan and implement classroom procedures that fit within the plan. Operating within the plan will maximize student success and be easier for everyone (Strout, 2005).

- ✘ **STOP using punishment as the first strategy to decrease undesirable behaviors.** Punishment is a strategy that involves negative consequences (e.g., time out, detention, suspension, and negative reports to parents) in an effort to decrease maladaptive behaviors (Alberto & Troutman, 2013) that often disrupts instructional time. Always use the least intrusive measure to decrease negative behavior (Sugai & Horner, 2009).

- ✘ **STOP sending students to the office and using suspensions without exploring the reasons for misbehavior.** Suspensions lead to increased dropout rates and missed instruction (Walker & Hott, in press) that translate to devastating consequences such as poor grades, decreased graduation rates, and increased likelihood of entering the juvenile justice system. If the student is looking to avoid instruction, a suspension just gives him what he wanted in the first place!

✖ **STOP working in isolation.** Effective PBS systems require active involvement of *all* stakeholders including students, parents, staff, teachers, and administrators (Gage & McDaniel, 2012). If a social or behavioral challenge is affecting one student, the behavior impacts an entire school's progress (e.g., riding the bus safely, transitioning between classes).

✖ **STOP using elementary materials.** Using smiley faces, cartoons, or primary materials in secondary settings decreases student buy-in and impedes social progress. Figure out what works for the students in your school. That doesn't mean you can't use a gold star; it just means you have to know your students and what motivates them.

✖ **STOP lowering expectations and waiting for students to fail.** School rules and expectations must be taught and consistently reinforced to maintain a safe learning environment. View behavioral challenges as teachable moments. Focus on setting individual goals and determining the supports needed to meet the goal.

✖ **STOP blaming students, families, staff, teachers, and/or administration.** PBS systems are rooted in prevention, instruction, and data-based decision-making (Eber, Sugai, Smith, & Scott, 2002). Placing blame on individual or groups of stakeholders will decrease PBS implementation fidelity and effectiveness.

✖ **STOP making decisions based on feelings or perceptions.** Use schoolwide, classroom, and individual data to make decisions. Implement a plan to prevent, deal with, and follow up on common behavioral infractions. If an adjustment or correction is needed, develop and communicate the plan. Yes, data collection and plan making can take time, but we'll give you strategies for this in the next section. The time will be worth it!

GO PBS: RECOMMENDATIONS FOR SECONDARY SETTINGS

While there are some barriers that need to stop, there are many strategies that if implemented with fidelity will improve outcomes for students and staff.

✓ **USE data to make decisions.** When starting a schoolwide PBS system, collect baseline data. Student, parent, and staff surveys are a means of providing stakeholder input. Review disciplinary data for the most common locations, infractions, times of the year with the highest infractions, and infraction patterns between students with and without disabilities (Office of Special Education Programs, 2014). After implementing a PBS model, continue to review data for patterns and make adjustments. Data collection can seem daunting with the many other daily responsibilities. A quick weekly review of data (e.g., incidents that occurred, location, and time) during team meetings can help identify patterns and develop a plan of action. Check out some of the websites listed at the end of the chapter to provide additional examples, templates, and easy progress monitoring tools.

✓ **DO implement the PBS plan with fidelity.** Fidelity refers to the degree that a program or intervention is implemented as designed (Smith, Daunic, & Taylor, 2007). All members of the team should have an in-depth understanding of the PBS plan and how to implement and monitor the plan. It is important to determine who will teach expectations and how progress will be monitored. A process for addressing problems helps to avoid small issues snowballing to more systematic challenges. Lane and Beebe-Frankenberger (2004) offer many concrete suggestions to strengthen fidelity.

✓ **HAVE a universal set of rules and clearly defined procedures for each area of the school** (e.g., bus, cafeteria, gym, hallways, and classrooms). Recognize that all areas and classrooms will not have the same expectations. For example, a chemistry classroom will have the same rules, but different expectations, than a band room. However, procedures for both the chemistry classroom and band room should fit within the schoolwide PBS system and rules. Check out the Classroom Rules and Procedures Planning Form that can be used as a guidance document for developing individual classroom procedures.

✓ **COLLABORATE to develop, enhance, and evaluate the PBS model.** Involve and clearly communicate with the *entire* PBS team. Expectations, rules, and consequences should be developed collaboratively with representatives from the student body, families, staff, faculty, and administration. Visual displays such as posters can be used to provide reminders of rules and positive consequences for demonstrating prosocial behaviors.

✓ **CONTINUE to involve parents and families at the secondary level.** At a minimum, send home letters to *all* families describing rules, expectations, and both positive and negative consequences. Maintain a system where parents are members of the PBS team and have a means to voice concerns as they arise. Remember to involve parents when students demonstrate positive behaviors and/

Making Connections

Check out Chapter 20 on Family Collaboration

or make progress. A quick e-mail, note, or phone call to share positive behavior or academic success is often well received and helps to foster a positive relationship with students and families.

✓ **EMPOWER specialists (e.g., school psychologists, reading specialists, and behavior specialists) to support students, staff, families, teachers, and the administrative team.** As with all initiatives, challenges will arise and some members of the team will need more support. Seek out the advice of colleagues who have expertise. Two (or more) heads are always better than one!

✓ **PROVIDE ongoing quality professional development for all members of the school team.** Best practice is to draft a plan and then make adjustments as needed. Differentiate staff development to meet the needs of team members. For example, support personnel (e.g., secretaries, nurses, and custodians) will need to be aware of the entire PBS system as well as procedures that impact areas of responsibility. A clear plan for requesting assistance and follow-up professional development should be in place.

✓ **FOCUS on preventative measures as a first line of defense against problematic behaviors.** Examples include (a) actively supervising students at all times, (b) clearly stating objectives and assessments, (c) consistently checking for student understanding of both academic and social expectations, (d) providing opportunities for students to respond in multiple ways, (e) allocating the majority of time for instruction, and (f) providing frequent positive interactions with students (Lewis & Sugai, 1999). See the Three Tiered Model of Prevention we provide in the Resources section of this chapter.

✓ **MAINTAIN high expectations for all students.** Simple steps like incorporating a variety of response tools can maximize student participation, decrease student disruptions, and ensure assessment of each student. When using traditional lecture formats with hand raising, only one student has the opportunity to respond. Free online student response systems such as Infuse Learning (www .infuselearning.com) allow *all* students to use mobile devices or iPad technology to answer every question the teacher poses. The software calculates total correct and incorrect responses, allowing the teacher to make quick instructional decisions and keep students engaged. No technology, no problem. A quick trip to the hardware store to purchase shower board is another option. Shower board can be cut in to 8.5in x 11in squares for a small fee. Simply duct-tape the edges and provide dry erase markers. Voila, instant whiteboards. For more strategies, check out the tiered intervention strategies list provided.

✓ **DO collaborate.** Involve colleagues and support personnel in developing and evaluating a plan of action for students experiencing difficulty. Functional Behavior Assessment (FBA) and Behavioral

Intervention Plans (BIP) are legally required for students with special needs with frequent suspensions (see Brigham & Hott, 2011; Hott, Walker, & Brigham, 2014; Walker & Hott, in press). Don't know what those are or how to create them? Don't worry. . . . There are special educators and other specialists in your school who do. Collaborate with them. A few websites and resources are provided below to help.

✓ **RECOGNIZE students when they make good choices.** Praise is free and highly effective! Verbal praise, loud praise, soft praise, group praise, individual praise, "shout out" cards. . . the list is enormous! Remember to ensure that praise is specific (e.g., "Michael, you have fantastic ideas. . . . Your persuasive essay included detailed, descriptive sentences. This will draw the reader to your paper. Excellent work!"). "Shout out" cards can be created with index cards or printed on colored paper. Simply write a praise statement and provide a student with a copy. If you know that a student is working on a specific goal, keeping track of praise statements provided is important. The Student Goals template on page 133 can be a helpful way to monitor corrections and praise provided to students experiencing difficulty or needing extra support.

SAMPLE POSITIVE
BEHAVIORAL SUPPORT MODEL

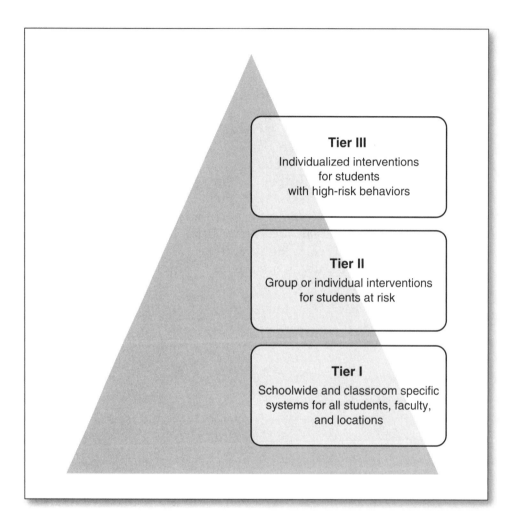

Tier III

Individualized interventions
for students
with high-risk behaviors

Tier II

Group or individual interventions
for students at risk

Tier I

Schoolwide and classroom specific
systems for all students, faculty,
and locations

TIERED STRATEGIES AND INTERVENTIONS

Tier 1 Strategies (Goal—reach 80%–90% of students)

- High rates of positive teacher-to-student interactions
    - Provide at least four positives to one negative (Daly, Martens, Barnett, Witt, & Olson, 2007)
    - Aim for a positive interaction every 5 minutes (Gunter, Jack, DePaepe, Reed, & Harrison, 1994)
- Active supervision in ALL areas
    - Monitor building entry/exits, hallways, bathrooms, cafeteria, gym
    - Praise positive behaviors
    - In classrooms, move around and continuously scan the classroom
- Facilitate smooth and efficient transitions between classes and activities
- Develop and teach routines (e.g., 2 minute transition time, walk directly to classes)
    - When an issue arises, be consistent and "business-like"
- Focus on quality planning and instruction
    - Minimize transitions, noninstructional time
    - Ensure each lesson has a focus
    - Majority of class time is devoted to instruction rather than behavioral correction
    - Have additional activities in case the class session is completed quicker than planned
    - Materials are available
    - Lesson pace is brisk
- Promote active responding
    - Incorporate a variety of response tools (Hott & Walker, 2012)
    - Allow multiple ways of responding (e.g., individual, choral, written vs. gestures, cooperative learning groups)
    - Embrace technology (Beard Carpenter, & Johnston, 2011)
    - Regularly check for student understanding
    - Provide opportunities for guided and independent practice throughout the lesson
    - Outline next activities and transitions

- Use preventative and proactive measures
  - Follow school rules and classroom procedures
  - Post rules and procedures
  - When issues arise, be consistent and "business-like"
  - Deal with minor problem behaviors immediately and positively

Tier 2 Strategies (impacts 10%–15% of students)

- Consider academic supports
- Provide social skills instruction
- Incorporate self-management strategies
- Emphasize parent training and collaboration
- Monitor progress, ongoing individual or small group assessment
- Use Evidenced-Based Interventions (see Anderson & Borgmeier, 2010)

Tier 3 Strategies (impacts 1%–5% of students)

- Functional Behavior Assessment (FBA; see Herschfeldt, Rosenberg, & Bradshaw, 2010; Scott et al., 2004)
- Behavior Intervention Plan (BIP; see Maag & Katsiyannis, 2006)
- Parent training and collaboration
- Alternatives to suspension and expulsion
- Evidenced-Based Interventions (see Regan & Michaud, 2011)

CLASSROOM RULES AND PROCEDURES PLANNING FORM

This template can be used as a guide to create and develop classroom rules and expectations.

School Rules	Classroom Procedures
1.	1.
2.	2.
3.	3.

Procedures Check

If the answer to one or more questions is no, revise procedures accordingly.

Yes   No   Classroom procedures fit in the school rules

Yes   No   Classroom procedures are MOO (Measurable, Observable, Objective)

Yes   No   Classroom procedures are stated positively

Yes   No   Classroom procedures state what a student should do

Yes   No   Classroom procedures are limited (three to five are sufficient)

Instruction

Who will teach procedures?

When will procedures be taught?

How will procedural compliance be monitored?

Source: Adapted from Herschfeldt et al. (2010); Lewis et al. (2010).

DEALING WITH PROBLEM BEHAVIOR

Common Minor Behavioral Infractions

Infraction	Procedure
Dress code violations	
Cursing	
Gum chewing	
Tardy	
Use of unapproved technology devices	
Other	

Major Behavioral Infractions

Infraction	Procedure
Fighting	
Repeated refusals to comply with teacher directions	
Damage to school property	
Ongoing minor behavioral infractions	
Other	

Source: Adapted from Herschfeldt et al. (2010).

STUDENT GOALS AND POSITIVE/NEGATIVE CORRECTIONS

Student Goals			
Student Name	Goal #1	Goal #2	Goal #3

Source: Adapted from Gardner & Hott (2014).

Student Progress Toward Goals												
	(Student Name)			(Student Name)			(Student Name)			(Student Name)		
	Shout Out Card Sent	+	−	Shout Out Card Sent	+	−	Shout Out Card Sent	+	−	Shout Out Card Sent	+	−
M												
T												
W												
R												
F												

(+) improvement toward goal behavior
(−) behavior negatively affected (blank) no change

Source: Adapted from Gardner & Hott (2014).

REFERENCES

Alberto, P. A., & Troutman, A. C. (2013). *Applied behavior analysis for teachers* (9th ed.). Upper Saddle River, NJ: Prentice Hall.

Anderson, C. M., & Borgmeier, C. (2010). Tier II interventions within the framework of school-wide Positive Behavior Support: Essential features for design, implementation, and maintenance. *Behavioral Analysis and Practice, 3*, 33–45.

Beard, L. A., Carpenter, L. B., & Johnston, L. B. (2011). *Assistive technology access for all students.* Upper Saddle River, NJ: Pearson.

Brigham, F. J., & Hott, B. L. (2011). A brief history of education for children and youths with emotional and behavioral disorders. In F. E. Obiakor, J. P. Bakken, & A. F. Rotatori (Eds.), *Advances in special education: Historical context of special education* (Vol. 21, pp. 151–180). Bingley, United Kingdom: Emerald Group.

Centers for Disease Control and Prevention. (2011). *Youth risk behavior survey.* Atlanta, GA: U.S. Department of Health and Human Services. Retrieved from www.cdc.gov/yrbs

Coffey, J. H., & Horner, R. H. (2012). The sustainability of school-wide Positive Behavior Interventions and Supports. *Exceptional Children, 78*(4), 407–422.

Daly, E. J., Martens, B. K., Barnett, D., Witt, J. C., & Olson, S. C. (2007). Varying intervention delivery in response to intervention: Confronting and resolving challenges with measurement, instruction, and intensity. *School Psychology Review, 36*, 562–581.

Eber, L., Sugai, G., Smith, C. R., & Scott, T. (2002). Wraparound and Positive Behavioral Interventions and Supports in the schools. *Journal of Emotional and Behavioral Disorders, 10*, 171–180.

Fenning, P., Pulaski, S., Gomez, M., Morello, M., Maciel, L., Maroney, E., . . . Maltese, R. (2012). Call to action: A critical need for designing alternatives to suspension and expulsion. *Journal of School Violence, 11*, 105–117.

Fitzgerald, C. B., Geraci, L. M., & Swanson, M. (2014). Scaling up in rural schools using positive behavioral interventions and supports. *Rural Special Education Quarterly, 33*(1), 18–22.

Flannery, K. B., Fenning, P., Kato, M. M., & McIntosh, K. (2014). Effects of school-wide positive behavioral interventions and supports and fidelity of implementation on problem behavior in high schools. *School Psychology Quarterly, 29*(2), 111–124.

Gage, N. A., & McDaniel, S. (2012). Creating smarter classrooms: Data-based decision making for effective classroom management. *Beyond Behavior, 22*(1), 48–55.

Gardner, J. & Hott, B. L. (2014). *Positive Behavioral Supports at the classroom level: Tips and tricks for high school teachers.* Unpublished manuscript, Texas A&M University—Commerce.

Grant, B. F. (2000). Estimates of US children exposed to alcohol abuse and dependence in the family. *American Journal of Public Health, 90*, 112–115.

Gunter, P. L., Jack, S. L., DePaepe, P., Reed, T. M., & Harrison, J. (1994). Effects of challenging behaviors of students with EDB on teacher instructional behavior. *Preventing School Failure, 38*, 35–46.

Herschfeldt, P. A., Rosenberg, M. S., & Bradshaw, C. P. (2010). Function-based thinking: A systemic way of thinking about function and its role in changing student behavior problems. *Beyond Behavior, 19*(3), 12–21.

Horner, R. H., Sugai, G., & Anderson, C. M. (2010). Examining the evidence base for school-wide Positive Behavior Support. *Focus on Exceptional Children*, 42(8), 1–15.

Hott, B. L., & Walker, J. D. (2012). Five tips to increase student participation in the secondary classroom. *Learning Disabilities Forum*. Retrieved from http://www.cldinternational.org/Publications/LdForum.asp

Hott, B. L., Walker, J. D., & Brigham, F. J. (2014). Implementing self-management strategies in the secondary classroom. In A. Cohan & A. Honingsfeld (Eds.), *Breaking the mold of classroom management: What educators should know and do to enable student success* (pp. 19–26). Lanham, MD: R & L Education.

Lane, K. L., & Beebe-Frankenberger, M. (2004). *School-based interventions: The tools you need to succeed*. Boston, MA: Allyn & Bacon.

Lewis, T. J., Barrett, S., Sugai, G., & Horner, R. H. (2010). *Blueprint for school wide positive behavior support training and professional development*. Retrieved from www.pbis.org

Lewis, T. J., & Sugai, G. (1999). Effective behavior support: A systems approach to school-wide management. *Focus on Exceptional Children*, 31(6), 1–24.

Maag, J. W., & Katsiyannis, A. (2006). Behavioral intervention plans: Legal and practical considerations for students with emotional and behavioral disorders. *Behavioral Disorders*, 31, 348–362.

Miller, J. A., Tansy, M., & Hughes, T. L. (1998). Functional behavior assessment: The link between problem behavior and effective interventions in schools. *Current Issues in Education*, 1(5). Retrieved from http://cie.ed.asu.edu/volume1number5

Nocera, E. J., Whitbread, K. M., & Nocera, G. P. (2014). Impact of school-wide positive behavior supports on student behavior in the middle grades. *Research in Middle Level Education Online*, 37(8), 1–14.

Office of Special Education Programs Technical Assistance Center. (2014). *Positive Behavioral Interventions and Supports*. Washington, DC: Author.

Regan, K. S., & Michaud, K. M. (2011). Evidenced-based practices for students with emotional or behavioral disorders. *Beyond Behavior*, 20(2), 40–47.

Scott, T. M., Bucalos, A., Liaupsin, C., Nelson, C. M., Jolivette, K., & DeShea, L. (2004). Using functional behavior assessment in general education settings: Making a case for effectiveness and efficiency. *Beyond Behavior*, 29, 189–201.

Smith, S. W., Daunic, A. P., & Taylor, G. G. (2007). Treatment fidelity in applied educational research: Expanding the adoption and application of measures to ensure evidence-based practice. *Education and Treatment of Children*, 30, 121–134.

Strout, M. (2005). Positive Behavioral Support at the classroom level: Considerations and strategies. *Beyond Behavior*, 27(1), 3–8.

Sugai, G., & Horner, R. (2009). Responsiveness-to-Intervention and school-wide Positive Behavior Supports: Integration of multi-tiered system approaches. *Exceptionality*, 17, 223–237.

U.S. Department of Health and Human Services. (2000). *Report of the Surgeon General's Conference on Children's Mental Health: A national action agenda*. Rockville, MD: Author.

Walker, J. D., & Hott, B. L. (in press). Navigating the Manifestation Determination process: A teacher's perspective. *Beyond Behavior*.

RECOMMENDED READINGS

* Kauffman, J. M., & Brigham, F. J. (2009). *Working with troubled children*. Verona, WI: Attainment.
* Lane, K., Wehby, J., & Cooley, C. (2006). Teacher expectations of students' classroom behavior across the grade span: Which social skills are necessary for student success? *Exceptional Children, 72*, 153–167.
* Lee, D. L., Vostal, B., Lylo, B., & Hua, Y. (2011). Collecting behavioral data in general education settings: A primer for behavioral data collection. *Beyond Behavior, 20*, 22–30.
* Scheuermann, B. K., & Hall, J. A. (2012). *Positive Behavioral Supports for the classroom* (2nd ed.). Upper Saddle River, NJ: Pearson.

GO EVEN FURTHER WITH THIS TOPIC ON THE WORLD WIDE WEB

* www.pbis.org/
* www.apbs.org/new_apbs/genintro.aspx
* flpbs.fmhi.usf.edu/
* www.osepideasthatwork.org/toolkit/behvr_pos.asp
* iris.peabody.vanderbilt.edu/iris-resource-locator/

THE Apps WE LOVE

* Interval Minder
* Behavior Tracker Pro (BTP)
* Behavior Assessment Pro (BAP)
* Tallymander
* D.A.T.A.

9

Classy Classroom Management

Rebecca Mieliwocki
2012 National Teacher of the Year

WHAT REALLY WORKS IN CLASSROOM MANAGEMENT IN THE SECONDARY CLASSROOM

Creating a Classroom Kids Love Coming To

Walk into any classroom in America and within 2 minutes you'll be able to ascertain three important things: (a) how the teacher feels about students, (b) whether the classroom is well run, and (c) how engaged students are in their learning. These powerful atmospheric indicators are hallmarks of a classroom that is successful. Or conversely, a classroom that is in chaos.

Well-run classrooms are simply a joy to be in. A quick look around reveals that everyone seems to know what to do from moment to moment, they know what's expected of them in a variety of situations, and they have some awareness of what might happen next. The start of the class, the transitions, and the closing appear to be smoothly orchestrated. There are routines and systems in place that guide nearly every action. It's as if everyone is operating at the highest possible level. Sounds simple, but creating a classroom like this isn't simple at all. In fact, it takes an enormous amount of deliberate planning and follow-through to create the invisible infrastructures that guide teacher actions and the student experiences while in the room.

Teachers are decision-making machines. From how kids move about the room, to routines for collecting or disseminating work, to absent students getting missed homework, to classroom discussions, to behavior issues—there are dozens of decisions teachers must make each day. These decisions amount to your classroom management plan. Failure to have plans in place spells certain disaster and can threaten to bog down your instruction, debilitate you as a teacher, or even worse, create a climate of chaos and uncertainty for you and your students. No one wants to have the frightening classroom they show on TV. You know the one. Oh the kids are busy all right; busy aiming spitballs at one another, listening to music on their headphones, or making out in the back of the room as the poor, harried teacher scribbles away on the whiteboard, seemingly oblivious to the destruction behind her.

The good news is that there is plenty we can do to keep that from happening. It begins by designing a classroom that runs beautifully because you have created it to do just that. Your classroom, the one you take the time to build from scratch, is one where your unique personality shines, where your love and support of all of your students is immediately evident. It is equitable and fair, and it operates so efficiently that student learning is optimized. It's a place you and your students love being. Ah, doesn't that sound lovely? It's not just a dream though.

All of this takes a tremendous amount of thought. Before you've written one lesson plan or designed one learning activity or field trip, you've got to mastermind the nuts and bolts of running your room. You've got to solidify how you feel about your role as teacher, how you feel about students and learning, what kind of vibe you want your room to feel like, how and when kids can move about the room, protocols for group work, absent students . . . you name it, it needs to be sorted out BEFORE you teach. At first, you might resist pinning yourself down to so many rules or routines or "if this happens, then I'll do that" kind of planning. Don't. Trust me. There's no better use of your time than figuring it all out before the first bell rings.

The purpose of this chapter is to help you find your way as you design that smart, effective infrastructure that will underpin your terrific instruction. It is brimming with practical, relevant, kid- and teacher-friendly solutions that you can employ right away to make sure you are free to do the thing you do best: TEACH!

WHAT IS CLASSROOM MANAGEMENT AND WHY DOES IT MATTER?

A preponderance of recent studies confirms this fact: Effective teachers are the single biggest in-school contributor to student success (Marzano, 2003;

National Commission on Teaching and America's Future, 1996). Even President Barack Obama has stood before the nation and said as much. "From the moment students enter a school, the most important factor in their success is not the color of their skin or the income of their parents, it's the person standing at the front of the classroom. . . . America's future depends on its teachers" (Office of the Press Secretary, 2009). On the surface it sounds so simple. An effective teacher must be someone who knows his or her content thoroughly and has a firm grasp on the many ways students learn best. Surely, if these two qualities exist, then academic success will be an automatic end result.

Not so fast. Being a great teacher requires much, much more than just subject matter competency. It requires more than a love for students and a passion for helping them learn. To be the kind of teacher considered highly effective, there's a third underlying skill that all teachers MUST master if they hope to succeed. You have to be an effective manager of your classroom. You must run a classroom that supports your instruction, which amicably and easily governs the transactions which occur within it, and that provides a safe space for students to engage, learn, and apply the content. Without classroom management, even the most knowledgeable and caring teachers cannot succeed. With it, you and your students can be unstoppable.

According to the Glossary of Education Reform (Great Schools Partnership, 2013), classroom management refers to the wide variety of skills and techniques that teachers use to keep students organized, orderly, focused, attentive, on task, and academically productive during a class. When classroom-management strategies are executed effectively, teachers minimize the behaviors that impede learning for both individual students and groups of students, while maximizing the behaviors that facilitate or enhance learning. Generally speaking, effective teachers tend to display strong classroom-management skills, while the hallmark of the inexperienced or less effective teacher is a disorderly classroom filled with students who are not working or paying attention.

When planning out how you want your classroom to operate, there are three key realms of classroom management that I have personally discovered need your focus and attention: how you approach students individually, the systems you design so that your room functions effectively, and the culture you create with your class collectively.

First, students want to know three things: that you care about them; that your classroom is a safe, fair place for all learners; and that you are in charge. This requires teachers to build strong relationships with the young people they teach. It requires that we display a personal interest in students (Marzano, 2003), have an understanding of what motivates students to behave the way they do so that we can guide them in making smart choices (Glasser, 1999), and that we understand implicitly and without reservation that our students want leadership from us (Chiu & Tulley, 1997). When we work to create warm, accepting, vibrant places for students to spend their time, they are primed for our most important work and theirs: teaching and learning.

Second, strong classrooms are those that feature a predetermined set of structures to govern teacher and student activity. That's not to say that every single possible interaction is preplanned, or that there is no room for epiphany, the aha! moment, or for a wonderful student-led academic diversion. It means that the teacher has spent time to put structures in place that guarantee learning has a strong chance to occur in a space that is safe and well run. Research by Emmer (1984) and Emmer and Evertson (2012) clearly conveys the value of establishing rules and procedures for general classroom behavior, group work, seat work, transitions and interruptions, use of materials and equipment, and beginning and ending the period or the day. Clear expectations for behavior, as well as explicitly stated learning targets or goals, are also key to establishing an environment conducive to student success (Marzano, 2003).

Making Connections

Check out Chapter 8 on Positive Behavior Supports

Third, how you view your students collectively and how you approach the work you do with them can create a culture of inclusiveness, care, and cohesion that makes the school-going experience positive for everyone. In Froyen and Iverson's (1999) study on schoolwide classroom management, there is importance placed on the idea of covenant management which asserts that each classroom in a school is its own unique social system shaped by the expectations and behaviors of the teacher along with the norms present in both the learning community and surrounding one. That means you've given a great deal of careful thought about your own personal teaching philosophy, how you want to see your students, and how you want to be seen by them. You communicate this feeling and philosophy TO your students early on, and each action you take in class amplifies it. Kids know you're firm, fair, and perhaps fun because you've told them those things matter to you. They know you see the entire class as a group of amazing kids with a lot of potential. They know you care about their mental strength and their emotional health. They know you see them collectively AND individually, and your decisions and actions are based on what's best for all of you and for the mission at hand: academic and personal success. This is the covenant and compact you weave with your kids. When teachers welcome diversity and have the ability to differentiate their management strategies for unique students, groups, and situations (Brophy, 1996), they begin to build strong, positive classroom communities that provide an enormous return on investment. Students from classrooms like this begin to internalize the expectations placed upon them, govern themselves more appropriately, and work hard to preserve their learning environment.

As you work to build your own classroom into one where great and wonderful things happen every day, keep in mind how important it is that your approach to students and the strategies you choose to run your room support and encourage excellence from both of you.

LET'S PRETEND THIS NEVER HAPPENED: THINGS WE CAN STOP DOING IN THE CLASSROOM

- ✖ **STOP flying by the seat of your pants and leaving classroom organization to whim and chance.** Certain situations may present the need for on-the-fly decision-making, but truly effective classroom operating systems are designed thoughtfully and deliberately so that both the students and the teacher can thrive.
- ✖ **STOP confusing rules with procedures.** Teachers should have fewer than five core statements about behavior and class culture that are inviolable and merit disciplinary consequences if broken. Everything else about how your classroom operates should be considered a procedure and one that needs to be modeled, taught, and retaught as often as is needed for it to become routine. When students break your rules, apply discipline. When they don't follow routines or procedures, reteach them (Wong & Wong, 1998).
- ✖ **STOP expecting others to care more about your students than you do, especially when it comes to behavior requiring disciplinary consequences.** Too many times, teachers reach a boiling point with students and cast them out to be dealt with by administrators. Administrators, having no context for all that emotion, often assign a consequence that teachers don't feel appropriate. The best solution is to handle virtually everything yourself in house. There will be the rare occasion when other authorities will need to do this work, but they are rare. Only you truly understand what happened, why it happened, and the best course of corrective action. Only you will be able to convey this process to parents appropriately to seek a solution that resolves the situation. Absolutely inform your administrators of your process so they are in the loop, but handle your business yourself whenever possible (hint: it's nearly always possible).
- ✖ **STOP sending students out of your classroom.** Typically, at the secondary level, students enjoy a respite from class and some even seek to misbehave in the hope that they'll be sent out and not have to complete the work of the day. Let that be something that NEVER happens in your room. Teach with the implicit belief that there is NOTHING a student can do to keep you from teaching or keep them from your instruction, the work you assign, or the community

of learners they are a part of. When you send kids away, you are subconsciously transmitting the idea that your class, the content, and student learning are not a priority.

✘ **STOP letting students get away with not doing the work you assign.** There should be nothing that gets in the way of your assignment and a student turning it in. Whether a student needs extra time, extra help, a differentiated task, or just a bit of nagging, hound students to get their work done. This conveys a powerful message that learning WILL happen in your class. No matter how hard they wish to make that process, you will make certain of it.

✘ **STOP talking over students who are talking.** I know it's hard, but a great learning environment is one where students listen to the teacher when teaching is occurring and converse when it's appropriate to communicate with classmates. Make sure you teach students when it's okay to talk and when it isn't. Stand still, go quiet, and wait for your class to quiet when you are ready to teach and do NOT continue until you have their attention. If they begin to chat it up again, pause and return to that earlier pose until they quiet. You may have to do this frequently at first, but eventually, they get the message. Trust me, it's incredibly awkward to have your teacher standing still at attention in the middle of the room not talking to them and staring straight ahead.

✘ **STOP forging ahead when it's clear students are not ready for the material you planned to teach.** That's a recipe for behavior problems during the lesson. Instead, go back and make sure they have foundation knowledge and skills before plunging into what's next.

✘ **STOP adhering so tightly to planning or pacing guides that you let a spontaneous learning moment pass by.** It might screw up your lesson a bit, but those "teachable moments" are often the ones students walk away remembering.

✘ **STOP trying to do all the work yourself.** Use the humans in the room to help make your classroom run beautifully. More on this in the next section.

✘ **STOP using sarcasm or snarkiness to engage students.** I learned this the hard way, by reading end-of-year student evaluations (I created these myself as I LOVE to know what my "customers" think of me) and finding out that what I thought was hilarious ribbing of kids was actually hurtful. You may not realize it, but your words and deeds are incredibly powerful and have the capacity to wound students deeply if you're not careful. It's okay to use humor. Kids love that and it's a great facilitator for learning. Just make sure it's content-related or self-effacing. Make sure the class is *in* on the joke, not *part* of the joke.

✘ **STOP refusing to take late work or allowing students to redo work.** If you really want your students to learn, you have to accept that they won't all do so in lock-step on your timetable. You also have to accept that life happens and that school is difficult for many, many kids. The best way forward is by building in flexibility and providing opportunities for kids to get you their work within a reasonable period of time after you may have collected it from the majority of the class. Teaching timeliness and responsibility cannot happen if students get to opt out of doing the work. Teaching responsibility happens when you demand that students DO the work and that you will follow up with them over and over and over again until it's in. You won't have to do this for every student forever. It's the few who need this kind of special attention, but they need it the most. Great teachers will go that extra mile.

✘ **STOP teaching for long swaths of time without brain breaks.** Kids can only process so much before they shut down, and you can only teach for so long without reflecting on how it's going and still be effective. In fact, research tells us that students can only pay attention for about one minute per year of age (Murawski, 2009). So middle school teachers have about 10 to 15 minutes and high school teachers have about 15 to 20 minutes before they need to shut up and engage the students in a different learning activity or reflection.

✘ **DON'T lose your cool and say something you'll regret.** Take a deep breath. Close your eyes. Do a yoga pose. I'm serious. I do these in front of kids and they see me doing the whole "count to ten" strategy. It gives you time to construct a measured and appropriate response to whatever has happened in class, and it alerts the class that they've crossed a line and need to rein themselves back in.

✘ **DON'T pit students against each other.** To create true community, all students have to appreciate and accommodate one another's uniqueness. That means you need to model tolerance, appreciation, and togetherness. Strengthen the bonds among your pupils by constantly attending to team-building. Pitting kids against one another in contests featuring lopsided praise or public shaming is the fast lane to a classroom culture that is toxic.

THE GREAT TEACHER TOOLBOX: IDEAS AND STRATEGIES TO EMPLOY TODAY!

Teachers, DO This

✓ **SAY hello and goodbye to your students.** I know you are stunned that this is number one. Stunned. And yet, how few teachers do this. In all my travels, the thing that shocked me the most was how few teachers started and ended their classes without any real emotional welcome for their students. They are so swamped that they don't realize they've dispensed with the essentials of human niceties such as an honest "Good morning" or "Hey, thanks for coming . . . see y'all tomorrow." Do it. It will make you stand out as a teacher who cares.

✓ **NAME your classroom.** The Brain Cave! The Fortress of Stumpitude! (my friend Josh Stumpenhorst's classroom name). The 4th Dimension! Create cohesion and belonging by making your classroom more than just Room 203.

✓ **CREATE a warm, welcoming classroom environment that conveys your personality and provides space to display your students' pictures or schoolwork.** Use posters, lighting, plants, and interesting furniture groupings to make it seem less of an institutional space and more of a home/hub for learning. Change it up frequently.

✓ **AVOID overstuffing your classroom walls and shelves.** It is possible to overstimulate kids when every square inch of classroom real estate is covered with pictures and words. Plus, where are you going to put their work and creations throughout the year?

✓ **KEEP your classroom clean, tidy, and fresh smelling.** There are a lot of stinky classrooms out there. Make fresh air a priority. Kids appreciate it. This actually does lead to better classroom management. Trust me on this.

✓ **DO design, label, and maintain the areas of your classroom where kids can get missed work, turn in or pick up work, and collect handouts.** Create dedicated shelves/files for each class period, color code each class period, and label things so it's a system that's easy for you AND your students to grasp.

✓ **KEEP your daily learning targets visible for students and in kid-friendly language.** It's important that kids understand what they are expected to learn each day and how you will both know they've been successful.

✓ **LINK today's learning with yesterday's, and preview how it will set them up for success with tomorrow's lesson.** Weave them together. I do this, and it is literally called "Yesterday, today, and tomorrow." I explain what we did yesterday, how it will inform today's work, and then tease tomorrow's work by telling them how success today will help them tackle tomorrow's challenge.

✓ **DO end each period by recapping what was learned.** Have the students take this over after you've modeled it. In classrooms where the teacher explicitly states what students learned that day, retention rates can almost double among students in the room. Sounds crazy, but telling students what they learned actually helps them hang on to that knowledge.

✓ **USE student employees to do the bulk of the classroom operations for you.** Create three to five separate jobs for students to do in class each period that free you up to teach. Make a job application, a time card, job descriptions, and a payment scheme. Rotate the jobs every few weeks so that many students have a chance to work for you. This is the single best thing I ever created for my classroom, and it works so well that the class can run itself whenever I am gone. My jobs are: Teacher's Assistant, Class Manager, Librarian, Host, Technology Director, and Circulation Director. They do everything: greet guests, answer phones, collect and pass out all papers, run all the tech, work the AC/windows, prep class for dismissal. We have a team currency called Dynabucks that we pay students with and which they can use to purchase things such as snacks, school supplies, free reading books, and toys.

✓ **HAVE an easy, effective system for getting work missed to absent students.** I use a daily agenda binder that holds the agenda for the period plus any handouts or posted due dates. When absent students return, they look at the binder and jot notes into their planners. Then, they visit the TA to schedule new due dates or get clarification on something they missed. After those two steps, they can linger at the end of class to check in with me if they have additional needs or questions. Visiting the binder first is their responsibility and one they need to be taught to do. You don't even have to take the time to write the agenda or put in a copy of the notes; make that a student job or use carbon paper so that a student who takes good notes can simply put a copy in the binder at the end of the period.

✓ **USE "repeat after me"s when correcting student behavior.** This is a light-hearted way of showing kids what they did wrong and what you expect them to do next. I came up to a kid flicking his pencil at a neighbor. I silently placed a hand on the pencil and pressed it to the desk. Then I said, "Eric, please repeat after me. I'm sorry I was flicking my pencil when I was supposed to be recording my group's answers to the grammar challenge. I'm keeping my team from completing their work and I know better than that. We can't be successful unless I get back on track, which I plan to do right now. Sorry team. Let's get back to it." I paused after each sentence so the team could hear Eric's recitation. There were smiles and chuckles from all of us, but it made the point that their work is important and they need to get to it. You can do this for minor infractions all the way up to far more serious situations, and it works to diffuse anger and hostility and get kids back to their learning.

✓ **USE humor to create unity or to create a positive emotional connection to the learning.** Like I mentioned before, be careful of using snarkiness or sarcasm; however; 40 years of research have shown that humor promotes learning (Banas, Dunbar, Rodriguez, & Liu, 2011). When kids are laughing, they are learning. If you are not inherently funny, find a daily cartoon to start the day or allow a student to tell an (appropriate) joke in the middle of class.

✓ **USE cards/sticks/apps/clothespins to randomize how you call on kids.** There are many, many ways to make sure you are calling on the WHOLE class, not just the eager beavers. Find a system that works for you, and stick faithfully to it. I use fun, graphic playing cards with the students' names on them and have invented several strategies for calling on kids with them. It's so successful that kids ask to take their cards home with them on the last day of the school year.

✓ **USE the "I don't know, yet" technique so that every kid answers every time.** Kids, especially older students, are terrified of looking bad in front of their peers so it's easier for them to say "I don't know" when you call on them instead of trying to answer and being wrong. His or her hope is that you will move on to someone who DOES know. Don't move on. Tell them, "Okay. You don't know YET, but you will. I'm going to call on two more students who will share their thoughts. I'll come back to you to see if that helps you with your own answer. Okay, Kwame? Please be prepared to share after you hear Sharon and Tim's thoughts." Call on Sharon and Tim. Hear them out, and then return to Kwame. Ask him to provide his own answer or to repeat what Sharon and/or Tim said. The point of this strategy is so that kids learn that every kid will be required to contribute something to the conversation (Morris, 2010). No one gets out without learning, and if that's the one and only thing your students remember about you after they've gone, how great is THAT?

✓ **ALLOW a 2-minute period of Q and A at the start of instruction to connect with kids.** Let them tell you what's going on at school, at home, in their lives. Ask them about books they're reading, movies they're seeing, and how their families are. Touch base. Answer their questions about you. Show them you are human and that you laugh, get scared, worry, and have friends. You're going to rely on this human connection when the learning gets tough and they fear you don't really see them as people, just scores. If you take the time to be real with them, even for 2 minutes a day, it pays huge dividends.

✓ **USE the "Ask 3-Then Me" rule.** Students love to check in with the teacher obsessively to see if they are doing things right or just to pick up a detail they missed hearing. You'll be stopped dead if you take all these questions, so I tell students that when they are stuck they can quietly ask up to three students their question before they come to me. The point is for them to become self-sufficient and not need the teacher for simpler, procedural details.

✓ **USE timers to keep track of activities/students during the period.** It's far too easy to let time slip away because we aren't keeping closer track of it. Decide in advance how long each activity/work time should last. Set a timer that students can see (many tech timers are available for free online), and stick to it. It's okay to give students more time for things as they need it.

✓ **DESIGNATE a space for supplies, and allow students to use them.** So many teachers refuse to provide extras of what kids need to succeed because they want kids to be responsible themselves. I get it. However, your students will use a too-stringent teacher's approach to keep them from having to actually DO anything while in class. You can't let that happen. Keep extra pens, handouts, and textbooks on immediate hand so that there's nothing standing between any student and success. The bottom line in your life as a teacher is that kids WILL learn in your class no matter what because you have removed all the barriers you possibly could.

✓ **DO use IN/OUT boxes.** Designate two bins, one for work that has been turned in to be looked at/marked by you and one for graded work that is ready to be returned. Use folders or files for each class period. Glue, tape, or paste a class roster to the inside of each folder so you can quickly see after grading a set of papers who owes you this assignment. Follow up with that student as soon as possible to establish a new due date for him/her.

✓ **FORECAST your actions.** As you teach, tell students what you are doing and where you're going next. Kids love to feel like they know what's happening so they can prepare to succeed. When you engage in visible thinking routines, it primes them to be successful.

✓ **DO keep and use TGIF cards.** Keep student contact information somewhere in your car. On your way home on Friday afternoons, choose three random students to call. Tell their parents something positive about that student, even if you must leave a message. Next week, do three more. Continue until the year is over, and by then, you will have contacted nearly every family and spread wonderful news throughout your classroom community. Your students will be shocked and awed by this and wait excitedly for their "turn."

✓ **BE WILLING to negotiate, compromise, and be flexible when it comes to how to do things.** If your students protest something in your class, pause and ask for a discussion of the issue. Listen to their concerns, and see where you can negotiate or change course. They need to see this process of careful contemplation and flexibility modeled so they can do it in their own lives.

Making Connections

Check out Chapter 20 on Family Collaboration

✓ **ALLOW student voice and choice in designing activities and rules.** Whenever and wherever possible, build in choice moments where you allow kids to chart the direction of the class, whether it is in the mode of instruction, the method for completing the work, the due date, the criteria for a scoring rubric, or your classroom rules. You want kids to invest and engage with the work of your classroom, so why not make them decision makers in the process? Research demonstrates that students, especially at the secondary level, crave choice and power (Erwin, 2004); they will fight you for it. Allowing them this input gives them exactly what they want—but on your terms.

✓ **USE music or tunes during setup/passing/transitions.** You can use TV themes, commercial jingles, or pop music to keep you both alert, happy, engaged, and on track. Musical chairs is also a great way to help with transitions between stations or centers. Kids get to talk while the music plays, and they sit in their new stations as soon as it ends (Murawski, 2009).

✓ **HAVE weekly FOCUS students that you devote at least 5 minutes to each day.** Stand by them, ask them questions, and listen to what they are up to. Pick the students who don't automatically seek out or get much attention . . . the ones who hide in plain sight. They need you more than ever. Find them. Connect.

✓ **HAVE office hours.** Allocate 1 hour a week to helping students with their work (any work, even from another class) and 1 hour a week to having fun with them. Do PE with your kids, have a lunch club (Scrabblers! The Movie Critics Colloquy, Sittin' N' Knittin'!), visit them in their other classes during your conference just to see them in a new context. Putting yourself in their orbit makes them want to do good work for you.

✓ **REPEAT an instruction or task so that students know exactly what to do.** Write it once on the board, and then state it out loud twice.

✓ **DO get out of the way.** Listen and observe your kids closely. When students are working hard, but it seems a little chaotic, don't worry. A hive of activity is a good thing. Try with all your might to stay out of it. Sometimes a teacher's constant interruptions keep kids from firing on all cylinders. Similarly, when you've tried to explain something tough and kids just aren't catching on, ask a student to take over and tell it to kids. Oftentimes, a voice from a peer who DOES get it can do more good than you trying a third time.

✓ **TEACH students how to apologize and how to accept an apology.** Model this in front of students. They don't always know, so talk them through it so it feels less intimidating.

✓ **MOVE around the room and teach "in the wild."** Use proximity to control misbehavior and sustain attentiveness.

✓ **USE silence as much as possible.** Communicate your behavior expectations with eye contact, proximity, a soft shoulder tap, a sticky note or See Me Later card you press on a student's desk as you pass by, or a gesture. Try not to add noise pollution to a situation you are trying to correct or manage.

✓ **DO explicitly plan your transitions and state out loud what kids are to do next.** Transitions are hands down the number one killer of classroom management (Smith, Polloway, Patton, & Dowdy, 2001). Know that. Plan for it, model, and be consistent.

✓ **DO discipline with dignity so that the outcome is a win for both you and the students.** Bend down so that you are at eye level with kids. Use eye contact. Soften your voice so that the conversation is as private as possible. Take students outside if you must. Ask the student what she was doing, what she was supposed to be doing, and what she will do next. This refocuses the student away from what they were doing wrong and back onto what they should go do now.

✓ **DO publicly praise students; privately discipline them.** Anytime a teacher is about to lay something as heavy as praise or a correction on a student, it's got to be done just right. The best advice is to know your students. Know who wants the big fuss. Know who'd prefer a sweet sticky note tucked into their reading book. Know who can handle the stink-eye or the insistent tone. Know who needs a gentler hand. Do the best you can to deliver exactly what each kid needs. If things go wrong, and they occasionally will, see below.

✓ **When students or classes have gone awry, MAKE SURE they know that tomorrow is a new day and a fresh chance to do or be better.** Tell them out loud, with an arm on their shoulder, "Today wasn't your best day, but I know you've got a great tomorrow in you. I'll be here, and I can't wait to see it." Allow them to leave your room with hope, not heartache.

✓ **Finally, GIVE yourself the same mercy.** Teaching is darn hard work. For all the effort and heart we put into it, sometimes things will go wrong. It's the nature of the business. Don't dwell on the mistakes. Put each day to bed once the sun is down, and give yourself some hope and the promise of a great tomorrow. You earned it.

MASTER TEMPLATES FOR EMPLOYEE JOB APPLICATIONS AND TIME CARDS

Employee Time Card

Student: _____   Period: _____

Position: _____

Each day you work, bring your time card to your teacher for an initial.

Each initial adds to your overall salary.

When you have 25 initials, you qualify for one homework pass.

Add up all of your initials at the end of 6 weeks, and turn in your timecard.

You'll receive your salary within 48 hours of your last day of work.

WEEK 1: M:_____   T:_____   W:_____   TH:_____   F:_____

WEEK 2: M:_____   T:_____   W:_____   TH:_____   F:_____

WEEK 3: M:_____   T:_____   W:_____   TH:_____   F:_____

WEEK 4: M:_____   T:_____   W:_____   TH:_____   F:_____

WEEK 5: M:_____   T:_____   W:_____   TH:_____   F:_____

WEEK 6: M:_____   T:_____   W:_____   TH:_____   F:_____

30 initials	=	100 dollars*
25–29 initials	=	80 dollars
20–24 initials	=	60 dollars
10–19 initials	=	50 dollars
5–9 initials	=	25 dollars

STUDENT EMPLOYEE JOB APPLICATION

Student: _____

Period: _____

AVAILABLE JOBS	
• Teacher's Assistant • Technology Director • Room Manager • Circulation Director	1st Choice Job:
• Librarian • Host	2nd Choice Job:

REFERENCES

Banas, J. A., Dunbar, N., Rodriguez, D., & Liu, S. (2011). A review of humor in education settings: Four decades of research. *Communication Education, 60*(1), 115–144.

Brophy, J. E. (1996). *Teaching problem students*. New York, NY: Guilford.

Chiu, L. H., & Tulley, M. (1997). Student preferences of teacher discipline styles. *Journal of Instructional Psychology, 24*(3), 168–175.

Emmer, E. T. (1984). *Classroom management: Research and implications*. (R & D Report No. 6178; ERIC Document Reproduction Service No. ED251448). Austin, TX: Research & Development Center for Teacher Education, University of Texas.

Emmer, E. T., & Evertson, C. M. (2012). Classroom management for middle and high school teachers (9th ed.). Upper Saddle River, NJ: Pearson.

Erwin, J. C. (2004). *The classroom of choice: Giving students what they need and getting what you want*. Alexandria, VA: Association for Supervision and Curriculum Development.

Froyen, L. A., & Iverson, A. M. (1999). *Schoolwide and classroom management: The reflective educator-leader* (3rd ed.). Upper Saddle River, NJ: Prentice Hall.

Glasser, W. (1999). *Choice theory: A new psychology of personal freedom*. New York, NY: HarperCollins.

Great Schools Partnership. (2013). Classroom management. *Glossary of Education Reform*. Retrieved from http://edglossary.org/classroom-management/

Marzano, R. J. (2003). *Classroom management that works*. Alexandria, VA: Association for Supervision and Curriculum Development.

Morris, R. (2010). *New management handbook* (3rd ed.). San Diego, CA: New Management.

Murawski, W. W. (2009). *Collaborative teaching in secondary schools*. Thousand Oaks, CA: Corwin.

National Commission on Teaching and America's Future. (1996). *What matters most: Teaching for America's future*. New York, NY: Author.

Office of the Press Secretary. The White House. (2009, March 10). Remarks by the President to the Hispanic Chamber of Commerce on a complete and competitive American education. Retrieved from http://www.whitehouse.gov/the_press_office/Remarks-of-the-President-to-the-United-States-Hispanic-Chamber-of-Commerce

Smith, T. E. C., Polloway, E. A., Patton, J. R., & Dowdy, C. A. (2001). *Teaching students with special needs in inclusive settings* (2nd ed.). Boston, MA: Allyn & Bacon.

Wong, H. K., & Wong, R. T. (1998). *First days of school: How to be an effective teacher* (2nd ed.). Mountain View, CA: Harry K. Wong.

RECOMMENDED READINGS

* Fay, J., & Funk, D. (1995). *Teaching with love and logic*. Golden, CO: Love & Logic Press.
* Kohn, A. (2006). *Beyond discipline: From compliance to community*. Alexandria, VA: Association for Supervision and Curriculum Development.
* Mackenzie, R. J. (2003). *Setting limits in the classroom: How to move beyond the dance of discipline in today's classrooms*. Roseville, CA: Prima.
* Payne, R. K. (2006). *Working with students: Discipline strategies for the classroom*. Highlands, TX: Aha! Process.
* Rubinstein, G. (1999). *Reluctant disciplinarian: Advice on classroom management from a softy who became (eventually) a successful teacher*. Fort Collins, CO: Cottonwood Press.
* Whitaker, T. (2004). *What great teachers do differently*. Larchmont, NY: Eye on Education.

GO EVEN FURTHER WITH THIS TOPIC ON THE WORLD WIDE WEB

- www.educationworld.com/a_curr/archives/classroom_management.shtml
- www.smartclassroommanagement.com
- www.web.calstatela.edu/faculty/jshindl/cm/
- www.incredibleart.org/links/toolbox/discipline2.html
- www.scholastic.com/teachers/unit/classroom-management-everything-you-need

THE Apps WE LOVE

- ClassDojo
- Kahoot
- Nearpod
- Socrative
- Too Loud/Best Sand Timer
- Remind 101

10

Cool Cooperative Learning

Scott Mandel

Los Angeles Unified School District

WHAT REALLY WORKS IN COOPERATIVE LEARNING IN THE SECONDARY CLASSROOM

Implementing Cooperative Learning Into Your Common Core Classroom

Businesses today expect their employees to be able to work together in project groups. This is very different from the way they normally learn in school, which is based on individualized learning—especially in secondary education. Luckily, the writers of the new Common Core recognized this in creating their view of education. In fact, a major aspect of the new Common Core State Standards (CCSS) initiative is the implementation of "inquiry-learning" or "project-based learning." The basic concept is that students will delve deeply into curricular material, and subsequently incorporate higher order critical thinking into their discussions—a primary tenet of the Common Core (Burris & Garrity, 2012). Those of you whose states have not adopted Common Core aren't exempt from reading this chapter, however! Fortune 500 companies don't care which schools graduated their applicants; they want employees who can collaborate, communicate, and problem-solve. They want folks who can work well with others, ask questions, lead, and follow. It is our job to not only teach our content but to also make sure we are creating these types of learners and thinkers. I know you know this already; this type of teaching is nothing new in the educational world. In fact, before the onset of No Child Left Behind (NCLB) in 2002, this methodology had a different name and was highly popular and widely successful. It was called "Cooperative Learning," and pre-NCLB, its implementation could be found in most classrooms in some form or another. So why are we spending a whole chapter on it in this day and age?

Unfortunately, with the advent of No Child Left Behind and the new nationwide focus on teaching primarily to pass an end-of-the-year test, Cooperative Learning virtually vanished in many classrooms. Whereas thousands of publications were written on the subject in the late 1980s and 1990s, between 2002 and 2014, scarcely a book or article appeared focused on cooperative learning, and fewer and fewer secondary teachers have incorporated it into their classrooms. However, with the teacher freedom promoted by the Common Core, Cooperative Learning has the opportunity to flourish once more. Call it "inquiry-learning" or "project-based learning," in its essence, it is all Cooperative Learning. In fact, you will find that your students will flourish, whether they are gifted, special education, English language learners, or even the "typical" student.

So what is cooperative learning, if it's not just throwing a bunch of kids together in a group? In its most basic form, it involves two or more students working with curricular material in a way that their discussion provides them with new insights into the material. It may indeed be as simple as pairs of students working together for 20 minutes on a problem you've given them. It may also be as complex as a group of students working together over a 2- to 3-week period on a special project. Whenever learning happens between two or more students, rather than directed by the teacher, you have a form of Cooperative Learning. Anyone who has worked with kids before knows that it takes way more than throwing them together; there is actually an art to doing this correctly so that the students learn and the teacher doesn't go crazy. This chapter will help you know what really works in making cooperative learning activities successful at the secondary level.

This chapter will focus on one of the more extensive forms of Cooperative Learning so that you can adapt the strategies to a variety of types of cooperative learning activities. The type that we will be looking at is an adaptation of the Group Investigation Model developed by the Sharans in the 1980s and 1990s at the height of the Cooperative Learning movement (Sharan, 1994; Sharan & Sharan, 1992). In this version, students are normally placed into groups for three or more days as they work to solve an academic problem presented by the teacher. This is the type of activity that you will find yourself implementing in your classrooms as your school adopts the Common Core State Standards. And if you are not, you certainly should be!

RESEARCH ON COOPERATIVE LEARNING

Cooperative Learning was extensively researched from its popular origins in the mid-1980s through 2002. The research demonstrated that using this teaching method significantly raised students' levels of higher order critical thinking skills across the board, regardless of their intellectual level, race, ethnicity, or special needs (Slavin, 1995). That's good for us all, right? Letting kids work in cooperative learning groups was actually shown to help students think divergently, work together to generate and test hypotheses, reason causally, master complex bodies of information, analyze social situations, and develop flexible social skills (Joyce, Calhoun, & Hopkins, 2002). In addition, this was also found to be highly successful in including special education students (Slavin, 1995). You can't argue against those kind of results, can you?

Cooperative learning is project-based by its very nature, and more importantly, prepares students for the real working world as adults. Too often, secondary education concentrates solely on "content." But by the time these students graduate in today's information society, that content will be obsolete. Instead, today's businesses increasingly want workers who can function successfully and productively with others on projects (Carnevale, 1996, 2002). Cooperative Learning provides students with the basic skills necessary to succeed in this type of environment—one that is very different from the "traditional" sit-and-take-notes classroom.

Cooperative Learning is also based on inquiry-based learning. Since this type of learning is the basis of the CCSS (Dana, Burns, & Wolkenhauer, 2013; Wolk, 2008), Cooperative Learning is expected to be regularly implemented into the Common Core classroom. Kids need to actually be taught to think, to question, to problem-solve, and not just to regurgitate facts. Many secondary students can find an answer online on their smartphone before the teacher finishes explaining the question! In today's society, we need to focus on teaching the kids how to *use* that data and how to *work with others* to fulfill a goal. This is a critical skill for students as they prepare to join the workforce. And it's an even greater reason to implement Cooperative Learning in all departments.

Unfortunately, most published models of Cooperative Learning require teachers to drastically change their teaching styles to fit a particular model. We all know that that is not reality. How many middle or high school teachers do you know who are ready to change the way they teach overnight? Each of us has a particular style based on our experiences, personalities, and classroom. Luckily, extensive classroom research has identified a number of key concepts central to Cooperative Learning success that can be easily transferred and implemented into your classroom situation and teaching style—without requiring wholesale changes to your repertoire (Mandel, 2003). It's those basic core concepts of Cooperative Learning implementation that will be the focus of this chapter—hence, what really works.

As stated earlier, the type of Cooperative Learning that will be the primary focus is the Group Investigation Model. Based on the work of educational pioneer H. A. Thelen (1954, 1960), the Sharans further developed this specific practice years later. This methodology allows students to delve into greater detail, where they can spend more time using higher order critical thinking skills than they would in short, one-day Cooperative Learning experiences (as found in most of the other models). It can be applied across all disciplines and continued for multiple class periods. Therefore, this model is the most appropriate for reaching the goals of the Common Core and for any educator interested in truly engaging and challenging diverse students and preparing them to enter the workforce.

WHAT YOU NEED TO AVOID AT ALL COSTS

Teachers

- ✖ **STOP using Cooperative Learning lessons as a substitute for frontal teaching.** Cooperative Learning is meant to replace seatwork, not directed lessons. There is still a need for students to learn the content from qualified teachers. This doesn't mean that students can't learn new information during their Cooperative Learning group time, but that teachers shouldn't completely abdicate their role as instructional leader.

- ✖ **STOP rejecting Cooperative Learning because you don't want to change your teaching style.** You have your own personal style and your unique group of students. An "expert" across the country can't determine what's best for your classroom (even me, unfortunately!). Nor can an out-of-classroom district person. Use the basic concepts of group formation, teacher questioning, group leadership, and so forth, and apply them to your individual style and situation (see Mandel, 2003). Basic tips are provided for you on page 164.

- ✖ **STOP refusing to try Cooperative Learning** because you don't believe that your special education students or English language learners can handle it. Cooperative Learning has been found to be extremely successful with these students who are included into your classroom (Slavin, 1995). In fact, the research on these groups emphasizes the positive outcomes when

Making Connections

Check out Chapters 12, 16, and 17 on Inclusion, English Language Learners, and Autism they are able to work collaboratively with heterogeneous groups (Murawski & Spencer, 2011).

✗ **STOP making groups of three students.** When students are in a group of three, most decisions come as a result of social relationship reasons—especially among secondary students, whose lives often revolve around their social groups and status. Four or six students are actually the best size because all decisions have to be decided by a sizable majority of the group, rather than a one-person margin.

✗ **STOP assigning students randomly to long-term group projects (those lasting more than one or two periods).** Groups require certain skills and abilities of its members to ensure success in whatever project you have assigned. Random grouping equals random success. See the Group Formation Chart on page 165 for assistance with this.

✗ **STOP using a problematic classroom setup as an excuse to not use Cooperative Learning.** If your classroom setup (desks, tables, open space) leads to barriers to group work, create a solution! Move around desks and chairs—use open floor spaces if necessary. Reserve the multipurpose room or auditorium if necessary.

✗ **STOP rotating jobs among the group members.** Research has shown that students with "leadership" skills will always take leadership—and will unknowingly sabotage the group if they are not allowed to "lead" (Mandel, 1991). This is especially true in secondary, where leadership roles are fairly well defined among the students. Don't worry; I'll give you the key to doing this in the next "DO THIS" section.

✗ **STOP assuming that higher order critical thinking will automatically happen in the group discussions.** Research has shown that the critical thinking level of the teacher's questioning or assignment of task is the primary determinant of the level of thinking that the group will incorporate into their discussions (Mandel, 1991). That means you need to model what you are looking for!

✗ **STOP having students spend so much time finding their own research.** Determine whether or not this is a content-related or a research-related lesson. Even in secondary, students will often spend more of their time conducting research to locate materials than discussing the data itself. More time spent analyzing is preferable to more time spent searching.

✗ **STOP assuming that "one lesson fits all of my classes."** Even if you teach the same subject all day, what works during the day may not work well the first or last periods. Be adaptable.

Administrators

✗ **STOP thinking that teaching isn't happening or standards aren't being covered during a Cooperative Learning lesson.** When entering a classroom, it is important not to make any decisions on the level of teaching or learning that is occurring without listening to the discussions taking place and asking the teacher about how the Cooperative Learning project fits in within the overall curricular unit.

✖ **STOP worrying about "noise" or "chaos" during a Cooperative Learning lesson.** If you observe a Cooperative Learning session, the more talking you hear, the more students are actively engaged in the lesson. Spend some time and listen to what the students are saying.

STRATEGIES FOR SUCCESS WITH COOPERATIVE LEARNING

Teachers, DO This

✓ **USE Cooperative Learning to eliminate busy seatwork, not directed teaching.** Cooperative Learning projects should always begin with the teacher giving some form of directed lesson to provide students with the background and context for the project. Directed lessons don't need to always be long boring lectures, but students do need to be provided with instruction before being asked to work collaboratively with peers to solve a problem. Core material from the standards should be presented during this time in order to ensure that all students cover it, rather than hoping that groups will touch on the necessary subjects.

✓ **MAKE groups of four to seven students.** As stated above, in secondary, groups of three have social issues as the primary determinant of decisions (two-to-one). Groups of more than seven become a "committee" and lose effectiveness. Again, the best groups are four or six, because decisions have to be by general consensus versus a one-vote majority.

✓ **DETERMINE the specific skills necessary for each group's success.** It is critical that groups are not put together randomly. Especially in long-term secondary-level projects, you need to match skills and traits of students to the requirements of that particular group's work. For example, if there is higher level reading required for the group, ensure that at least one member of the group can read at that level. If graphic design is required, then ensure that a student with a high Spatial Multiple Intelligence is a member (see Mandel, 2003, for a discussion on group formation and how to use Multiple Intelligences for determining student traits). Want ways to get kids in groups that seem heterogeneous but are still thoughtful and teacher-designed? Check out "Tips for Creating Cooperative Learning Groups" on page 164.

✓ **LET the leadership of the group develop on its own rather than predetermining group roles.** Studies have demonstrated that students with strong leadership personalities will naturally take over the leadership of the group (Mandel, 1991). What's worse, a student with a strong leadership personality who is not able to take a "positive" leadership role will inevitably take on a "negative" leadership role and disrupt the group. This is especially prevalent in secondary classrooms. Similarly, a student who does not have a strong leadership personality but is put in that position will either be highly uncomfortable and not do the job or will allow someone else to take over. Instead of assigning jobs, provide a list of jobs required of each group (such as a "recorder," "presenter," and "materials-getter") and let the group determine how best to hand out roles (Mandel, 2003). Turn to page 166 for a list of potential jobs.

✓ **PREPARE higher order critical thinking questions to use with students.** Studies have shown that the critical thinking level you leave the students with at the end of your directed lesson is the level in which they will work for the remainder of the lesson. This is true on all levels, including secondary. Likewise, if you talk to an individual group while they are working, whatever critical thinking level you last use will be the level in which they operate after you leave (Mandel, 1991). For example, if you ask the students a low-level critical thinking question such as, "How did the war in Europe end in WWII?" they will locate facts such as American and allied victories, Hitler's suicide, and so forth. However, if you ask them a higher order critical thinking question such as, "Determine the causes of the Nazi defeat," the students will investigate factors such as military and Nazi policy decisions, resources, Allied strengths, and other relevant variables (see Mandel, 2003). Also, be aware of asking too many questions as students work or of hanging around groups for too long; they will tend to want to defer to the teacher as opposed to listening and communicating with one another.

Making Connections

Check out Chapter 15 on Gifted Education

✓ **REMEMBER that special education students can be full members of your groups.** Many students who receive special education services have a discrepancy in particular learning areas. Always predetermine those discrepancies when planning, and then ascertain if adaptations are needed. If a student has a discrepancy in reading comprehension, make sure that he is in a group where reading at a level above his ability is not a requirement for all group members. If a student has behavioral problems due to her disability, ensure that she is in a group with other students with whom she has positive relationships, and avoid those who may pose a problem. Being proactive is a major component of universally designing strong differentiated and successful lessons (Murawski & Spencer, 2011).

✓ **REMEMBER that English language learners can be full members of your groups.** English language learners have difficulty with the use of the English language; that does not mean, however, that they also have cognitive problems. Therefore, many can fully integrate the use of higher order thinking skills once you account for their language barrier. This can be accomplished in many ways: You can partner an ELL student with another fluent in the primary language, and they can serve as a "translator" in the discussion back and forth. (However, be aware of problems with "social group status" of the partners—they need to be willing to work with each other.) Materials from the Internet can easily be translated using Google Translate. Just type in the web address (translate.google.com), select your language, and print out the material for the students to read in their primary language. Finally, if you have enough students who speak the same language, you can create groups of them and let them discuss the material and work with it in their primary tongue, using their higher order thinking skills. If the goals of your lesson are content-based versus English language-based, this is a perfectly acceptable accommodation. Also consider collaborating or co-teaching with an ELL coach or teacher to come up with more helpful adaptations.

Making Connections

Check out Chapter 16 on Working With English Language Learners

✓ **CREATE packets of materials for the students to use in their investigation.** For Cooperative Learning sessions to be successful, students need sufficient material to investigate—even in secondary classrooms, where the students are more advanced in research skills. Simply using textbooks and/or encyclopedias are not enough. Students will spend a significant amount of their time looking for material when asked to do their own research. Therefore, it is imperative that you acquire material that you can put into file folders and give to the appropriate groups. The students can then concentrate their time on discussing and manipulating the material, rather than on a search for the data. The Internet is the ultimate resource center (see Mandel, 2003)! Even though this may initially be time consuming, once it is complete, you can save the material for Cooperative Learning sessions in the future. A list of some of the best curricular sites for materials is listed later in this chapter.

✓ **USE an "Adapted Group Grade" system if you are giving grades for group work.** Too often one student does not get credit for doing more work than the others, and another student gets the credit for doing less than the average. This is especially a problem with many high school students who are overly focused on their G.P.A. for college admissions. They tend to immediately reject any form of cooperative work where their grade may be dependent on an outside person. Therefore, if you give a group grade, use that as a basis—but then adapt it. For example, you determined that a group should receive a B for their work. Then determine—by observation throughout the work sessions and by questioning the students as a whole—who did work above and beyond. You raise that student's grade to an A. At the same time, you determine someone did little. You give that student a new grade of C. The students immediately see that you are being "fair" in your grading, and that all are held responsible for their individual efforts toward the collective group work.

Administrators, DO This

✓ **ENCOURAGE creativity with your teachers.** Promote Cooperative Learning methodologies with your staff, especially with your more experienced teachers. After a dozen years of the limitations of No Child Left Behind (scripted curricula, strict timelines), teachers may need encouragement to try something as different as Cooperative Learning. This will also assist your school with the upcoming Common Core exams, as they are largely based on higher order critical thinking and often will have a group inquiry work component.

✓ **SET UP a Cooperative Learning Materials Center for your teachers.** Set aside a couple of file cabinets in a central location and encourage teachers to deposit copies of their Cooperative Learning materials. This way, they can share with each other and not have to recreate materials every time they have a Cooperative Learning session.

A COOPERATIVE LEARNING LESSON FORM

TITLE OF LESSON:

COMMON CORE STANDARDS ADDRESSED:

    1.

    2.

    3.

WHERE DOES THIS LESSON OCCUR IN THE OVERALL UNIT (How does it relate to the directed lesson)?

MATERIALS NEEDED FOR THE GROUPS:

INTERNET SITES TO USE TO ACQUIRE MATERIAL:
TITLE:
URL:
Content Description:

TITLE:
URL:
Content Description:

TIPS FOR CREATING COOPERATIVE LEARNING GROUPS

Cooperative learning projects, which are fairly short (under 5–6 hours of work), do not require a lot of group determination.

- Look in your gradebook at the last major test/project in the subject matter of the Cooperative Learning lesson you're about to begin. Then assign every group an equal number of students at the various ability and achievement levels. Be flexible, and make slight adjustments for students who do not work well together or students with specific special needs.
- Use your roster and knowledge of students to create groups in advance that will serve different purposes. For example, for large heterogeneous groups, create color groups (e.g., Red, Blue, Green, Yellow), number groups (1–6), and shape groups (e.g., Circle, Square, Triangle). Be thoughtful about who is in each group and why, but create them proactively. Now, whenever you want students to get in groups of four to six for shorter projects, you can ask them to get in their number, color, or shape groups.

For long-term Cooperative Learning projects, it's much more important to construct groups that you know will work and achieve your desired long-term goals. For more complex or longer tasks, take the following steps in creating your groups:

1. *Determine the basic traits and skills you need students in each particular group to possess.* For example, you may determine that "high-level reading" is important for one particular group; "graphic design skill" may be critical for another group.

2. *Go through your roll book, and start to place students in the groups based on what you know of their personal abilities.* Important—not every group member must possess every skill! They will help each other with the tasks. For example, if there is high-level reading required, you simply must have at least one or two high-level readers in that group. The rest will still participate in the group discussions and other tasks. Using the students' Multiple Intelligence levels is an excellent tool here. (For easy "tests" for determining M.I. level, you can copy the appendices in *Cooperative Work Groups*, Mandel, 2003).

3. *Fill out the Group Formation Chart (included here), and adjust membership in each* based on social considerations. For example, pay extra attention to students who should not be with each other and to the

abilities and areas of concern or strength of students with disabilities, special needs, language differences, or giftedness.

The following chart will help you in listing the requirements of your groups and creating them.

GROUP FORMATION CHART

Group 1	Group 2	Group 3	Group 4	Group 5
Traits and Skills Required for Each Group				
1-	1-	1-	1-	1-
2-	2-	2-	2-	2-
3-	3-	3-	3-	3-
Group Members				

GROUP GOALS

Group 1—*Their Main Task:*   *Extra Tasks:*

Group 2 —*Their Main Task:*   *Extra Tasks:*

Group 3—*Their Main Task:*   *Extra Tasks:*

Group 4—*Their Main Task:*   *Extra Tasks:*

Group 5—*Their Main Task:*   *Extra Tasks:*

Teacher Notes

POSSIBLE GROUP MEMBER ROLES

Facilitator: Your job is to keep the process moving.

Recorder: Your job is to keep notes on what you are doing and who is doing what.

Reporter: Your job is to report on what your group did.

Timer: Your job is to help with time management for the group.

Member: Your job is to help complete the tasks given.

Cheerleader: Your job is to keep up the motivation and morale of the group.

Materials Manager: Your job is to get and disseminate any materials necessary for the task.

Tech Consultant: Your job is to help with any technological needs of the group.

Consultant: Your job is to help the group "solve" the task, without giving them the answers.

Housekeeper: Your job is to ensure all materials get put away and that group members have cleaned up after the task.

Questions Asker: Your job is to be a liaison with the teacher if the group has any questions about the process or task.

Source: Adapted from Murawski (2003) with permission from author.

MORE COOPERATIVE LEARNING TIPS!

Here are a number of "extras" for you to consider as you start to use cooperative learning strategies listed above:

How Do You Identify
Students With a Strong Leadership Personality?

The easiest way to determine those with strong leadership personalities is by observation. Who leads the school clubs, sports teams, or arts programs? Who do the students gravitate to in the class or outside after school or during lunch? In the classroom, who are the students who are the first to raise their hands in a discussion? This is whether or not they know the correct answers! Leadership and academic achievement are not connected.

What Happens if Someone Refuses to Work?

After a number of warnings and discussion as to the reason for their actions, students who refuse to work should be given an alternate assignment that covers the same material. Usually, this comes in the form of a written assignment/report. Be very careful, however, to determine the function of their behavior. If their purpose is to avoid working in groups, they may choose to continue their negative behavior. For most students, however, they will often soon determine that group work is preferential to this boring paper-pencil type of alternative!

How Do I Assess the Lesson?

What are your original goals for the lesson? If students are supposed to be learning core material for the unit, then test them on the content to be learned. If you want to grade group work and process, then use the "Adjusted Group Grade" mentioned earlier. Above all—you know your curriculum and you know your students. Assess them in whatever way you feel is most appropriate and fair. However, with secondary students, it always helps to let them know in advance how you are assessing and why you are assessing it that way!

REFERENCES

Burris, C. C., & Garrity, D. T. (2012). *Opening the common core: How to bring all students to college and career readiness.* Thousand Oaks, CA: Corwin.

Carnevale, A. P. (1996). Liberal education and the new economy. *Liberal Education, 82*(2), 4–11.

Carnevale, A. P. (2002). Preparing for the future. *American School Board Journal, 189*(7), 26–29, 47.

Dana, N. F., Burns, J. B., & Wolkenhauer, R. (2013). *Inquiring into the common core.* Thousand Oaks, CA: Corwin.

Joyce, B., Calhoun, E., & Hopkins, D. (2002). *Models of learning: Tools for teaching* (2nd ed.). Buckingham, England: Open University.

Mandel, S. (1991). Responses to cooperative learning processes among elementary-age students. ERIC Clearinghouse on Elementary and Early Childhood Education, ED 332808.

Mandel, S. (2003). *Cooperative work groups: Preparing students for the real world.* Thousand Oaks, CA: Corwin.

Murawski, W. W. (2003). *Co-teaching in the inclusive classroom: Working together to help all your students find success.* Medina, WA: Institute for Educational Development.

Murawski, W. W., & Spencer, S. (2011). *Collaborate, communicate, and differentiate! How to increase student learning in today's diverse schools.* Thousand Oaks, CA: Corwin.

Sharan, S. (1994). *Handbook of cooperative learning methods.* Westport, CT: Greenwood Press.

Sharan, Y., & Sharan, S. (1992). *Expanding cooperative learning through group investigation.* New York, NY: Teachers College Press.

Slavin, R. E. (1995). *Cooperative learning: Theory, research, and practice* (2nd ed.). Englewood Cliffs, NJ: Prentice Hall.

Thelen, H. A. (1954). *Dynamics of groups at work.* Chicago, IL: University of Chicago Press.

Thelen, H. A. (1960). *Education and the human quest.* New York, NY: Harper & Row.

Wolk, S. (2008). School as inquiry. *Kappan, 90*(2), 115–122.

RECOMMENDED READINGS

* Armstrong, T. (2009). *Multiple intelligences in the classroom* (3rd ed.). Alexandria, VA: Association for Supervision and Curriculum Development.

* Johnson, D. W., & Johnson, R. T. (1986). *Learning together and alone* (2nd ed.). Englewood Cliffs, NJ: Prentice Hall.

* Kagan, S. (1990). The structural approach to cooperative learning. *Educational Leadership, 47*(4), 12–15.

* Mandel, S. (2003). *Cooperative work groups: Preparing students for the real world.* Thousand Oaks, CA: Corwin.

GO EVEN FURTHER WITH
THIS TOPIC ON THE WORLD WIDE WEB

- teachershelpingteachers.info
- people.ucalgary.ca/~dkbrown/index.html
- mathforum.org
- besthistorysites.net
- www.eduq.com/Sites/Codys-Science-Education-Zone.aspx

THE Apps WE LOVE

- Collaborate
- Edmodo
- Vine
- Google Drive
- Hashtag-based storytelling for 21st century

11

Unique Universal Design for Learning

Tamarah M. Ashton

California State University, Northridge

WHAT REALLY WORKS IN UDL IN THE ELEMENTARY CLASSROOM

Adopting the UDL Frame-of-Mind

Walk into any middle school or high school classroom in the country and what do you see? Different genders, colors, heights, abilities, clothes, and different . . . well, everything. Secondary school teachers today are working with the most diverse set of students our country has ever experienced (National Center for Education Statistics, 2009). These are exciting educational times. As a citizenry, we have made the choice to teach everyone—no matter what (e.g., Individuals with Disabilities Education Improvement Act, 2004). Diversity, of course, includes not just ethnicity.

Consider all the students with disabilities who are now included in general education classrooms; they have special needs in learning, cognition, physicality, emotions, health, and more. What about those with gender identification issues or those in need of second language skills? Socioeconomic issues, sexual orientation, homelessness—the list goes on and on. Additionally, in some places, physical classrooms are a thing of the past and are rapidly becoming virtual educational experiences (see Connections Academy, 2014). How do educators even begin to address all of these elements in the daily design of their class instruction?

Incorporating Universal Design for Learning (UDL) into their planning, instruction, and assessment can make all the difference in the world for a secondary teacher. Adopting a UDL frame-of-mind means recognizing that we all learn differently (Chiasson, 2005) and that we can use those differences to enhance instruction, rather than hinder it.

> Universal Design for Learning (UDL) is a set of principles and techniques for creating inclusive classroom instruction and accessible course materials. At its core is the assertion that *all* students benefit when they are given multiples ways to take in new information, express their comprehension, and become engaged in learning. (Access Project, 2012, para. 1)

Therefore, UDL minimizes barriers and maximizes learning for all students (Center for Applied Special Technology, 2010). That certainly sounds like a good plan, doesn't it?

UDL: WHAT THE RESEARCH SAYS

> The intent of universal design is to simplify life for everyone by making products, communications, and the built environment more usable by as many people as possible at little or no extra cost. Universal design benefits people of all ages and abilities. (Center for Universal Design, 2008, para. 2)

Universal design (UD) was first conceived to address the barriers created in the original development of architectural elements, methods of communication, and many everyday products (Rose & Meyer, 2002). For example, using curb cuts to ease our shopping cart out of the market and into the parking lot has become routine. Most of us probably do not even think about why those indentations in the pavement were originally put there (i.e., smoother mobility for those who use walkers or wheelchairs). And what about television remote controls? It seems everyone, even the youngest of us, now knows that the CC button stands for closed captioning used primarily by those who are deaf. Instead, kids can turn it on to indicate that their parents are talking too loudly on the phone while they are watching an important reality TV show.

It is not surprising that soon after UD was recognized as an important contribution to our society, the need for a broader access to learning became a point of focus with educators. The term UDL was developed in the 1990s by the Center for Applied Special Technology (CAST) (Ashton, 2005). It was defined as "the practice of embedding *flexible* [italics added] strategies into the curriculum during the *planning* process so *all* students can access a variety of learning solutions" (DeCoste, n.d., p. 3).

Flexible planning [for] all. Those are the words italicized in the previous quote, and if you walk away from this chapter with nothing else, let it be the notion that UDL equates with flexible planning for all. We must continue to emphasize that there is not one kind of learning! Learning differs across tasks, development, and individuals (Rose, 2014).

Thus were born CAST's UDL Guidelines. The three guiding principles of UDL, are more fully described on page 177, are: (a) Provide multiple means of representation, (b) provide multiple means of action and expression, and (c) provide multiple means of engagement. This may sound daunting, but hang in there. I'll explain this so you'll see how to do it easily. After you've finished reading this chapter, take a look at the sample UDL lesson plan. The items that fall under representation, action and expression, and engagement are highlighted so you can see the thought processes that go into creating a good UDL lesson.

Plugged In
www.cast.org

Proactive Nature of UDL. UDL means making things accessible before they occur (Rose & Meyer, 2002), rather than adapting them afterward. In other words, if you think about how to reach all of your learners *after* teaching a lesson, you will only be reacting to the problems created by not thoroughly thinking them through before you began. For example, a ninth-grade teacher must take into account that his second period class of 30 students with mixed ethnicities, several of whom have disabilities, as well as a variety of levels of English learning, is not going to require the identical planning as his colleague's class across the country with 22 students of all one ethnicity and one language background. Planning proactively is a necessity.

When physical structures were the main target of UD, architects and other designers focused on avoiding the retrofit (Rose & Meyer, 2002). They front-loaded their planning as much as possible to save time, money, and other resources. So why is this early planning important in Universal Design for *Learning*? Researchers and practitioners alike say it is more efficient (e.g., Basham, Israel, Graden, Poth, & Winston, 2010), it benefits more students (e.g., Basham & Marino, 2013), and it is more acceptable to students (e.g., Chita-Tegmark, Gravel, Serpa, Domings, & Rose, 2012). Great. So UDL is good. "Got it," you think, "but how exactly does that look in my class and my planning?" In these next sections, I provide you with concrete actions to avoid and those actions you should engage in instead.

AVOID THESE UDL BLUNDERS IN SECONDARY EDUCATION

- ✘ **STOP dismissing UDL as a viable option for your instructional design because you already know a lot about modalities and multiple intelligences.** Learning modalities (visual, kinesthetic, tactile) and multiple intelligences (spatial, linguistic/verbal, musical, etc.) have been introduced to teachers for years. These are interesting to think about regarding your students, but UDL is much more than just adding pictures to your lessons or having kids listen to recorded books. UDL is about design—instructional design. A lot of thought and many elements go into really well-designed lessons. Modality preference and intelligence strengths might come into play in informing your design, but it is not the design itself.

- ✘ **STOP confusing UDL with differentiation.** Differentiation allows teachers to design instruction to meet the broadest range of students possible. It is simply one piece of UDL. For example, you may plan to start the lesson with a warm-up activity, followed by 5–10 minutes of direct instruction through lecture, then move to a few stations for application of the new content. For UDL, you are proactively planning to mix up your representation of the material and the way the kids engage with it; well done! However, just because you have stations doesn't mean you have differentiated for the students with special needs. You may still need to incorporate some additional accommodations or modifications.

Making Connections

Check out Chapter 12 on Inclusion

- ✘ **STOP thinking this will take too much time.** What you've been having to do thus far is to fix problems you have created *after* it is too late. That actually takes more time than doing it right the first time. Remember that UDL's origins are based in architecture. Addressing possible problem areas *before* instruction saves everyone a lot of time and heartache.

- ✘ **STOP "teaching to the middle."** No teacher wants to leave students who process more slowly in the dust or punish the ones who pick up quickly by boring them to tears. Yes, the majority of your class probably will be in "the middle." Consider *all* students in your flexible planning!

- ✘ **STOP buying into the idea that there is one true, effective, and proven way to teach something.** No one would ever discover anything new if we all felt that way. Think out-of-the-box, and have fun with teaching. Engaging students is the hardest part of any lesson.

✖ **STOP pointing out to the whole class that you have created something in a special way so Reynoldo can participate.** This kind of behavior defeats the purpose of UDL. UDL values diversity. Remember that old adage: "If you want to give students equal opportunity, you must treat them all differently."

✖ **STOP defining UDL as "just good teaching."** UDL is good teaching, but good teaching is not necessarily UDL. Do not forget the three basic components: (a) Provide multiple means of representation, (b) provide multiple means of action and expression, and (c) provide multiple means of engagement. Still not sure what that means? Look at page 177.

✖ **STOP thinking that UDL is a "special ed thing."** UDL is about providing access to the curriculum for *everyone*. If you keep in mind that all students are *your* students, you will start thinking of them all as special. Aw . . . isn't that sweet?

STEPS TO UDL SUCCESS IN SECONDARY EDUCATION

✓ **EXPLAIN to your students what UDL is and why you are doing it.** Remember that those hormone-laden brains are much more clever than we give them credit for. Use *all* your resources. Students have great ideas, too! This helps them to see diversity in a positive light. Ask them for ideas . . . and then be open to them.

✓ **REMEMBER that it is acceptable to go deep with differentiation for a few while planning instruction for the needs of many.** Consider making yourself a copy of the magnifying glass on page 178. Post it near your workstation to continually remind yourself of this concept. Here's an example: Imagine you are teaching a class Algebra I, and you're working on addition of quadratic equations. Some students might be just fine practicing the way we were all taught (i.e., complete all the odd numbered problems by themselves while the teacher circulates and assists as needed). But what about those who just aren't getting it? If you could find a way to have them access the content in a variety of ways, it just might help their magnifying glasses hone in on the way adding quadratic questions makes most sense to them. Try setting up areas in your classrooms so students can rotate through centers. One could focus on basic skill development, one could have some manipulatives available for hands-on practice, and one could have them explain the process through journal writing.

✓ **TELL students that we all learn differently and that it is okay.** Give them an example of someone who does one thing well but really struggles with another. Short-term memory versus long-term memory is a good way to introduce this topic. Maybe you can recall a student who memorized information quickly and got perfect scores on every test. But you also remember he or she had difficulty remembering that information for very long. You might actually want to use yourself as an example; students love learning the strengths and weaknesses of their teacher. Okay, so you have no weaknesses . . . make one up.

✓ **OFFER options for students to show they understand the concept or can do the task.** Whenever possible, ask kids to work in their preferred modes (e.g., acting, rap, dancing, puppetry, multimedia). You will feel better knowing they understand the topic, and they will feel more successful for having demonstrated it *their* way. Don't worry about the fact that they'll have to demonstrate their learning on standardized tests; they'll have plenty of opportunity to practice traditional test taking. If your goal is to see if they've learned the material, then let them show you they have!

Making Connections

Check out Chapter 6 on Arts Instruction

✓ **MAKE learning fun and engaging.** Promise right now that you will never stand in front of your class again and simply lecture in a dry monotone. Even adult students enjoy humor, variety, and an appealing presenter. Teens deserve even MORE of that!

✓ **THINK back on your own educational experiences in secondary school.** Who were your favorite teachers? Why? Consider using some of their "magic." Did you have a history teacher have the class act out Washington crossing the Delaware, and you had so much fun you'll never forget it? What about an English teacher who let you sing, draw, rap, or sculpt, as long as you could demonstrate you understood and could identify the main themes in *To Kill a Mockingbird*? That's what I'm talking about!

✓ **ASK, "What are the *essential* elements of your standards? How could you teach something in a different way?"** Teaching in the same format, using essentially the same words, day in and day out, cannot be very much fun for teachers. Just assume the students do not like it either. Feeling brain dead? Ask a colleague for some ideas. Collaborate, communicate, share—these are encouraged words in today's schools!

✓ **USE tiered lessons and menus to proactively provide options.** Go online and look up tiered lessons and lesson plan menus. There is so much out there! Teachers can give a Tic-Tac-Toe board with nine options and ask students to choose three (that, of course, need to go either horizontally, vertically, or diagonally). Or give different points to different activities and allow students to

Plugged In

daretodifferentiate
.wikispaces.com/
Tiering

choose. For example, if they need to do 10 points for a novel in English class, they could choose to write an essay (10 points), *or* write a poem (5 points) *and* draw a new cover to the book (5 points), *or* draw three characters (2 points each) *and* create a song about the book (4 points), and so on. You could also create lessons that have MUST DO sections that the whole class needs to complete, while a variety of options for MAY DO sections. Let the class know they need to select at least one MAY DO in addition to the MUST DO.

✓ **INSERT variety and choice without too much work.** A simple example of this is to stop telling your class WHAT they have to write about. A little autonomy goes a long way. When the content isn't the point of your lesson, allow students choice whenever possible. You create the guidelines for those choices, but ultimately, they've chosen themselves.

✓ **FOCUS on the idea that UDL is based in design elements.** Educators call that "planning." FLEXIBLE PLANNING for ALL!

UNIVERSAL DESIGN FOR LEARNING GUIDELINES

I. Provide Multiple Means of Representation

1: Provide options for perception
1.1 Offer ways of customizing the display of information
1.2 Offer alternatives for auditory information
1.3 Offer alternatives for visual information

2: Provide options for language, mathematical expressions, and symbols
2.1 Clarify vocabulary and symbols
2.2 Clarify syntax and structure
2.3 Support decoding of text, mathematical notation, and symbols
2.4 Promote understanding across languages
2.5 Illustrate through multiple media

3: Provide options for comprehension
3.1 Activate or supply background knowledge
3.2 Highlight patterns, critical features, big ideas, and relationships
3.3 Guide information processing, visualization, and manipulation
3.4 Maximize transfer and generalization

Resourceful, knowledgeable learners

II. Provide Multiple Means of Action and Expression

4: Provide options for physical action
4.1 Vary the methods for response and navigation
4.2 Optimize access to tools and assistive technologies

5: Provide options for expression and communication
5.1 Use multiple media for communication
5.2 Use multiple tools for construction and composition
5.3 Build fluencies with graduated levels of support for practice and performance

6: Provide options for executive functions
6.1 Guide appropriate goal-setting
6.2 Support planning and strategy development
6.3 Facilitate managing information and resources
6.4 Enhance capacity for monitoring progress

Strategic, goal-directed learners

III. Provide Multiple Means of Engagement

7: Provide options for recruiting interest
7.1 Optimize individual choice and autonomy
7.2 Optimize relevance, value, and authenticity
7.3 Minimize threats and distractions

8: Provide options for sustaining effort and persistence
8.1 Heighten salience of goals and objectives
8.2 Vary demands and resources to optimize challenge
8.3 Foster collaboration and community
8.4 Increase mastery-oriented feedback

9: Provide options for self-regulation
9.1 Promote expectations and beliefs that optimize motivation
9.2 Facilitate personal coping skills and strategies
9.3 Develop self-assessment and reflection

Purposeful, motivated learners

Source: © 2011, CAST. Used with permission. All rights reserved.

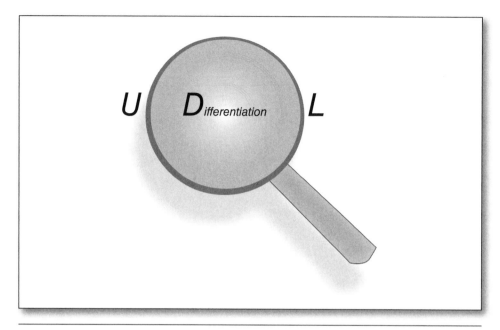

Source: Phillip Bell, 2014—San Pedro High School, CA. Used with permission.

UDL LESSON PLAN EXAMPLE

Fractals, an Inquiry: Day 1

Middle School Science

UDL components of this lesson have been highlighted.

Essential Question: What are the steps in scientific inquiry?

- Students will gain an understanding of the steps in a scientific inquiry.
- Students will become aware that scientific inquiries can happen anywhere and are a natural part of exploring the world.

Overview: This unit is designed to support student understanding of scientific inquiry. Students experience each step firsthand in the inquiry process and how the steps systematically build toward understanding. Then, a case study is used to guide students' understanding of the steps in a scientific inquiry. A simple art activity that involves creating fractals with paint serves as the context for the inquiry (Day 2).

Anticipatory Set: Whole Class (10 minutes)

Ask students to rate a series of statements (e.g., to conduct a scientific inquiry, you need a science lab with precise equipment, including microscopes, Bunsen burners, test tubes, and proper chemicals—F) as true or false. Students write down a "T" or "F" as the statements are read aloud. Then, ask for a show of hands for numbers of students who answered true or false to each question. Finally, discuss the implications for each statement as a class.

Introduce and Model New Knowledge: Whole Class (10 minutes)

Provide an overview of the steps of scientific inquiry: asking good questions, testing the question, observing closely, collecting and organizing data, interpreting the results to develop conclusions, and reporting on them. Explain that by making their own fractals (Day 2), students will have an opportunity to engage in scientific inquiry.

Guided Practice: Whole Class (20 minutes)

Guide students through a case study as a model of an inquiry. Use highlighters to accentuate important points in the case study. Using a graphic organizer, share the following example of an inquiry with students. For each step, have students fill out the corresponding section of their graphic organizers.

Peer Conferencing: Think-Pair-Share (10 minutes)

Ask students to turn to a partner and share any questions they might have about today's activities. Have one partner share a question that came up for him or her, then both should discuss what they believe to be a possible answer(s). Next, have one partner share his or her question and possible answer with the whole class. Call on volunteers to add their ideas and information to what the student thinks is the answer. Be sure to correct any misinterpretations and to refine student understanding through feedback and elaboration. Repeat the process with other pairs of students.

Assessment: During the activity that models Max's Inquiry, be sure to note which students have trouble charting the steps of the inquiry process in their graphic organizers. Collect their responses in order to study them in detail.

Be prepared for the Think-Pair-Share activity with a sheet of paper divided into three columns: Confused, With Partner, With Rest of Class. Then, note which students seemed confused, those who were able to generate answers to their own questions with the help of a partner, and those who needed the added insights of the rest of the class. Use this information for later grouping purposes so you can pair novice learners with those who seem more versed in the scientific inquiry process.

Max's Inquiry

I am a scientist, but most people think I am just a dog. They see me at the pond and throw sticks in the water for me to fetch. I am curious about how many sticks get thrown in the pond during the year. So the topic of my inquiry is investigating how many sticks people throw in the pond.

I wrote one sentence in the form of a question to help me focus on my inquiry: *How many fetching sticks do people throw in the pond?* I needed to make **observations** and **record** how, what, when, and how often I made them. I also needed to record **other information** that might be important.

I counted the number of fetching sticks in my favorite pond. That's the **what** and **how** of my observations. Every afternoon for a week, I counted the sticks on the pond—that's the **when** and **how often** of my observations. I also needed to know the weather conditions in the park on the days I counted sticks in the pond. This is the **other information** that could be helpful as a part of my observations.

I made a chart that organized and recorded all my data. Each column on my chart has a label: Day, Time, How Many Sticks, and Weather Condition. Here's an example of one entry:

Day	Time	How Many Sticks	Weather Condition
9/24	**3:30**	**16**	**sunny**

I studied all of my entries and noticed a pattern. On days when the weather was warm and sunny, there were more sticks in my pond. This is the **conclusion** part of my inquiry. Now I'm wondering whether the warmer weather brings out more people to play fetch with their dogs on these days, and if that's why there are more sticks on sunny days. This is the **now I need to do another inquiry** part of my inquiry. *These inquiries can go on forever!*

Source: adapted from a lesson presented on the CAST UDL Lesson Builder website (lessonbuilder.cast .org/explore.php?op=static&pid=fractals_1).

REFERENCES

Access Project. (2012). *Universal design for learning*. Colorado State University. Retrieved from http://accessproject.colostate.edu/udl/

Ashton, T. M. (2005). Students with learning disabilities using assistive technology in the inclusive classroom. In D. Edyburn, K. Higgins, & R. Boone (Eds.), *The handbook of special education technology research and practice* (pp. 229–238). Whitefish Bay, WI: Knowledge by Design.

Basham, J. D., Israel, M., Graden, J., Poth, R., & Winston, M. (2010). A comprehensive approach to RTI: Embedding universal design for learning and technology. *Learning Disability Quarterly, 33,* 243–255.

Basham, J. D., & Marino, M. T. (2013). Understanding STEM education and supporting students through universal design for learning. *Teaching Exceptional Children, 45*(4), 8–15.

Center for Applied Special Technology (CAST). (2010). *UDL at a glance.* Retrieved from http://www.youtube.com/watch?v=bDvKnY0g6e4

Center for Universal Design. (2008). *Environments and products for all people: About UD.* North Carolina State University. Retrieved from http://www.ncsu.edu/ncsu/design/cud/about_ud/about_ud.htm

Chiasson, P. (2005). Peirce's design for thinking: An embedded philosophy of education. *Educational Philosophy and Theory, 37*(2), 207–226.

Chita-Tegmark, M., Gravel, J. W., Serpa, M. deL. B., Domings, Y., & Rose, D. H. (2012). Using the universal design for learning framework to support culturally diverse learners. *Journal of Education, 192*(1), 17–22.

Connections Academy. (2014). *Your child deserves a superior K–12 education at home.* Retrieved from http://info.connectionsacademy.com/

DeCoste, D. C. (n.d.). Universal Design for Learning in the classroom [Presentation slides]. Retrieved from https://www.montgomeryschoolsmd.org/departments/hiat/udl/UDL_intro.pdf

Individuals with Disabilities Education Improvement Act of 2004, Pub. L. No. 108-446.

National Center for Education Statistics. (2009). *Projections of education statistics to 2018* (37th ed.). Washington, DC: Author.

Rose, D. H. (2014). *UDL guidelines—version 2.0.* Retrieved from http://www.cast.org

Rose, D. H., & Meyer, A. (2002). *Teaching every student in the digital age: Universal design for learning.* Alexandria, VA: Association for Supervision and Curriculum Development.

RECOMMENDED READINGS

* Goeke, J. L., & Ciotoli, F. (2014). Inclusive STEM: Making integrative curriculum accessible to all students. *Children's Technology and Engineering*, *18*, 19–22.

* McGuire, J. M., Scott, S. S., & Shaw, S. F. (2006). Universal design and its applications in educational environments. *Remedial and Special Education*, *27*(3), 166–175.

* Rappolt-Schlichtmann, G., Daley, S. G., Lim, S., Lapinski, S., Robinson, K. H., & Johnson, M. (2013). Universal design for learning and elementary school science: Exploring the efficacy, use, and perceptions of a web-based science notebook. *Journal of Educational Psychology*, *105*(4), 1210–1225.

* Smith, S. J., & Basham, J. D. (2014). Designing online learning opportunities for students with disabilities. *Teaching Exceptional Children*, *46*(5), 127–137.

* Spooner, F., Baker, J. N., Harris, A. A., Ahlgrim-Delzell, L., & Browder, D. M. (2007). Effects of training in universal design for learning on lesson plan development. *Remedial and Special Education*, *28*(2), 108–116.

* U.S. Department of Education, Office of Special Education Programs. (n.d.). OESP ideas that work: Tool kit on Universal Design for Learning. Retrieved from https://www.osepideasthatwork.org/udl/instrpract.asp

GO EVEN FURTHER WITH
THIS TOPIC ON THE WORLD WIDE WEB

- www.cast.org/udl/
- www.udlcenter.org
- www.cec.sped.org
- marylandlearninglinks.org/1021
- udltechtoolkit.wikispaces.com

THE Apps WE LOVE

- UDLinks
- Toontastic
- Geoboard
- Scribble press
- Bitsboard

12

Incredible Inclusion

Erin Studer

CHIME Institute

Amy Hanreddy

California State University, Northridge

WHAT REALLY WORKS IN
INCLUSION IN THE SECONDARY CLASSROOM

They Are All OUR Students

A principal is on a morning tour of classrooms at her school. In chemistry, she sees students working collaboratively to create molecular models of various compounds using 3-D atomic models. The general education and special education teacher are both facilitating centers in which students identify the atomic weights of their creations. In the English classroom next door, students are working on a "Reader's Theater" lesson in which students recreate scenes from the novel they are reading. One of the students assists another student, who is nonverbal, by inputting text into a speech-generating device for their performance. In history class at the end of the hall, the teacher is about to preview a unit on World War II. Before displaying his PowerPoint, he gives the students the option of three different styles of guided notes that he and his special education co-teacher developed based on the needs of the students in the class. The principal returns to her office, pleased at what she has observed and excited that she is leading a school that provides its students with wonderfully differentiated lessons and opportunities to learn in inclusive environments.

Increasingly this kind of education at the secondary level is not the exception but is becoming what is expected. Students of all abilities are expected to learn together, have access to the general education classroom, and engage in innovative differentiated curriculum to help them learn to their full potential. While this can sometimes seem daunting, given the proper strategies and supports, this approach to teaching all students is highly effective. Research shows that taking an approach of differentiating instruction and including all learners is beneficial to all students in a classroom (Cole, Waldron, & Majd, 2004; Ghandi, 2007; Sailor & Roger, 2005).

Differentiation is an approach to planning and instruction that asks teachers to know their students well and use that knowledge to develop options for students to take in information and to show what they know (Center for Applied Special Technology, 2008; Edyburn, 2010). Differentiation is often seen as a key component for creating an inclusive classroom environment.

Inclusive teaching means considering the wide range of learners in every step of the teaching process and ensuring that all students have a way to access the curriculum, express what they know, and remain engaged and motivated. If I am beginning to teach a lesson that involves reading from a textbook and Sam struggles to decode text, I could consider other ways for him to access the material (e.g., audio, pictures), provide him with text written at his reading level, deliver a presentation that includes the textbook content, or support students in finding material online (including videos) that addresses the same content. The strategy that I choose might depend on Sam's interests and skills, my goal for the lesson, and the needs of other students in the class, with the expectation that whatever strategy I pick, Sam can implement it in the general education classroom.

Inclusive teaching also means considering the social needs of our students—yes, even in middle and high school. Inclusive teachers facilitate a sense of membership and belonging in their classrooms, support students' ability to resolve conflicts, and teach communication and social skills as a key piece of the curriculum. This culture of inclusion in the classroom provides the benefits of ethical and social development and provides true access to education for all students.

Making Connections

Check out Chapter 19 on Social Skills

Secondary schools have their own unique impediments to differentiation and inclusion than elementary schools, such as graduation requirements, grading policies, and the rigors of college preparation courses. However, secondary teachers don't need to fear that differentiation leads to watered-down standards or that including students with special needs prevents all learners from achieving rigorous academic standards. When implemented properly, differentiation and inclusive educational approaches support *all* learners to gain required knowledge and skills and allows teachers to be effective and engaging instructors for their students.

RESEARCH SUPPORTS PRACTICES OF DIFFERENTIATION AND INCLUSION

Inclusive education is actually a collection of several research-based instructional practices that support learning, belonging, and positive behavior for diverse classrooms (Sailor & Roger, 2005; Theoharis & Causton, 2014).

Benefits to students without disabilities. Yes, believe it or not, being in an inclusive class with students with special needs actually provides benefits to students who do not have disabilities. This is important for general education teachers to know but may be something for parents of students without disabilities to learn as well. When considering the benefits of including students with disabilities in general education classes, the learning of *all* students must be considered. Several studies have explored the impact of inclusion on students without disabilities and have found that nondisabled students have achieved improved academic outcomes as a result of being in an inclusive class (Cole et al., 2004; Ghandi, 2007). This may be due to the increased supports (such as a special education teacher or paraprofessional) that may be in place or the increased attention to individual needs. Sailor (2008) noted that inclusive practices such as Universal Design for Learning, Positive Behavior Interventions and Supports, and co-teaching have the potential to result in reduced special education referrals schoolwide, because struggling students receive assistance before they fall too far behind.

Benefits to students with disabilities. Evidence also suggests that students with disabilities demonstrate improved academic and social outcomes as a result of increased time spent in general education classes (Cosier, Causton-Theoharis, & Theoharis, 2013; Rea, McLaughlin, & Walther-Thomas, 2002; Vaughn, Moody, & Schumm, 1998), including improved social skills, communication skills, and increased interactions with typical peers (Boyd, Conroy, Asmus, McKenney, & Mancil, 2008; Carter, Siseo, Brown, Brickham, & Al-Khabbaz, 2008). Although time spent in general education is linked to improved academic and social outcomes for students with disabilities, additional supports such as accommodations, modifications, peer supports, and co-teaching are all critical strategies associated with the success of students with disabilities in inclusive settings. Clearly, it is not enough to just schedule a few students with disabilities into a few general education content classes and call it inclusion.

Practices to support inclusive education. Universal Design for Learning considers the wide range of student strengths and needs when planning instruction by ensuring multiple means of representation, expression, and engagement (Center for Applied Special Technology, 2008; Edyburn, 2010). Accommodations and modifications (changes to the curriculum such as increased visuals, use of technology, and enhanced content) are critical tools to support student engagement and learning in general education classes (Dymond & Orelove, 2001; Suk-Hyang, Wehmeyer, Soukup, & Palmer, 2010). Even when a lesson has been developed using a "universally designed" approach, some students will continue to require individualized adjustments. For example, Joey has a physical disability and needs adequate space to move his wheelchair through the classroom. Samantha has a challenge in graphomotor (writing) skills and so is given the option to type her assignments. Max has an intellectual disability and so uses a version of the story assigned in class that includes simplified text and less pictures. These adjustments are carefully designed based on individual needs, with an emphasis on access to the general education curriculum and environment. If you are concerned that you don't have the background knowledge to figure out what adjustments, accommodations, or modifications will be needed, you don't need to worry. That's why we emphasize collaboration between general educators and special education teachers and specialists!

> **Making Connections**
>
> Check out Chapters 7 and 11 on Technology and UDL

Special education is defined in the Individuals with Disabilities Education Improvement Act (IDEIA, 2004) as "specially designed instruction" (Sect. 300.39). This definition does not state *where* this instruction can take place, and thus, individualized instruction can occur in a wide range of settings. When students who receive special education services spend all or part of their day within a general education classroom, one way to ensure that these students are receiving "specially designed instruction" is for a special education teacher to co-teach with the general education teacher (Murawski & Lochner, 2011). With strong evidence demonstrating improved outcomes for a wide range of students (Solis, Vaughn, Swanson, & McCulley, 2012), co-teaching is a critical piece to the puzzle of inclusive classrooms. Yes, this book has you covered in this regard as well! Check out Chapter 13 to read about how to effectively co-teach with a partner.

At times, additional adults (typically known as paraprofessionals, aides, or paraeducators) might be assigned to a classroom, a group of students, or even an individual student based upon an administrator and/or Individualized Education Program (IEP) team's determination that a higher level of support is needed than can be provided by a general education teacher in collaboration with a special education teacher. These paraprofessionals can be important components to ensuring that all students receive adequate supports and access to the curriculum and are viewed as essential in many inclusive classrooms and schools (Giangreco, 2010). Despite the benefits, however, there are also many drawbacks. Giangreco, Edelman, Luiselli, and McFarland (1997) examined the trend of assigning paraprofessionals in inclusive classrooms and noted common challenges: increased reliance on adults, interference with social relationships, and reduced access to instruction from credentialed teachers. In order to avoid these negative impacts, it is critical that paraprofessionals are well trained to support all students, that teachers provide high-quality supervision, and that paraprofessionals do not provide the majority of instruction for students with identified disabilities (Giangreco & Doyle, 2002).

Positive social relationships play a key role in student success, and yet students with intellectual disabilities, autism, and multiple disabilities may be less skilled at the social nuances of middle and high school interactions, leading to less access to unstructured social opportunities (Wagner, Cadwallader, Garza, & Cameto, 2004). Peer supports can support the development of positive social relationships while reducing reliance on adults. Although these arrangements often begin with some adult facilitation, students with and without disabilities generally become comfortable with one another over time and often develop friendships as a result (Carter, Bottema-Beutel, & Brock, 2014).

Inclusive teachers will consider the idea of "inclusion" as the process of refining differentiation skills, engaging in reflection on student learning, and collaborating with others to meet the needs of their students. Want to engage in this process? Great! Then make sure you are not engaging in any of the common pitfalls. If you are, simply stop and make sure that instead you are actively practicing more from our "DO" category.

STOP "WHAT YOU NEED TO AVOID AT ALL COSTS"

Teachers

- ✖ **STOP assuming that "there is nothing" a student with a moderate to severe disability can gain from academic high school classes.** Students can learn a wide range of embedded skills within core content instruction, are able to gain contextual knowledge about subjects that can be applied to functional aspects of the curriculum, and are able to gain social and developmental benefits from engaging with typically developing peers (Downing & Peckham-Hardin, 2007).
- ✖ **STOP believing that it is not your job to teach self-management, organization, and social skills.** All students develop these kinds of

skills at a wide variety of ages. In fact, brain research tells us that the human brain does not finish developing the frontal cortex (the part responsible for discernment and high-level decision-making) until humans are 25 years old. Given that organization, social skills, and self-management are highly necessary skills for being considered "Career and College Ready," secondary teachers need to work collaboratively to embed instruction and practice opportunities concerning social learning.

- ✘ **STOP confusing mere placement in a general education classroom with inclusive teaching practices.** True inclusion means that students benefit from a comprehensive approach to their educational program. This comprehensive approach includes (a) planned adult supports in co-teaching, and if necessary, paraprofessional support, (b) access to universally designed and appropriately differentiated curriculum, (c) use of carefully considered accommodations and modifications, and (d) supports by peers and any needed service providers. Placement in a general education class for students with special needs without these supports and considerations is not inclusion; it is just assigning a seat.

- ✘ **STOP assuming that if a student with a disability is to be included in general education, they will need full-time paraprofessional support.** Carefully considered accommodations, modifications, differentiation, co-teaching, and peer supports often eliminate the need for paraprofessional supports. In fact, if these additional supports are provided without first trying less restrictive approaches, we may actually hamper students' development and growth as independent students. Yes, it feels helpful to have another set of hands, but consider that it might actually be detrimental to the student in the long run.

- ✘ **STOP relying on paraprofessionals to provide instruction to students with disabilities.** Students deserve to receive instruction from highly qualified and well-trained teachers (that's you!). When assigned to classrooms or students, paraprofessionals should not be the primary deliverers of instruction. According to Giangreco, Suter, and Doyle (2010), this amounts to assigning "the least qualified personnel to students who present the most challenging learning and behavior characteristics" (p. 51). Instead, paraprofessional supports should be utilized to help students who require a higher level of support to access the carefully designed and appropriately differentiated lessons presented by the classroom teacher. While paraprofessionals can play an integral role in the instruction of all students in the classroom, teachers should always consider themselves the primary educator of all students.

- ✘ **STOP seating students with disabilities together or in the back of the classroom.** Assigned seating for students with disabilities should be determined like that of any other student in the class-room with any special consideration taken into account (e.g., field of vision consideration, access and mobility challenges). Grouping of students with disabilities in close proximity to one another for the ease of providing support during independent work time is really just a symptom of a larger instructional issue. Students of any one group (high achieving, English language learners, students with special needs) shouldn't all be working together all of the time. Heterogeneous groups provide learning opportunities for all students that cannot be achieved in homogeneous groupings. Keep this in mind when planning group work and when creating your seating chart.

✘ **STOP calling students "my kids" and "your kids" when referring to students with and without disabilities.** In many secondary classrooms, general education teachers are identified as the "teacher of record" because they are the "highly qualified content teacher." This doesn't mean you are on your own however or that you pull rank on your special education colleagues. Caseloads and class rosters are of secondary importance compared to who is sitting in your classroom. In inclusive classrooms, as soon as a student sits down in your classroom, they are "our" students. You don't have to be singularly responsible for their well-being and education; you have your special education teachers, Title I teachers, paraprofessionals, counselors, and other service providers to help you.

✘ **STOP considering individual learning needs *after* a lesson has been planned and developed.** Co-planned, universally designed lessons take into consideration the needs of the class prior to deciding "how" a lesson is going to play out. All lessons are driven by the general education curriculum ("what") and are guided by the needs present in the classroom ("who"). By taking student strengths and needs into account, you are better able to create a cohesive lesson plan that is accessible to all of your students, rather than attempting to develop "retrofitted" solutions to help a student be a part of a preexisting lesson.

✘ **STOP using a "one-size-fits-all" behavior management system in the classroom.** Fair isn't equal; fair is getting what you need (Lavoie, 2004). It is true for instruction, and it is true for behavior management. Every class should have rules and a comprehensive Positive Behavior Support program in place. There will be occasions when individual students need something slightly different or in addition to your established system. Students might need a personalized checklist, reward system, or opportunities to take breaks. These adjustments are not unfair to the other students (remember those students don't *need* the additional supports) nor is it mollycoddling the student who requires the additional support. It is providing the child with a system they need to learn new behavioral skills.

✗ **STOP establishing prerequisites for membership in your classroom.** For example, some teachers say students are only "ready" to enter their class when they can sit quietly or work independently. Prerequisites to be included in a general education class are the classic traps of a segregated special education delivery model. Students cannot learn how to "sit quietly and work independently" in your classroom by going down the hallway and learning how to do it in the resource room with another teacher.

✗ **STOP treating special educators like an aide in the classroom.** Special education teachers are highly trained professionals with critical knowledge about the needs of a wide variety of learners. They are trained in strategies and approaches that help children who are struggling. Too often, they are used to merely "support" students or pull a small group of learners off to the side for help while the general education teacher instructs the "rest" of the class. This is a misuse of their expertise and an underutilization of the adult resources in a room. Times when both a general education and special education teacher are present in a classroom should be treated as highly valuable and important time; it should be planned for, and the teachers should be using one of several co-teaching methods so students get the maximum benefit from their teachers.

✗ **STOP structuring your groups solely by ability levels.** There are times for ability or "readiness level" groupings in a classroom, but there is also ample time and reasons for mixed-ability level groupings. Merely utilizing heterogeneous ability groupings often leads teachers to recommend more restrictive placements for students because they feel there "isn't a group" in their room available for students with more significant needs.

✗ **STOP working like an independent contractor when it comes to planning instruction.** Too many teachers work in isolation when it comes to planning instruction for their classrooms. The task of differentiating meeting individual needs is too much for just one teacher to take on. We know that! We agree completely. To truly be effective, teachers must work with their colleagues to plan their instruction and their lessons.

✗ **STOP believing that only students with special needs will benefit from an inclusive approach.** Students from low socioeconomic backgrounds, students who have had limited access to early education programs, English language learners, students from migrant families, students who are high achieving/gifted, and students who are merely struggling because of prior gaps in their instruction can all benefit from inclusive education environments with carefully designed and differentiated curriculum and instruction.

✘ **STOP relying so heavily on lecture for delivery of instruction.** Lecture formats can be effective, efficient, and appropriate when used sparingly and purposefully. Let's repeat: sparingly and purposefully. However, when used too frequently, it can lead to passive instruction and, even worse, passive learners. Differentiated instruction and universally designed lessons would dictate that instruction be active, engaging, and represent multiple pathways to obtain and express knowledge.

Administrators

✘ **STOP integrating and including students after general education rosters are created.** This continues the sense that students with disabilities create additional work. Students with disabilities need to be placed within the master schedule before general education students, not after. In addition, if a maximum class size is 30 students, then any student with an IEP included in the class should be included within that 30; the class should not be made twice as big, even if its co-taught. In fact, inclusive classes should include no more than 30% of the class as students with special needs (Murawski & Dieker, 2013); too many schools are now "clustering" students into general education classes and calling a class wherein 70% of the class has IEPs as "inclusive." This is antithetical to our goal of heterogeneity.

✘ **STOP making placement decisions based on students' eligibility category.** Not only is this not in compliance with IDEIA and other state and federal guidelines, it is ultimately limiting to the growth and development of children. Each child's Least Restrictive Environment (LRE) requires individual considerations about his strengths and needs. Each IEP team must also consider if and how the supports and accommodations any one child needs can be implemented in the general education classroom. A presupposition of a child's placement based solely on the disability category listed on their IEP is *not* legal, educationally appropriate, or ethical.

GO STRATEGIES FOR SUCCESS

Teachers, DO This

✓ **KNOW the definition of co-teaching** so you can differentiate it from in-class support, monitoring, and what a paraprofessional might do. True co-teaching requires "co-planning, co-instructing, and co-assessing" (Murawski, 2003, p. 10). If teachers are walking in the room and saying, "So, what are we doing today?" they are not co-teaching; they need to know what it is and how to do it so that students truly benefit (Murawski, 2009).

✓ **BREAK direct instruction (especially whole-group instruction) into small chunks.** Delivering instruction in smaller chunks and providing time in between for students to work with and create meaning out of the instruction provided is good practice for all learners. It provides additional benefit for children with special needs and struggling learners. Leveraging active learning, social interaction, and increased time to build and consider new knowledge allows a variety of learners to access the curriculum through a wider range of learning pathways than mere lecture or demonstration.

Making Connections

Check out Chapter 13 on Co-Teaching

✓ **USE a Positive Behavior Support system in your classroom.** Teachers often cite issues of classroom management as a reason for seeking segregated settings for students with special needs. However, challenging behavior is not solely attributable to students with special needs. Teachers who develop and implement Positive Behavior Support systems find that any classroom environment becomes more manageable and effective, creating an environment in which all learners can succeed.

Making Connections

Check out Chapter 8 on Positive Behavior Supports

✓ **PURPOSEFULLY PLAN for ways to utilize peer supports in your classroom.** Peer modeling may be one of the most powerful and effective tools that a teacher in an inclusive classroom has at her disposal. And, let's face it—in middle school and high school, peers are far more important and powerful than any curriculum, teacher, book, or PBS technique! In a certain sense, the power of peer modeling and interaction is at least half the point of inclusive classrooms. So now that you have all of the students of wide ranging abilities together, put them to work helping, teaching, and modeling for one another. The old teacher adage, "Never do anything a student can do for you; it's their learning experience, not yours," is never more true than in an inclusive classroom. Peer support, peer modeling, and peer collaboration are often more welcome and desired by students than support from a teacher or paraprofessional.

✓ **COLLABORATE, co-teach, co-plan, and co-assess with your colleagues.** The style of work required to include a wide variety of learners in a classroom and to develop universally designed and differentiated lessons must be a collaborative working style. You can't do it on your own. It's true—even as a content specialist, you must be willing to accept and in some cases seek out the support, collaboration, and genuine shared responsibility of your colleagues.

✓ **CREATE a system for adaptations to the curriculum or instruction.** Too many teachers and schools recreate the wheel every year. Instead, have a repository for all of your adapted materials at each grade level. That way, if your biology teacher has to teach chemistry as well next year, she can look at all the materials that have already been adapted for chemistry students over the years. Certainly, students are different and she may need to continue to make adaptations, but at least she doesn't have to start from scratch.

✓ **START to become well informed about the needs and concerns for students with a wide range of disabilities.** Everyone naturally has differing levels of knowledge and expertise about how to support learners across the range abilities (gifted learners, English language learners, students who have reading disabilities, etc.). One of the positives of co-teaching and collaboration is that no single teacher has to know everything. By putting all of our heads together, we are able to teach all students. When teachers engage in this kind of quest for a deeper understanding about the needs of their students, they are more likely to feel prepared to work with their colleagues to meet those needs and less likely to recommend that a student with special needs has to be educated by "an expert" in some other classroom.

Administrators, DO This

✓ **CREATE a schedule that supports teachers in spending time together for co-planning and co-teaching.** Everyone knows that time is an especially limited resource at schools. The worst thing you can do is add to the burden by not making effective use of meeting time or scheduling too many staff meetings. Consider trading out some staff meeting time for co-planning time in your master schedule for teachers (Murawski & Dieker, 2013).

✓ **MODEL an inclusive environment.** If you talk about "those" students as different and support segregated placements, your teachers will often do the same. Show them all that you believe in taking whatever steps—even baby steps at first—to become a more inclusive site. Ask for help. Show parents, students, faculty, and staff that you are open to ideas for becoming the most inclusive school you can be.

SAMPLE GOAL/ACTIVITY MATRIX

Class Activities: Goals:	English	Math	Social Studies	Science
Correctly respond to comprehension questions after reading a short selection of text.	Embed comprehension questions into independent and group reading activities.	When completing a word problem, highlight key words and identify what a problem is asking.	After decoding information from a selection of a nonfiction text (online or textbook), identify key facts.	Correctly follow written directions for science activities.
Use a checklist of assignment steps and self-monitoring strategies to complete class assignments at a similar pace as her peers.	Follow a writing checklist to monitor progress on an extended writing assignment.	Use a timer to "check in" on her own progress every 5 minutes while working independently on a worksheet.	When working on a group project, act as a "project manager" to ensure the group has completed all required steps and has followed the given timeline.	Follow steps to the completion of a science activity by checking off each step on a checklist.

Cecilia is a student whose goals emphasize reading comprehension and the completion of assignments in a timely manner.

Class Activities: Goals:	English	Math	Social Studies	Science
Use pictures to represent the understanding of modified reading material.	Identify pictures that represent the main idea and characters in a novel read in class.	Correctly identify pictures to match a word problem.	Use an image search engine to select at least three pictures that represent a key topic discussed in class, and share these with peers.	Follow a materials checklist using pictures to prepare for a science lab activity.
Count items with 1:1 correspondence up to 20.	Count the number of books needed for his table group, and distribute these to students.	Use manipulatives to solve simple addition and subtraction problems to 20.	Identify materials needed for group members when creating a diorama.	Act as "materials manager" in lab activity. Gather and count needed materials for his small group.

Rodrigo is a student whose goals emphasize using pictures as a form of communication and counting items up to 20. Even in a middle school or high school classroom, he can be an active member of the class while working on his own individual goals and objectives.

SELF-ASSESSMENT OF INCLUSIVE EDUCATIONAL PRACTICES

Complete the self-assessment for your classroom, indicating the degree to which each practice is currently being implemented. Once the assessment is completed, highlight two rows that will be prioritized in the weeks that follow. Continue choosing items and moving them closer to being "fully" implemented!

	Fully	Partially	Not Yet
Teachers differentiate for a variety of learners by using visual, tactile, and kinesthetic materials and experiences.			
Teachers use a variety of student groupings, such as pairs, small groups, and whole class.			
Teachers choose groupings on the basis of learning styles, abilities, interests, and curricular focus, and not on the basis of ability alone.			
Teachers plan accommodations for students with disabilities, based on their IEP, and incorporate those accommodations into lesson plans and everyday instruction.			
Teachers plan modifications to classroom instruction for students with disabilities who need it, using the same or similar, age-appropriate materials for assignments, homework, and tests.			
Teachers provide direct instruction on IEP goals, infused across subject areas within the general education curriculum.			
All students receive positive reinforcement and feedback (i.e., at least 75% positive; no more than 25% corrective).			
Teachers interact with students in ways that allow for positive peer relationships and personal dignity.			
Teachers work with paraprofessionals who are assigned to individual students to a) provide appropriate supports and b) fade adult support to increase student independence.			
Instructional staff select co-teaching methods on the basis of student need and curriculum content when two adults are instructors in the class.			
Instructional planning teams welcome parents as active team members.			

Revised from the (2006) Quality Indicators of Inclusive Education. *Maryland Coalition for Inclusive Education.* Retrieved online at http://www.mcie.org/usermedia/application/8/quality-indicators---building-based-practices-2011%28accessible-by-berman%29.pdf

GOAL/ACTIVITY MATRIX

Directions

1. At the head of each column in the top row, identify four main activities to target throughout the day.

2. Summarize two IEP goals to be prioritized for an individual student. List these at the start of each row on the left.

3. For each goal, describe how it might be addressed within each of the main activities. Share this chart with all team members (special ed and general ed teachers, family, related service providers).

As routines are established for addressing these first two skills throughout the day, continue to add more goals and more activities!

Class activities: → ↓ Goals:	Activity 1	Activity 2	Activity 3	Activity 4

REFERENCES

Boyd, B. A., Conroy, M. A., Asmus, J. M., McKenney, E. L. W., & Mancil, G. R. (2008). Descriptive analysis of classroom setting events on the social behaviors of children with autism spectrum disorder. *Education and Training in Developmental Disabilities, 43*, 186–197.

Carter, E. W., Bottema-Beutel, K., & Brock, M. E. (2014). Social interactions and friendships. In M. Agran, F. Brown, C. Hughes, C. Quirk, & D. Ryndak (Eds.), *Equity and full participation for individuals with severe disabilities: A vision for the future* (pp. 197–216). Baltimore, MD: Paul H. Brookes.

Carter, E. W., Siseo, L. G., Brown, L., Brickham, D., & Al-Khabbaz, Z. A. (2008). Peer interactions and academic engagement of youth with developmental disabilities in inclusive middle and high school classrooms. *American Journal on Mental Retardation, 113*, 479–494.

Center for Applied Special Technology. (2008). UDL Editions by CAST. Retrieved from http://udleditions.cast.org/

Cole, C., Waldron, N., & Majd, M. (2004). Academic progress of students across inclusive and traditional settings. *Mental Retardation, 42*(2), 136–144.

Cosier, M., Causton-Theoharis, J., & Theoharis, G. (2013). Does access matter? Time in general education and achievement for students with disabilities. *Remedial and Special Education, 34*(6), 323–332.

Downing, J. E., & Peckham-Hardin, K. D. (2007). Inclusive education: What makes it a good education for students with moderate to severe disabilities? *Research and Practice for Persons with Severe Disabilities, 32*(1), 16–30.

Dymond, S. K., & Orelove, F. P. (2001). What constitutes effective curricula for students with severe disabilities? *Exceptionality, 9*, 109–122.

Edyburn, D. (2010). Would you recognize Universal Design for Learning if you saw it? Ten propositions for new directions for the second decade of UDL. *Learning Disability Quarterly, 33*, 33–41.

Ghandi, A. (2007). Context matters: Exploring relations between inclusion and reading achievement of students without disabilities. *International Journal of Disability, Development, and Education, 54*(1), 91–112.

Giangreco, M. (2010). One-to-one paraprofessionals for students with disabilities in inclusive schools: Is conventional wisdom wrong? *Intellectual and Developmental Disabilities, 48*(1), 1–13.

Giangreco, M., & Doyle, M. (2002). Students with disabilities and paraprofessional supports: Benefits, balance, and band-aids. *Focus on Exceptional Children, 34*(7), 1–12.

Giangreco, M., Edelman, S., Luiselli, T., & McFarland, S. (1997). Helping or hovering? Effects of instructional assistant proximity on students with disabilities. *Exceptional Children, 64*, 7–18.

Giangreco, M. F., Suter, J. C., & Doyle, M. (2010). Paraprofessionals in inclusive schools: A review of recent research. *Journal of Educational & Psychological Consultation, 20*(1), 41–57.

Individuals with Disabilities Education Improvement Act. (2004). 20 U.S.C. § 1400.

Lavoie, R. (2004). *How difficult can this be? The F.A.T. City Workshop: Understanding learning disabilities* [DVD]. United States: PBS Videos.

Murawski, W. W. (2003). *Co-teaching in the inclusive classroom: Working together to help all your students find success.* Medina, WA: Institute for Educational Development.

Murawski, W. W. (2009). *Collaborative teaching in secondary schools: Making the co-teaching marriage work!* Thousand Oaks, CA: Corwin.

Murawski, W. W., & Dieker, L. A. (2013). *Leading the co-teaching dance: Leadership strategies to enhance team outcomes.* Arlington, VA: Council for Exceptional Children.

Murawski, W., & Lochner, W. (2011). Observing co-teaching: What to ask for, look for, and listen for. *Intervention in School and Clinic, 46*(3), 174–183.

Rea, P. J., McLaughlin, V. L., & Walther-Thomas, C. (2002). Outcomes for students with learning disabilities in inclusive and pullout programs. *Exceptional Children, 68*(2), 203.

Sailor, W. (2008). Access to the general curriculum: Systems change or tinker some more? *Research and Practice for Persons with Severe Disabilities, 33/34*(4-1), 249–257.

Sailor, W., & Roger, B. (2005). Rethinking inclusion: Schoolwide applications. *Phi Delta Kappan, 86*, 503–509.

Solis, M., Vaughn, S., Swanson, E., & McCulley, L. (2012). Collaborative models of instruction: The empirical foundations of inclusion and co-teaching. *Psychology in the Schools, 49*(5), 498–510.

Suk-Hyang, L., Wehmeyer, M. L., Soukup, J. H., & Palmer, S. B. (2010). Impact of curriculum modifications on access to the general education curriculum for students with disabilities. *Exceptional Children, 76*(2), 213–233.

Theoharis, G., & Causton, J. (2014). Leading inclusive reform for students with disabilities: A school- and systemwide approach. *Theory Into Practice, 53*(2), 82–97.

Vaughn, S., Moody, S., & Schumm, J. (1998). Broken promises: Reading instruction in the resource room. *Exceptional Children, 64*(2), 211–225.

Wagner, M., Cadwallader, T. W., Garza, N., & Cameto, R. (2004). Social activities of youth with disabilities. *NLTS2 Data Brief, 3*, 1–4.

RECOMMENDED VIDEOS

Fabrocini, J., Adler, M., & San Giacomo, L. (2007) *Accessible IEPs for all: Gathering the experts around the table* [DVD]. Baltimore, MD: Paul H. Brookes.

Habib, D. (2007). *Including Samuel* (DVD). Concord, NH: Author.

Habib, D. (2007). *Thaysa.* Available at https://www.youtube.com/watch?v=HHYur2c3N8&index=11&list=TLaazIdxYLjh5XhMuAdgDiSXQ1NXPfmPjY

Habib, D. (2014). *All means all.* SWIFT Center. Available online at https://www.youtube.com/watch?v=v1MaeQqaygg&index=8&list=TLaazIdxYLjh5XhMuAdgDiSXQ1NXPfmPjY

RECOMMENDED READINGS

* Artiles, A., Kozleski, E., & Waitoller, F. (2011). *Inclusive education: Examining equity on five continents.* Cambridge, MA: Harvard Education Press.
* Carter, E. W., Cushing, L. S., & Kennedy, C. H. (2009). *Peer support strategies: Improving all students' social lives and learning.* Baltimore, MD: Paul H. Brookes.
* Downing, J. (2010). *Academic instruction for students with moderate and severe disabilities in academic settings.* Thousand Oaks, CA: Corwin.
* Halvorsen, A. T., & Neary, T. (2009). *Building inclusive schools: Tools and strategies for success.* Boston, MA: Pearson.

GO EVEN FURTHER WITH
THIS TOPIC ON THE WORLD WIDE WEB

* www.mcie.org/pubs.asp
* njcie.net/tools_schools.asp
* www.csie.org.uk/index.shtml
* www.theinclusiveclass.com/
* www.projectparticipate.org/handouts/TipsforParaeducators.pdf

THE Apps WE LOVE

* Bitsboard
* Dragon Dictation
* Clicker Docs
* Educreations
* Pictello

13

Creative Co-Teaching

Wendy W. Murawski

California State University, Northridge

WHAT REALLY WORKS IN CO-TEACHING IN THE SECONDARY CLASSROOM

Let's Do More Than Just Play Nicely in the Same Room!

It's the day before school starts. You finally received your rosters and, as you stand in the mailroom cringing at the numbers of students in each class, the assistant principal (AP) walks by and says, "Oh, hey. Did I tell you that you'll be co-teaching for your first and second periods?" He gives you a happy thumbs-up and moves on. As he walks away, you look in disbelief and as the words sink in, you think, "What's co-teaching? Who am I co-teaching with? Why co-teaching? What the heck just happened?" Welcome to the world of co-teaching!

As schools move toward including more students with disabilities into general education classrooms, we seriously need to reform the instructional methods used to support both students and teachers. The call for reform in both general and special education is to include evidence-based practices that are interactive, multimodal, collaborative, dynamic, and real world. Yet, despite shared goals between general and special education organizations as well as legal mandates, there remains a mismatch between the learning needs of students and the traditional instructional delivery methods actually used in classrooms. Who hasn't seen the many teachers who still "stand and deliver" or even "say and spray?"

Co-teaching as a service delivery model is gaining ground both nationally and internationally. It offers a way to provide quality services to students with special needs in general education classrooms and to increase differentiation of instruction to benefit all students. Co-teaching occurs when two or more professionals teach a group of students together. They can't just be in the room together though. In fact, Murawski (2009) (yes, that's me!) clarified that in order for true co-teaching to occur, "co-planning, co-instructing, and co-assessing," are necessary (p. 8). Teachers and students can potentially get the best of all worlds. Think about it: Pair a specialist who is highly qualified to differentiate instruction with an educator who is highly qualified in specific grade-level content and . . . BAM! You get differentiating heaven. This chapter is about how to make that actually happen.

Let's get back to our opening scenario: You are standing there, dazed and confused. Then as you look back at your roster, imagining how you're going to try to fit that many students in your small classroom, you also notice how many students have different codes next to their names. Once you figure out the key to the codes, you now know that many of your students are English language learners, or gifted, or have disabilities of varying types. You start thinking back to what your AP said and begin to think, "Well, at least I don't have to face them all alone."

KEY RESEARCH YOU NEED TO KNOW ABOUT CO-TEACHING

Think of the typical secondary classroom. Are you imagining a room in which students are working collaboratively and critically analyzing problems, while two teachers joke as they facilitate fun and differentiated learning activities? Or . . . a room with a frustrated teacher, standing at the front whiteboard and raising her voice to ask kids to pay attention and take notes? I'm guessing it was the latter. That's the most common scenario, unfortunately.

Although findings demonstrated that students' standardized test scores were higher if teachers individualized and differentiated instruction (Pearl & Miller, 2007), research also shows that teachers continue to use traditional, whole-group teaching methods even as classes become more diverse and inclusive of students with disabilities (Kennedy & Ihle, 2012; King-Sears & Bowman-Kruhm, 2011). Individuals who want to co-teach are expected to work as equals, using parity, shared expertise, and resources to optimize outcomes for students (Cramer, Liston, Nevin, &

Thousand, 2010; Rea, McLaughlin, & Walther-Thomas, 2002). Co-teaching is described as resulting in smaller student-teacher ratios, more cooperative group work, an increase in the use of evidence-based practices, and a stronger emphasis on essential questions, big ideas, and real-world application of content (e.g., Austin, 2001; Friend & Cook, 2012; Murawski & Spencer, 2011). Thus, co-teaching meets the call for instructional reform in the fields of both general and special education. Woo-hoo! On board yet?

Co-teaching is in no way new, and many of you have probably heard of it before. However, research on actual implementation and outcomes remains confusing at best. Much has been written about the quality, or lack thereof, of existing research (McDuffie, Mastropieri, & Scruggs, 2009; Murawski & Goodwin, 2014). Unfortunately, it is rare for studies on co-teaching to meet all of the standards for sound, well-defined, outcome-focused research (Scruggs, Mastropieri, & McDuffie, 2007; Weiss & Brigham, 2000). In general, collecting data on a specific treatment should not pose a problem; however, co-teaching is a service delivery option in which collaboration, personality, and student characteristics play an integral role (Friend, Cook, Hurley-Chamberlain, & Shamberger, 2010; Zigmond, Magiera, Simmons, & Volonino, 2013). These are variables that are extremely difficult to tease out and quantify. In essence, this is a doozy to collect data on!

In 2001, I completed the first meta-analysis on co-teaching with Lee Swanson. A meta-analysis is essentially where you take all the quantitative research you have on an intervention and boil it down to one number called an effect size, to see if the intervention works or not. Ultimately, we reported an overall positive effect size of 0.40, though we called it an "apples and oranges" comparison (Murawski & Swanson, 2001). What that really means is that, while it seems like co-teaching has significant promise, at the time there were just insufficient studies to compare. Then, in 2007, Scruggs and colleagues offered the first meta-synthesis of qualitative co-teaching data; their results reinforced the components cited in most literature as critical to co-teaching effectiveness. Not surprisingly, those studies that included administrative support, professional development, planning time, and teacher voice yielded more positive results than those that did not. Anyone here surprised? Just recently, Vanessa Goodwin and I summarized the research on co-teaching as contradictory, confusing, and cautiously optimistic (Murawski & Goodwin, 2014). In a nutshell, those teachers who have the critical characteristics and logistics present for co-teaching success (i.e., parity, planning, personalities, professional development, and presence) are successful. Those who don't, often struggle. (Yes, a big collective "no duh" is allowed.)

My job then is to provide you with the DOs and DON'Ts for co-teaching by identifying actions that I've frequently observed that actually act as obstacles for co-teaching success, as well as those actions that maximize the chance of secondary co-teachers making a positive impact on middle and high school students. Data continue to be collected on the implementation and impact of co-teaching. In the meantime, this is your user-friendly reference for getting started or improving co-teaching at your school—unless, of course, you prefer buying a whole book called, *Collaborative Teaching in Secondary Schools: Making the Co-Teaching Marriage Work*, by Murawski (2009). I hear it's fabulous! No? Alright, I'll still provide you with resources for additional reading at the end of this chapter if you'd like to learn even more.

WHAT YOU NEED TO AVOID AT ALL COSTS RELATED TO CO-TEACHING

Teachers

- ✖ **STOP confusing "collaboration" and "inclusion" with "co-teaching."** They are not the same thing. Collaboration is a style of interacting; you can collaborate to accomplish a mutual goal, but that goal doesn't have to be related to co-teaching. Inclusion is the philosophy that students with special needs can have those needs met in the general education setting; co-teaching might help accomplish that, but co-teaching is not the only option. Co-teaching requires "co-planning, co-instructing, and co-assessing" (Murawski, 2003, p. 10); collaboration is a major requirement.

- ✖ **STOP thinking that all co-teaching takes is putting two people in the same classroom.** Even two phenomenal teachers may not co-teach well if they do not know what it requires or if both have been taught only how to "lead" a class and not how to collaborate. If this is a collaborative marriage, it'd be nice if your two teachers actually got along, wouldn't it?

Making Connections

Check out Chapter 12 on Inclusion

- ✖ **STOP calling the general education teacher the "teacher" and the special education teacher "the co-teacher."** He or she is not a copilot. Stop calling general education students "regular education"; the others are not irregular. Just say "co-teachers" and "general and special education students" or even just "students."

- ✖ **STOP expecting co-taught classrooms to look the same as solo taught classes.** By definition, two teachers should be interacting with each other and with students differently to get different outcomes.

- ✖ **STOP looking at co-teaching as *the* method for inclusion.** Inclusive schools use a variety of in-class service delivery options for students. Not all students with disabilities need to be in a co-taught class, nor do all teachers need to co-teach.

- ✖ **STOP blaming administrators, parents, or other teachers if they are not on board with co-teaching.** They may just not know what to do. Teach them. Get them on board.
- ✖ **STOP trying to wait to see if you'll be required to co-teach.** This train has left the station. It's happening. You'd be better off to try it now while there are resources and professional development offered, rather than when it's fait accompli.
- ✖ **STOP having the general education teacher lead and the special educator become the aide.** This is a major complaint in co-teaching, and it's worse in secondary schools where the content matter is more complex and the stakes are higher (Murawski & Dieker, 2004). Sure, the special educator may not have the same level of content expertise as the general educator, but that doesn't mean there aren't multiple opportunities for face time and lead instruction with the kids. We each need "face time" with the students, and we each have something to contribute.
- ✖ **STOP teaching one way 1st period and then expecting your co-teacher to replicate what you did in 2nd and 3rd periods.** Co-taught classes should be taught differently than solo-taught classes. Make sure your co-teacher had input in the planning of the lesson.
- ✖ **STOP complaining that you don't have time to co-plan.** If you're not co-planning, you're not truly co-teaching. It's as simple as that. So either quit calling it co-teaching (say "in-class support" instead) or go to your administrator and brainstorm ways to get co-planning time. Consider walking in with *Leading the Co-Teaching Dance: Leadership Strategies for Enhancing Team Outcomes* (Murawski & Dieker, 2013); have the chapter on finding time for co-planning bookmarked and highlighted.
- ✖ **STOP having some kids on one roster or gradebook and others on another.** They are all "your" (collective) kids. This may mean going and talking to your administrator again about how to accomplish this.
- ✖ **STOP making the room feel like it belongs to one of you.** Yes, the Biology teacher is in there for all six periods and the Special Education teacher only comes in for 4th period, but it is so simple to put both names on the door and inside the room. In 4th period, it will scream parity; in the other periods, the kids simply won't care.

Administrators

- ✖ **STOP breaking up great teams.** Just because they are good together, doesn't mean they will be equally effective with other partners (Murawski & Dieker, 2013). Leave them alone to keep doing their magic!

✗ **STOP evaluating co-teachers using the same rubrics and tools as solo-taught teachers.** Two teachers should be doing different things in the class. You want them to—you're paying for it! Want to know what to look for, listen for, and ask for during co-teaching observations? Check out Wilson (2005) or Murawski & Lochner (2011).

✗ **STOP using special education co-teachers to substitute classes where no sub is available.** These individuals are in the general education classes for a legal and academic reason. They need to stay there or you're asking for trouble.

✗ **STOP putting teachers into co-teaching teams with no opportunity or time for planning and expecting different outcomes.** What you will get is called merely "in-class support" in which the special educator shows up and asks, "What are we doing today?" If you want something different, they need time to plan for that.

STRATEGIES FOR MAKING YOU SUCCESSFUL WITH CO-TEACHING (OR "IF I COULD ONLY GET YOU TO DO THESE THINGS, ALL WOULD BE WELL WITH THE WORLD")

Teachers, DO This

✓ **KNOW the essential question for co-teaching!** Murawski and Spencer (2011) provide it as this: "How is what co-teachers are doing together substantively different and better for students than what one teacher would do alone?" (p. 96). We emphasized that instruction with two teachers should look differently than it does with one. I know I've said that frequently, but I'm hoping it's sinking in. Has it? Does your co-teaching look different? Self-evaluate. If not, what do you need to do? Figure it out, and get to it!

✓ **INTRODUCE the class as "being taught by two teachers,"** not as being taught by a special educator and general educator. Make sure parents know that a co-taught class can be a boon to all students, including those who are gifted, because teachers are more able to individualize and differentiate. Define co-teaching in your syllabus or letters home to parents.

✓ **READ "10 Tips for Efficient Use of Co-Planning Time"** (Murawski, 2012) to learn how to use time more effectively. Embrace the "What/How/Who" approach to co-planning.

✓ **USE the SHARE worksheet** (provided on page 210) to communicate your preferences, pet peeves, and ultimate desires for the classroom. Doing this proactively, before students enter the room, will help you be on the same page and reduce the chances of them "playing mom against dad." Reduce, not eliminate.

✓ **SHOW parity.** Have both names on the door, both names on report cards, and space for both of you to keep your things. Make sure both of you have access to the hard copy or electronic gradebook and both teachers' names are on materials sent home to parents. Practice using "we" language instead of "I" language to demonstrate that you are a team.

✓ **COMMUNICATE, communicate, communicate!** Talk to each other about *how* to talk to each other. How will you share problems, concerns, observations, and constructive criticisms before they become real obstacles? Remember, students will pick up on any negative vibes!

✓ **TRY new things.** Secondary teachers are notorious for sticking with lectures for direct instruction. Secondary co-teachers are notorious for sticking with "One teach/One support." Step away from the large group instruction, and embrace small groups. Mix it up, and try all of the different instructional approaches (Cook & Friend, 1995; see page 209) and then come up with some of your own!

> **Making Connections**
>
> Check out Chapters 1–6 on content areas, as well as Chapter 11 on UDL

✓ **INCREASE your toolbox.** In addition to professional development (PD) on co-teaching, the general educator should go to PD on differentiation, UDL, and other typically special education focus areas. The special educator should go to PD on the general education content area, especially as it relates to Common Core or other content areas.

✓ **DETERMINE your roles and responsibilities.** All teachers have preferred areas. Talk to each other. If one of you loves technology, that person can be in charge of updating the class website, creating the PowerPoints, and finding worthwhile YouTube videos. The other person might take on making all photocopies, creating the daily warm-up, and calling parents. When you've established basic roles, it will save you time in co-planning.

✓ **USE technology in planning.** There is never enough time to plan. It will rock if you are given a common planning period, but many don't get that at first. So turn to Google Docs, Skype, Facetime, Dropbox, or similar tools that will enable you to co-plan even when getting in the same room at the same time is a barrier.

✓ **LET GO of the reins.** We are teachers. We like control. It is very hard to let go and try something new—especially if you are the content teacher and you've been teaching something the same way for a while! But students learn differently, and to meet their individualized, differentiated needs, you may need to try something new. Listen to your co-teacher's ideas with an open mind. Try it. You may like it.

Administrators, DO This

- ✓ **When scheduling, PUT students with disabilities into the master schedule first.** This is critical. You can hold spots by calling up to 30% of the class "Ghosts" and filling in those spots with students with special needs later if needed. Do not have more than 30% of the class have special needs or you run the risk of the class feeling more like a special education class than an inclusive one (Murawski & Dieker, 2013).

- ✓ **GIVE planning time!** Make ways for co-teachers to have regular time together to plan (planning periods, lunch meetings, time in the week when students are at an assembly or a pep rally or in electives). Need more ideas? Check out *Leading the Co-Teaching Dance: Leadership Strategies to Enhance Team Outcomes* by Murawski & Dieker (2013).

- ✓ **BE strategic in scheduling.** Start by reducing the number of partners and subjects with which you are expecting your teachers to engage. Remember scheduling for successful co-teaching does not always require more faculty. It does typically require a lot of thought and often the willingness to try something new. Finally, be sure to work with special educators to make sure they know how to manage their entire workload while co-teaching. Help them with scheduling so that they can plan, assess, attend IEPs, make accommodations, talk to paraprofessionals, and otherwise manage their caseloads, in addition to co-teaching.

- ✓ **HOOK 'EM UP!** Give teachers who are co-teaching priority for new technology, access to the computer lab, perks in scheduling or planning, and first dibs on upcoming professional development. Co-teaching takes time and energy, and these teachers are often working with the most difficult population of students. Respect this by helping them in any way you can.

AT-A-GLANCE: CO-TEACHING APPROACHES TO INSTRUCTION

Co-Teaching Approach (Cook & Friend, 1995)	Class Setup	Quick Definition
One Teach, One Support (OT/OS)	Whole Class	One teacher is in front of the class leading instruction. The other is providing substantive support (e.g., collection or dissemination of papers, setting up labs, classroom management). Both are actively engaged.
Team Teaching	Whole Class	Both teachers are in front of the class, working together to provide instruction. This may take the form of debates, modeling information or note taking, compare/contrast, or role-playing.
Parallel Teaching	Regrouping	Both teachers take half of the class in order to reduce student-teacher ratio. Instruction can occur in the same or a different setting. Groups may be doing the same content in the same way, same content in a different way, or different content (Murawski, 2010).
Station Teaching	Regrouping	Students are divided into three or more small, heterogeneous groups to go to stations or centers. Students rotate through multiple centers, though teachers may rotate also. Teachers can facilitate individual stations or circulate among all stations.
Alternative Teaching	Regrouping	One teacher works with a large group of students, while the other works with a smaller group providing reteaching, preteaching, or enrichment as needed. The large group is not receiving new instruction during this time so that the small group can rejoin when finished.

Source: Murawski & Spencer (2011, p. 97).

S.H.A.R.E. WITH YOUR COLLEAGUES: SHARING HOPES, ATTITUDES, RESPONSIBILITIES, AND EXPECTATIONS

Directions: Take a few minutes to individually complete this worksheet. Be honest in your responses. After completing it individually, share the responses with your co-planning partners by taking turns reading the responses. Do not use this time to comment on your partners' responses—merely read. After reading through the responses, take a moment or two to jot down any thoughts you have regarding what your partners have said. Then, come back together and begin to share reactions to the responses. Your goal is to (a) agree, (b) compromise, or (c) agree to disagree.

1) Right now, the main *hope* I have regarding this co-planning situation with my colleagues is the following:

_____

_____

2) My *attitude*/philosophy regarding sharing my time, plans, and materials with my colleagues is the following:

_____

_____

3) I would like to have the following *responsibilities* in a co-planning situation:

_____

_____

4) I would like my colleagues to have the following *responsibilities:*

_____

_____

5) I have the following *expectations* for our co-planning relationship

(a) regarding punctuality:

_____

(b) regarding managing materials:

_____

(c) regarding homework (work prior to meeting):

_____

(d) regarding planning time:

_____

(e) regarding reflection on process and lessons:

_____

(f) regarding adaptations for individual students:

_____

(g) regarding grading/assessments:

_____

(h) regarding communication skills (listening, sharing, electronic, and in person):

_____

(i) regarding organization:

_____

(j) regarding giving/receiving feedback to each other:

_____

(k) other important expectations I have:

_____

Source: Murawski (2010, p. 71).

DO'S AND DON'TS OF CO-TEACHING

Co-Teaching Is . . .	Co-Teaching Is Not . . .
Two or more coequal (preferably credentialed) faculty working together.	A teacher and an assistant, teacher's aide, or paraprofessional.
Conducted in the same classroom at the same time.	When a few students are pulled out of the classroom on a regular basis to work with the special educator. It is also not job-sharing, where teachers teach different days.
Conducted with heterogeneous groups.	Pulling a group of students with disabilities to the back of the general education class.
When both teachers plan for instruction together. The general education teacher (GET) is the content specialist while the special education teacher (SET) is the expert on individualizing and delivery to various learning modalities.	When the general education teacher (GET) plans all lessons and the special education teacher (SET) walks into the room and says, "What are we doing today, and what would you like me to do?"
When both teachers provide *substantive* instruction together—having planned together, the SET can grade homework, teach content, facilitate activities, etc.	When the special education teacher walks around the room all period as the general education teacher teaches the content. Also, not when the SET sits in the class and takes notes.
When both teachers assess and evaluate student progress. IEP goals are kept in mind, as are the curricular goals and standards for that grade level.	When the GET grades "his" kids and the SET grades "her" kids—or when the GET grades all students and the SET surreptitiously changes the grades and calls it "modifying after the fact."
When teachers maximize the benefits of having two teachers in the room by having both teachers actively engaged with students. Examples of different co-teaching models include team-teaching, station-teaching, parallel-teaching, alternative-teaching, and one teach–one support (see Friend & Cook, 2000).	When teachers take turns being "in charge" of the class so that the other teacher can get caught up in grading, photocopying, making phone calls, creating IEPs, etc.—or when students remain in the large group setting in lecture format as teachers rotate who gets to "talk at them."
When teachers reflect on the progress and process, offering one another feedback on teaching styles, content, activities, and other items pertinent to improving the teaching situation.	When teachers get frustrated with one another and tell the rest of the faculty in the teachers' lounge or when one teacher simply tells the other teacher what to do and how to do it.

Source: Adapted from Murawski (2002, p. 19).

REFERENCES

Austin, V. L. (2001). Teachers' beliefs about co-teaching. *Remedial and Special Education, 22*(4), 245–255.

Cook, L., & Friend, M. P. (1995). Co-teaching: Guidelines for creating effective practices. *Focus on Exceptional Children, 28*(3), 1–16.

Cramer, E., Liston, A., Nevin, A., & Thousand, J. (2010). Co-teaching in urban secondary school districts to meet the needs of all teachers and learners: Implications for teacher education reform. *International Journal of Whole Schooling, 6*(2), 59–76.

Friend, M., & Cook, L. (2000). *Interactions: Collaboration skills for school professionals* (3rd ed.). White Plains, NY: Longman.

Friend, M., & Cook, L. (2012). *Interactions: Collaboration skills for school professionals* (7th ed.). Boston, MA: Pearson.

Friend, M., Cook, L., Hurley-Chamberlain, D., & Shamberger, C. (2010). Co-teaching: An illustration of the complexity of collaboration in special education. *Journal of Educational and Psychological Consultation, 20*, 9–27.

Kennedy, M. J., & Ihle, F. M. (2012). The Old Man and the Sea: Navigating the gulf between special educators and the content area classroom. *Learning Disabilities Research and Practice, 27*, 44–54.

King-Sears, M. E., & Bowman-Kruhm, M. (2011). Specialized reading instruction for adolescents with learning disabilities: What special education co-teachers say. *Learning Disabilities Research and Practice, 26*, 172–184.

McDuffie, K., Mastropieri, M. A., & Scruggs, T. E. (2009). Promoting success in content area classes: Is value added through co-teaching? *Exceptional Children, 75*, 493–510.

Murawski, W. W. (2002). Demystifying co-teaching. *CARS+ Newsletter, 22*(3), 19.

Murawski, W. W. (2003). *Co-teaching in the inclusive classroom.* Bellevue, WA: Bureau of Education and Research.

Murawski, W. W. (2009). *Collaborative teaching in secondary schools: Making the co-teaching marriage work!* Thousand Oaks, CA: Corwin.

Murawski, W. W. (2010). *Collaborative Teaching in Secondary Schools.* Thousand Oaks, CA: Corwin.

Murawski, W. W. (2012). 10 tips for using co-planning time more efficiently. *Teaching Exceptional Children, 44*(4), 8–15.

Murawski, W. W., & Dieker, L. A. (2004). Tips and strategies for co-teaching at the secondary level. *Teaching Exceptional Children, 36*(5), 52–58.

Murawski, W., & Dieker, L. (2013). *Leading the co-teaching dance: Leadership strategies to enhance team outcomes.* Arlington, VA: Council for Exceptional Children.

Murawski, W. W., & Goodwin, V. A. (2014). Effective inclusive schools and the co-teaching conundrum. In J. McLeskey, N. Waldron, F. Spooner, & B. Algozzine (Eds.), *Handbook of research and practice for inclusive schools* (pp. 292–305). New York, NY: Routledge.

Murawski, W., & Lochner, W. (2011). Observing co-teaching: What to ask for, look for, and listen for. *Intervention in School and Clinic, 46*(3), 174–183.

Murawski, W. W., & Spencer, S. (2011). *Collaborate, communicate, and differentiate! How to increase student learning in today's diverse classrooms.* Thousand Oaks, CA: Corwin.

Murawski, W. W., & Swanson, H. L. (2001). A meta-analysis of co-teaching research: Where are the data? *Remedial and Special Education, 22*(5), 258–267.

Pearl, C. E., & Miller, K. J. (2007). Co-taught middle school mathematics classrooms: Accommodations and enhancements for students with specific learning disabilities. *Focus on Learning Problems in Mathematics, 29*(2), 1–20.

Rea, P. J., McLaughlin, V. L., & Walther-Thomas, C. (2002). Outcomes for students with learning disabilities in inclusive and pull-out programs. *Exceptional Children, 72*, 203–222.

Scruggs, T. E., Mastropieri, M. A., & McDuffie, K. A. (2007). Co-teaching in inclusive classrooms: A metasynthesis of qualitative research. *Exceptional Children, 73*(4), 392–416.

Weiss, M. P., & Brigham, F. J. (2000). Co-teaching and the model of shared responsibility: What does the research support? In T. E. Scruggs & M. A. Mastropieri (Eds.), *Advances in learning and behavioral disabilities* (pp. 217–245). Greenwich, CT: JAI.

Wilson, G. (2005). This doesn't look familiar! A supervisor's guide for observing co-teachers. *Intervention in School and Clinic, 40*(5), 271–275.

Zigmond, N., Magiera, K., Simmons, R., & Volonino, V. (2013). Strategies for improving student outcomes in co-taught general education classrooms. In B. G. Cook & M. Tankersley (Eds.), *Research-based strategies for improving outcomes in academics* (pp. 116–124). Upper Saddle River, NJ: Pearson.

RECOMMENDED READINGS

* Conderman, G., & Hedin, L. (2012). Purposeful assessment practices for co-teachers. *Teaching Exceptional Children, 44*(4), 18–27.

* Dieker, L. A. (2001). What are the characteristics of "effective" middle and high school co-taught teams? *Preventing School Failure, 46*(1), 14–25.

* Dieker, L. A., & Murawski, W. (2003). Co-teaching at the secondary level: Unique issues, current trends, and suggestions for success. *High School Journal, 86*(4), 1–13.

* Magiera, K., Smith, C., Zigmond, N., & Gebauer, K. (2005). Benefits of co-teaching in secondary mathematics classes. *TEACHING Exceptional Children, 37*(3), 20–24.

* Murawski, W., & Dieker, L. A. (2008). 50 ways to keep your co-teacher. *Teaching Exceptional Children, 40*(4), 40–48.

* Villa, R. A., Thousand, J. S., Nevin, A., & Liston, A. (2005). Successful inclusive practices in middle and secondary schools. *American Secondary Education, 33*(3), 33–50.

GO EVEN FURTHER WITH
THIS TOPIC ON THE WORLD WIDE WEB

- www.cec.sped.org
- www.2teachllc.com
- www.coteach.com
- www.specialconnections.ku.edu
- www.coteachsolutions.com
- www.arcoteaching.com

THE Apps WE LOVE

- Edmodo
- Pinterest
- GoogleDocs
- Dropbox
- Thyme

14

Amazing Assessment

Brooke Blanks

Radford University

WHAT REALLY WORKS IN
ASSESSMENT IN THE SECONDARY CLASSROOM

I Know What I Taught, But What Did They Learn?

It is time to talk about something we love to hate: Assessment. What is it, and how should we use it? Some days it feels like everyone, everywhere, is talking about educational assessment. . . ALL THE TIME. The frustrating thing is that while everyone agrees that we need to know what kids learn when we teach them stuff, we actually don't get practical suggestions about what assessments are and how they should be used. What is most troublesome, however, is that while everyone is fussing about the importance of assessment, very little information is out there to describe how to use assessment to support the most important responsibilities we have as educators: teaching kids important stuff that (a) they don't know and (b) helps them become interesting, productive, happy people. It also does not help that the "experts" write about educational assessment in language that no one really understands. Never fear! In this chapter, we are going to explore assessments you can and should use in your classroom.

FORMATIVE ASSESSMENT VERSUS SUMMATIVE ASSESSMENT

Formative and summative assessments are very much connected to one another. Both are important to understanding students' learning in response to our instruction. But while most of the emphasis in policy discussions and mandates is on summative assessments (e.g., high-stakes testing), formative assessment is what really has the greatest impact on student learning (Hamilton et al., 2009). This actually makes a lot of sense when you think about it because formative assessment is assessment used *for* student learning while summative assessment is assessment *of* student learning (Fisher & Frey, 2010). A quick review of the following essential characteristics of each drives the point home:

Formative Assessment	*Summative Assessment*
Checks students' understanding in order to plan instruction	Offers teachers and students with information about mastery of content knowledge
Results inform next steps in instruction to ensure students' success, which means they have significant practical value but usually have low emotional impact or value	Results often inform grading which means they have significant evaluative importance and thus, often have high emotional impact and value
Must be part of an instructional framework that is responsive to students' ongoing growth and current needs	Evaluates students' learning at the end of an instructional unit and compares the results to some standard or benchmark
Examples of formative assessment: • Revision-based assignments, projects, and performances • Diagnostic interviews and asking questions	*Examples of summative assessment:* • Capstone assignments, final projects, senior recitals • Final exams

Source: Adapted from Kharbach (2014).

Our goal as teachers is to use formative assessment to learn about our students so that we know what and how to design and provide instruction that meets their needs. If we do that well, the summative assessments will show us, the kids, the parents, the school, and the state that indeed, the students did learn this material.

WHAT DOES THE RESEARCH TELL US?

Assessment can be one of our most challenging professional responsibilities. As teachers, we worry about the impact that testing may have on our students' academic, emotional, and developmental well-being. Nowadays we also worry about the impact the testing results will have on our careers and paychecks. Despite this, knowing how to effectively design, administer, and use assessments to improve our instruction is an essential element of our teaching practice.

Let's face it; testing is a political hot-button issue. Unfortunately, much of the discussion overlooks the fact that testing and assessment mean different things to different stakeholders. Politicians talk about using tests to evaluate the quality of teachers and schools. Community members and parents understand assessment to mean high-stakes tests that determine if students go on to the next grade. Students with disabilities and their families are familiar with testing that has been the path to receiving special education services. Two significant school improvement initiatives in the last decade, Positive Behavior Intervention and Supports (PBIS) and Response to Intervention (RTI) are grounded in the idea that we must use assessments to provide measures of students' behavior and/or learning in order to make decisions about what students need and how we will work to meet those needs. Finally, among students, assessment scores are often viewed as the means by which classmates compete against one another rather than mileposts on their path to knowledge and critical thinking. Clearly all of these stakeholders have legitimate perspectives on the form and function of assessment in our classrooms and schools. While it is important that we understand that no single assessment or type of assessment will address all of these purposes well, it is important (and I personally think it is also very cool) that much of the research on assessment indicates that what is really important is what we do with those results! Thus, for our purposes as teachers, we will focus on what research tells us are effective assessment practices that we can use to drive our instruction in our classrooms—yep, we're going to look at what really works in assessment. Over and over again, research tells us that effective teachers know how to use the results provided by the consistent use of classroom-based formative assessments (Hamilton et al., 2009; Hoover & Abrams, 2013). So let's figure out how to do just that.

Making Connections

Check out Chapters 8 and 12 on Positive Behavior Support and Inclusion

Focus on classroom assessments. Before we can plan instruction, we must explore and document what students already know. Understanding their knowledge is essential for planning instruction that will lead to their full understanding of concepts (Black & Wiliam, 1998). Using assessment information to ask questions and understand students' progress is the only reasonable way to mold your instruction to fit your students. That is, you should use assessment data to measure students' progress and to inform instructional practice (Stiggins, Arter, Chappuis, & Chappuis, 2004). And don't be afraid to put your older students to work! Middle and high school students can and should learn how to participate in ongoing assessment of their own learning.

Effective classroom assessments. Effective classroom assessments require skill and practice. However, remember that formative assessment is something most of us do every single day, without even realizing it sometimes. The following guidelines are a great way to explain all that we already know and do related to formative assessment.

Focus on teaching and the curriculum. All assessments should be tied to the curriculum, which is based on your state's academic standards (Randel & Clark, 2013). Most of us are already pretty familiar with which standards are assessed on our end-of-course tests. If you aren't, start looking into it now. Next, look at those standards and decide what skills and knowledge students need to meet those standards (Popham, 2006). This step is really important if your formative assessments are going to provide information you can use to plan instruction.

Know your objectives. High-quality objectives are directly and obviously linked to your instruction, and they provide your students with a road map of exactly what they need to do to demonstrate their mastery of those objectives (Marzano, 2009). By the way, this is a great activity for a team of teachers to work on throughout the year. Everyone can share ideas and work to develop a "bank" of assessment tasks that work for a variety of students with a range of strengths and needs. No need to recreate the wheel in every classroom!

Involve students. Making the invisible process of testing and assessment visible to students is a huge change in the way we think about and use assessment in our classrooms. Students should be taught to use rubrics and checklists that clearly describe how their work will be evaluated (Randel & Clark, 2013). Models of excellent work, work that needs revision, and work that is below standard are fabulous tools when we spend time unpacking them with our students. Transparency helps students realize that assessments are useful because they help us understand how to be successful (Stiggins et al., 2004).

Question frequently. Questioning is an excellent formative assessment (Burns, 2005). You can use verbal or written questions to probe students' knowledge and asking meaningful questions about how they understand what we're teaching helps us better understand their thinking. In turn, these insights guide our future planning for instruction (Center for Comprehensive School Reform and Improvement, 2014). Don't forget to differentiate your questioning based on the different learners you have. Your students can participate in this process. Go online, and check out the brief introduction to teaching kids to write essential questions on the Plugged In box. This is a win-win strategy. Kids learn to monitor their own learning, and teachers can quickly assess their depth of understanding by listening to their questions. Shallow questions often suggest that students have only a rudimentary understanding of your instruction.

Plugged In

www.teaching
channel.org/videos/
structure-learning-
essential-questions

Provide meaningful feedback. We provide students with a lot of feedback every day. The trick is to make sure we are providing feedback that helps students understand what they are doing now and what they can do in the future to increase and/or enhance their learning and performance. High-quality instructional feedback is timely, useful, and appropriate. Feedback is most helpful to students' learning when it emphasizes the features of the task (Brookhart, 2008) and shows students how their performance of the assessment task compares to the standard. This approach to feedback helps students see the gaps that exist between their goals and their current levels of performance and understanding. It also provides a guide to help students through the process of meeting those goals (Brookhart, 2008). The most effective feedback is that which occurs either during the learning experience or immediately after. Timing is everything! Our goal as teachers is to find that sweet spot in which we are giving students enough time to really work through the task they are trying to accomplish, but not so much time that we are allowing them to either practice doing things incorrectly or waiting until it's too late for them to correct course. Check out the Edutopia article in the Plugged In box; it provides practical examples of how to develop a culture of feedback in your middle and high school classrooms.

Plugged In

www.edutopia.org/
blog/grading-tips-
student-feedback-
heather-wolpert-gawron

Understand and use your data. The information you get from regularly using formative assessments provides a ton of information about your teaching: what worked, what did not, and what you should do next and with which students. Do not make this more difficult than it has to be! Fancy looking data that are hard to gather and impossible to read are useless. Use what you know how to use. . . . And if you don't know what to use, checklists and graphs are a great place to start. Create a checklist that captures the essential information you want all students to know, and write a series of conversational questions to use during conferences with your students. When you talk with your kids, use the checklist to keep track of their answers to the questions. These data will help you figure out which kids need additional instruction. Look for patterns or trends in your data over time. Ask yourself questions, such as, "Are all of the kids missing the same question?" If so, your response can be, "Great, now I know what I need to reteach!" The point is to use formative assessments so that students' responses, particularly errors, provide you with information about specific student needs that you can use to guide your instruction (Center for Comprehensive School Reform and Improvement, 2014; Popham, 2006).

Change your instruction based on your assessments. Knowing what to do with your data is one of the most challenging aspects of assessment. When your students' results indicate the need for reteaching, we need to provide instruction that is different from our initial instruction, as well as additional opportunities for students to demonstrate their learning (Guskey, 2007). After all, the definition of insanity (attributed to a range of thinkers from Benjamin Franklin to Albert Einstein so there must be something to it!) is doing the same things over and over while expecting different results! If lecture was used for the initial lesson, think about using manipulatives or an interactive center for your follow-up instruction. Use groups effectively! Tomlinson and Imbeau's (2010, pp. 90–91) recommendations include using multiple ability tasks, assigning individual roles, using accessible content, and assigning competence. Classwide peer tutoring is an excellent instructional approach for a range of students in a differentiated classroom (Maheady & Gard, 2010). The aim is to reach all students by using a variety of teaching strategies. Your assessments help you figure out how to do this.

STOP ASSESSMENT PRACTICES THAT TEST OUR PATIENCE!

Teachers

✗ **STOP confusing formative and summative assessments.** Summative assessments are snapshots of what students know at a particular point in time. They are spread out and occur after instruction. Summative assessments are too far removed from instruction to be helpful in adjusting your teaching and making intervention decisions. Formative assessments are for instructional planning. They provide information about how students are responding to instruction while there is still time to adjust your teaching. Formative assessment helps teachers determine the next steps in their instructional process and for whom.

✘ **STOP confusing assessment with grading.** The purpose of grading to get a measure of performance. Grades do not necessarily measure learning because they often include criteria such as attendance, participation, and effort, which are related to, but not indicative of, what students actually know. The purpose of assessment is to improve student learning by looking at multiple formal and informal indicators of what students know and what they can do as a result of your instruction and then using this information to improve instruction.

✘ **STOP using assessments that only test students' ability to memorize random snippets of information. . . that's what the Internet is for.** Classroom based assessments should measure students' abilities to *use* and *apply* what they have learned from you. So what if they need to look up some of the facts or use some tools—those are skills we all use in the REAL WORLD! Oh c'mon, admit it. How many times have you Googled something today alone?

✘ **STOP using assessments to play "gotcha" with kids, particularly kids who (let's be honest here) get on your nerves in the classroom.** Testing to reward "good" kids for paying attention, turning in homework on time, etc., is pretty useless, especially if the purpose of your assessment is to inform your instruction. If you already know that certain kids won't know the information you are assessing because they didn't engage with your instruction, punishing them with a bad grade is really just a form of bullying and a waste of everyone's time. Don't worry; I'll give you alternative strategies in the "DO" section.

✘ **STOP assuming that you have to do the same thing to assess all students.** We easily accept the idea that students are going to access and learn information in the different ways. The same is true for assessment. Differentiate your assessments to make sure that you are getting as comprehensive a picture as possible of what each student knows and what each student still needs from your instruction.

Administrators

✘ **STOP confusing preparation and motivation when it comes to high-stakes assessment.** There is little evidence to suggest that motivation strategies like pep rallies, pizza parties, and "Test Day" breakfasts on high-stakes assessment days result in improved achievement. Instead, focus your efforts and attention on supporting teachers' use of formative assessments for effective instruction throughout the year. That doesn't mean you can't keep motivating;

just be sure you aren't doing that in lieu of providing true value to your teachers.

✗ **STOP thinking about student assessments as an effective way to evaluate your teachers.** We have a substantial body of evidence to suggest that student achievement scores and "Value Added Models" are not valid and reliable measures of teacher effectiveness (Darling-Hammond, Amrein-Beardsley, Haertel, & Rothstein, 2012). Ask any teacher anywhere. Their work is so much more than their students' test results. And we'll be a very different society if we encourage teachers to look at their students as more than their test score.

GO ASSESSMENT PRACTICES THAT STAND THE TEST OF TIME

Teachers, DO This

✓ **THINK about assessment as a process that is directly and clearly useful with students rather than a tool that is used to fill in blocks in your gradebook.** Assessment is a process that helps students and teachers understand students' progress toward learning goals when it is ongoing and diagnostic. Remember, the goal is to make instruction more responsive to learners' needs (Tomlinson & Imbeau, 2010). Use formative assessments to determine what students have learned from your well-designed instruction.

✓ **OBSERVE your students.** Observation is an essential element of classroom-based assessment. Observation at a distance involves periodically taking 5 minutes or so to watch students (individually or in groups). Close-in observation involves observing an individual student for about 5 minutes (adapted from Venn, 2004). In fact, Friend and Cook (2012) suggest that teachers who are co-teaching occasionally use a model wherein one teacher leads instruction while the other observes and collects data on students.

✓ **USE a steady cycle of different assessments to identify students who need help in specific domains and/or with specific content.** We can always assess and monitor student learning in our classrooms. We do it pretty naturally; it's how we make decisions and judgments about our kids. Get deliberate and record these observations, thoughts, students' responses to your questions, and so on, and get creative about opportunities to provide more support and instruction when students need additional help to master the content.

✓ **USE different types of informal assessment to monitor students' progress.** Exit Cards, Response Cards, Diaries, Learning Logs, and

Student Progress Monitoring Charts are all excellent and easy to use informal assessments. Check out the "copy-me" resource pages at the end of this chapter.

✓ **TEACH students to be directly involved in the assessment of their learning.** Incorporate activities into your instruction that ask students to think and talk about (a) what they have learned and (b) how they have learned it. This can include answering a set of questions, visually representing their learning processes with pictures or other forms of visual media, talking with a partner, or keeping a journal. Check out the AssessmentforLearning site for some great advice and resources for teaching self-assessment to older students. I've also given the URL for one of my all-time favorite teacher blog posts, Larry Ferlazzo's *"We Should Celebrate Mistakes,"* in which he talks about a unit he did with his students on the mistakes they make in class.

✓ **DECIDE when to use checklists, rubrics, portfolios, annotated notes, or percentage accuracy.** These are all valuable tools for your assessment toolbox, but it can be overwhelming to think about when to use each one. The Calhoun AL link in the Plugged In box will take you to a great document that explains in detail how and when to use each tool.

Plugged In

www
.assessmentforlearning
.edu.au/professional_
learning/student_self-assessment/
student_strategies_enhance.html

larryferlazzo.edublogs
.org/2011/12/06/we-should-
celebrate-mistakes/

www.calhoun.k12.al.us/makes%20
sense/Adobe%20Reader/DO%20
NOT%20OPEN%20program%20
files/Assessment/Assessing%20
skills.pdf

www.teachingchannel.org/
blog/2013/06/10/formative-
assessment/

✓ **USE formative assessments to give students second (or more) chances to be successful!** Formative assessments should not be a one-time, high-stakes proposition for students. Students should have a second chance to demonstrate their new level of competence and understanding that results from differentiated reteaching. This not only benefits the students but it also helps teachers determine the effectiveness of the follow-up instruction (Guskey, 2003). Essentially, that second chance shows you how well you retaught that student.

✓ **GET CREATIVE about managing the time for and implementation of assessment and follow-up activities.** Use more student-directed learning activities to reduce the amount of time spent on review for formative assessments. Instead, shift that time to follow-up instruction and enrichment (Guskey, 2007). Check out the Teaching Channel link for ideas about how to incorporate assessment into your middle and high school classrooms.

Administrators, DO This

- ✓ **LOOK for classrooms where students can demonstrate what they know in a variety of ways.** We tend to dismiss instructional practices we are not familiar with. Talk with your teachers about their assessment practices. Tests are not always the answer.

- ✓ **PROVIDE ongoing professional development for teachers on multiple ways to assess student learning and how to move from data to instruction.** Support teachers with professional development opportunities to learn more about using formative assessments in their classrooms. Get creative about making space in the weekly or monthly schedule for teachers to collaborate over their data, and get creative about solving instructional problems.

- ✓ **RECOGNIZE AND CELEBRATE teachers' creative use of formative assessments.** Ask questions, spend time in classrooms, dig deeply into key assignments, and talk with students about their learning outcomes. Ask teachers who have evidence that their use of formative assessment is improving learning outcomes in their classrooms to share their ideas, experiences, and resources with their colleagues.

- ✓ **FOCUS your staff supervision and evaluation processes on teaching and learning.** Look for evidence in your classrooms of the following high-impact instructional activities that are based on the results of formative assessments: reteaching, individual and group tutoring, peer tutoring, cooperative teams, alternative textbooks/media resources, academic games, learning kits, learning centers and laboratories, and instructional computer activities (Guskey, 2007). Ask teachers how they determined who was going to do what, at what level, and why. Their responses should include words like "data, answers, responses, or assessments."

AWESOME IDEAS FOR QUICK AND EASY FORMATIVE ASSESSMENTS IN YOUR CLASSROOM

Methods for Observing and Recording

- *Anecdotal record*: A descriptive narrative of a student's behavior or learning; details are useful for teacher's planning, conferencing, etc.
- *Running record*: A sequential record recorded while the behavior or learning is occurring; documents what a child might do in a particular situation.
- *Checklist*: A list on which the teacher checks the behaviors, traits, or learning targets observed during a lesson or activity.
- *Rating scale*: A list of behaviors made into a scale that features frequency of behavior or level of mastery.

Whole Group Informal Assessments

- *Thumbs up/thumbs down*: Students give a thumbs up or a thumbs down to show their level of understanding with respect to a previous, current, or upcoming task.
- *Think-pair-share*: Students are given time to think about a question or prompt, then to share information with a partner, and finally to share their thoughts with the whole group for discussion.
- *Response cards*: Teacher-made or student-made cards used to show responses to teacher prompts. The following are some examples of *premade response cards*.

  - Multiple choice: students can show A, B, C, or D by clipping a clothespin on the letter of their choice.
  - Categories: good for comparisons such as mammal or reptile, fantasy or realism, dependent or independent, etc.

Individual Informal Assessments

- *Interview*: Talk to students individually, discussing HOW they arrived at their answers. This short video provides an excellent example of how quick and easy interviews can be in your classroom. www.scoe.org/pub/htdocs/data-formative.html
- *Tiered exit cards*: Present brief problems to solve or questions to answer at the end of a lesson. Students turn in their solutions prior to leaving class. Collected answers can be reviewed to create small groups for the next day and to assess understanding of the

presented lesson. www.teachingchannel.org/videos/student-daily-assessment

- *Keep the question going*: With this formative assessment technique, the teacher asks one student a question and then asks another student if that answer seems reasonable or correct. Then, he asks a third student for an explanation of why there is an agreement or not. This helps keep all the students engaged because they must be prepared to either agree or disagree with the answers given and provide explanations. depts.washington.edu/nwcenter/downloads/KeepQuestioning.pdf

- *3-2-1*: Ask students to jot down 3 facts they learned, 2 examples of their learning, and 1 question or confusion they still have. sites.google.com/a/eusd.org/kjosephson/home/formative-assessment/3-2-1-cards

- *Four Corners*: Pose a question and offer four possible answers. Students show their answers by traveling to the corresponding corner. Discuss why each group chose that corner and how they could convince others that they are correct. www.theteachertoolkit.com/index.php/tool/four-corners

- *One-Minute Paper*: Ask students, "What was the most important thing you learned in this lesson? What important question remains unanswered?" Allow 1 minute to write and 5–10 minutes to discuss the results. www.theteachertoolkit.com/index.php/tool/one-minute-note

SAMPLE OBSERVATION FORMS

Student Name: _____   Subject Area: _____

Date	Observations

Name	Reads fluently	Self-corrects missed words	Rereads when story is unclear	Describes main character	Retells story with accuracy
1.					
2.					
3.					
4.					
5.					

SAMPLE RESPONSE CARDS

AGREE

DISAGREE

NOT SURE

Source: Auton, Beck, & West (2010). Reprinted with permission.

REFERENCES

Auton, K., Beck, S., & West, T. (2010). Informal assessment strategies. Handout prepared for Summer 2010 (RES 5560-375) Appalachian State University—Dr. George Olson, Instructor.

Black, P., & Wiliam, D. (1998). Inside the black box. *Phi Delta Kappan, 80*(2), 139–148.

Brookhart, S. (2008). *How to give effective feedback to your students*. Alexandria, VA: Association for Supervision and Curriculum Development.

Burns, M. (2005). Looking at how students reason. *Educational Leadership, 63*(3), 26–31.

Center for Comprehensive School Reform and Improvement. (2014). *Using classroom assessment to improve teaching*. Retrieved from http://www.education .com/reference/article/Ref_Using_Classroom/

Darling-Hammond, L., Amrein-Beardsley, A., Haertel, E., & Rothstein, J. (2012). Evaluating teacher evaluation. *Phi Delta Kappan, 93*(6), 8–15.

Fisher, D., & Frey, N. (2010). *Enhancing RTI: How to ensure success with effective classroom instruction and intervention*. Alexandria, VA: Association for Supervision and Curriculum Development.

Friend, M., & Cook, L. (2012). *Interactions: Collaboration skills for school professionals* (7th ed.). San Francisco, CA: Pearson.

Guskey, T. R. (2003). How classroom assessments improve learning. *Educational Leadership, 60*(5), 6–11.

Guskey, T. R. (2007). The rest of the story. *Educational Leadership, 65*(4), 28–35.

Hamilton, L., Halverson, R., Jackson, S., Mandinach, E., Supovitz, J., & Wayman, J. (2009). *Using student achievement data to support instructional decision making* (NCEE Publication No. 2009-4067). Washington, DC: National Center for Education Evaluation and Regional Assistance, Institute of Education Sciences, U.S. Department of Education.

Hoover, N. R., & Abrams, L. M. (2013). Teachers' instructional use of summative student assessment data. *Applied Measurement in Education, 26*(3), 219–231.

Kharbach, M. (2014). A visual chart on summative vs. formative assessment. Retrieved from http://www.educatorstechnology.com/2014/02/a-visual-chart-on-summative-vs.html

Maheady, L., & Gard, J. (2010). Classwide peer tutoring: Practice, theory, research, and personal narrative. *Intervention in School and Clinic, 46*(2), 71–78.

Marzano, R. J. (2009). *Designing and teaching learning goals and objectives*. Bloomington, IN: Solution Tree.

Popham, W. J. (2006). All about accountability/phony formative assessments: Buyer beware! *Educational Leadership, 64*, 86–87.

Randel, B., & Clark, T. (2013). Measuring classroom assessment practices. In J. H. McMillan (Ed.), *SAGE handbook of research on classroom assessment* (pp. 145–164). Thousand Oaks, CA: SAGE.

Stiggins, R. J., Arter, J. A., Chappuis, J., & Chappuis, S. (2004). *Classroom assessment FOR student learning: Doing it right—using it well*. Portland, OR: ETS Assessment Training Institute.

Tomlinson, C. A., & Imbeau, M. B. (2010). *Leading and managing a differentiated classroom*. Alexandria, VA: Association for Supervision and Curriculum Development.

Venn, J. (2004). *Quick, easy, and accurate classroom assessment for all students: A resource guidebook for teachers*. Retrieved from http://www.johnvenn.com

RECOMMENDED READINGS

* Bennett, R. E., & Gitomer, D. H. (2009). Transforming K–12 assessment: Integrating accountability testing, formative assessment and professional support. In C. Wyatt-Smith & J. Cumming (Eds.), *Educational assessment in the 21st century* (pp. 43–61). New York, NY: Springer.
* Enger, S. K., & Yager, R. B. E. (2009). *Assessing student understanding in science: A standards-based K–12 handbook.* Thousand Oaks, CA: Corwin.
* Popham, W. J., & Popham, J. W. (2005). *Classroom assessment: What teachers need to know.* Boston, MA: Allyn & Bacon.

GO EVEN FURTHER WITH
THIS TOPIC ON THE WORLD WIDE WEB

- wvde.state.wv.us/teach21/ExamplesofFormativeAssessment.html
- www.nctm.org/uploadedFiles/Research_News_and_Advocacy/Research/ Clips_and_Briefs/Research_brief_04_-_Five_Key%20Strategies.pdf
- www.nwea.org/blog/2013/mapping-formative-assessment-strategies-to-the-common-core-state-standards-part-one/
- www.edutopia.org/blog/formative-assessments-importance-of-rebecca-alber

THE Apps WE LOVE

- For All Rubrics
- Voice Thread
- Formative Feedback for Learning
- Three Ring
- GoClass
- QuizCast

SECTION III

What Really Works With Special Populations

15

Great Gifted Education

Claire E. Hughes

College of Coastal Georgia

WHAT REALLY WORKS IN GIFTED EDUCATION IN THE SECONDARY CLASSROOM

Different, Not More

Have you heard the saying, "All children are gifted. They just open their packages at different times and in different ways?" Yeah, well. That may be simplifying the notion of giftedness just a tad. In fact, although teachers and parents might identify giftedness in students by the differences that they demonstrate in a classroom, the definition of *giftedness* is a challenging one. Students with gifts and talents are not required to be identified or served through federal law, so each state has a slightly different version of definition and service. Some theorists state that giftedness is an internal quality, one that is highly inheritable and measureable (Terman, 1925), while others say that it is a result of development of a combination of factors (Renzulli, 1978). Others have also noted that the idea of giftedness is very dependent on one's culture (Peterson, 1999). When we talk about a "gifted student," we tend to mean students who are precocious or learn very quickly, notice things faster and with greater intensity, have the ability to concentrate for long periods of time, have areas of significant interest, have strong memory and imaging skills, and who can work with abstract information and ideas—all above their age peers (Poh, 2008). In addition, they tend to be more flexible in their thinking and more intuitive in their learning than other students.

So if there is no standard way to identify a student with gifts and talents, why should we serve them? The reason is an ethical one: All students deserve an education that meets them where they are and moves them forward. In fact, in the case of gifted students, not doing so as a public school system leaves the development of talent up to parents, which means that only students from advantaged backgrounds would be provided advanced and enriched opportunities. That's certainly not okay. One of the greatest ways to provide equality of educational growth is to offer gifted education. There is an old adage out there, typically attributed to Rick Lavoie (2004), "Fair does not mean the same; fair means giving each student what he or she needs." You've heard this in the chapter on inclusion, UDL, and co-teaching; now you're hearing it again in a chapter on gifted education.

Making Connections

Check out Chapters 11, 12, and 13 on UDL, Inclusion, and Co-Teaching

This is particularly true, in my humble opinion, for gifted students because they are often the most frequently left out of education. A gifted student is more likely to be "left behind" than any other subgroup of children—meaning that they are the least likely to make a year's worth of gains in a year. They come into school ahead, but then their relative position slips. Students who begin school knowing 75%–85% of the content for that grade are the least likely to make significant academic gains over that year. In addition, particularly relevant for students in secondary schooling, most math and science advances were made by people in their early- to mid-20s, most of who graduated from undergraduate programs early. This implies that the students who end up changing the world have also been significantly advanced. Perhaps most concerning is that gifted students from poverty are the most likely to slip in their achievement levels over time (Spielhagen & Cooper, 2005). This loss of talent and ability is significant—both for the individual and for our nation. Developing the talents and abilities of *all* students is the work of education, which includes those students who learn faster than their age peers. No pressure, right?

There is no "one-size-fits-all" program or practice that is guaranteed to work. Often, a teacher just wants to keep a gifted student busy and out of trouble, so she or he may end up using materials that are marketed "for gifted kids," are attractive, and yet have no real substance. According to the book *Best Practices in Gifted Education* (Robinson, Shore, & Enerson, 2007) that detailed the results of a project sponsored by the U.S. Department of Education, there are 29 strategies that have been proven effective in identifying and serving gifted students. These research-grounded strategies offer specific guidance to teachers, administrators, policy makers, and parents. While many educational practices and packaged programs employ these strategies, there are even more that are based in pseudoscience, reputation, or just busywork with no substance. According to Robinson, Shore, and Enerson (2007, p. 2) these 29 strategies can be broken down based on where they are used: home, classroom, and school. While addressing each of these 29 strategies—or even just the ones in the classroom category—would be too much for this chapter to attempt, I do recommend you check out their book. It's an excellent resource for you and for parents. In the meantime, don't fret. This chapter will take many of these research-based strategies and make them "real" for you. I'm sure that you want to meet ALL of your students' needs; let's not let any group of students lag behind in their educational growth.

STOP "MORE" IS NOT BETTER! HERE ARE YOUR GIFTED "DON'TS"

Teachers

- ✗ **STOP thinking that gifted kids can do it all.** "Well, if you're so gifted, you should be able to ____" is a common statement that gifted kids hear all the time. *Giftedness* is a way of describing significantly strong performance in one area or a way of describing how fast their processing or memory might be. There are gifted students with learning disabilities, which means that it is fairly likely that there will be a gifted student in class who might be a very strong reader, but lousy at math . . . or a kid who knows everything about fusion and fission but can't remember the multiplication tables. Gifted students are strong learners—in their area of strength. C'mon, aren't *you* good at some things and lousy at others?
- ✗ **STOP thinking that you can do it all.** It takes lots of ideas to come up with new ways to advance and enrich material. It may mean collaborating with another teacher to help find the time, the material, and the ideas about what to do (Hughes & Murawski, 2001). It may mean that you're going to include the local college students and professors. Don't think you have to *be* a gifted ed teacher, or gifted yourself, to teach students who are gifted.
- ✗ **STOP having them be the "peer tutor" because they finish early.** Some gifted kids are great teachers and genuinely love to help others. But not all of them. Some of them are terrible tutors because they can't explain how they learned it. . . *they just "knew it."* They often end up doing the work for other kids, which doesn't help other students actually learn the content. Worst case scenario? They actually embarrass the other kids by saying, "Seriously? You don't know this? It's so easy!"

- **STOP having them do work that they already know how to do.** Every student deserves to learn something new every day. Gifted kids start each grade knowing approximately 75%–85% of that year's content. That means that there is only about 15%–25% of content that is new to them. Be sure to pretest them. If they can already do the work, let them go ahead.

- **STOP thinking that they're not "emotionally mature" enough to work with older children.** Often, a gifted kid is trying so hard to fit in with peers who are less developed than they are, they overdo it and their behavior looks silly. Or they're incredibly sensitive due to their giftedness rather than their chronological age. That won't go away with time. Research finds over and over again that students who are advanced (e.g., moving ahead in content or even skipping a grade) do much better—both academically and emotionally—than their gifted peers who are not advanced. Older kids tend to understand them better, and any sensitivities are put down to age, not to being "weird." Not so when they are with their age-level peers. It's also a way for them to break out of the secondary school "cliques" where everyone is organized by popularity.

- **STOP being intimidated if they know more than you do.** By the time gifted kids are in secondary school, they may actually know graduate level material in their content area. Of course you are wiser in the ways of the world than they are. You have experiences that they don't. But they are depending on you to be a mentor to them, not a competitor. Watch Robin Williams in "Good Will Hunting"—his speech is an excellent way to feel wiser!

- **STOP thinking that only kids who get As must be gifted.** Often, gifted students are unmotivated to learn grade-level material and will "check out" of school, do the minimum, or throw something together at the last minute. Gifted students who are not of the same cultural or language background of the teacher are particularly at risk for disengaging from content they do not see as relevant. Look at their content knowledge, abilities, and potential, not their grades.

Administrators

- **STOP spreading your gifted kids across classes.** It might help a teacher's test score average, but it doesn't help the student. Gifted students must have an opportunity to work together at some point during the day. That means that grouping has to be flexible. Heterogeneous groups are great for some things, but gifted learners need to have like-minded peers around to challenge them.

- **STOP holding kids back with policies that discourage advancement or programs that only focus on kids who are struggling.** All students deserve to have their needs met, and gifted students deserve the right to an education as well. Open your minds—and your policies.

✖ **STOP treating parents who ask for "more" as "pushy" parents.** They are asking for educational interventions that are appropriate for where their student is. This is what *all* parents ask. They are not asking for "more"; they are asking for "learning opportunities."

✖ **STOP saying "We don't have any gifted kids here."** If you are an administrator in a low-performing or low-socioeconomic school, or none of your students meet the state or district criteria, that doesn't mean you don't have gifted children. Giftedness is defined in context, and there will be students who are performing in the top 10% of your school. Treat them as "at-promise" students, and celebrate their strengths.

✖ **STOP identifying giftedness with one measure or a set of measures that use "teacher-pleasing" behaviors.** Oftentimes, gifted students are not the "good" kids but are the ones who ask questions, don't study but know the answers, exhibit leadership, and challenge authority. Untrained teachers are not very good at identifying giftedness separate from "good" classroom behavior that is typical of the majority culture.

GO "DIFFERENT" IS BETTER!

Teachers, DO This

✓ **DIFFERENTIATE *up* as well as down.** To differentiate means to change the instruction according to the characteristics of the child. Gifted students need differentiation as well. The "age-level/grade-level" expectations are frequently not appropriate. Remember, all kids have the right to an education that is focused where they are learning.

✓ **ASK higher order thinking questions.** The most important thing you can do to help a gifted student grow is to ask higher order thinking questions. These are questions without limits that force a student to use understanding and information to answer but can't be "looked up" and don't have a "right" answer. Try to avoid closed yes/no and multiple choice questions.

✓ **DO compact the curriculum.** Time is extremely important. You want to be able to use your time most effectively, and the best way to do this is spend a little time with your advanced learners. Get them started on projects that they can do independently. The critical element is the time you spend with them upfront. Gifted students need teachers; they cannot be expected to go in a corner and teach themselves.

✓ **USE flexible grouping.** Gifted students aren't gifted at everything. You may have a student who is gifted in math, but not in reading. You might have a student who is gifted in astronomy, but not in geology. You might have a student who is gifted in social leadership, but not in math. Grouping should follow the students, not their label. Similarly, you can't just "sprinkle" gifted kids throughout your class in the hope that they can teach other students. Often, they're terrible tutors because they already knew the information and can't remember learning it. Gifted students should spend part of their day with other gifted kids with differentiated curriculum. Beyond academic benefits, using gifted grouping provides social benefits. Often, a gifted kid will become arrogant when they're the only one with the answers. Being around other gifted students may be a shock, but they can then make friends with other students who have esoteric interests, too!

✓ **USE instructional technology.** Computers and other technology allow opportunities for gifted students to use their thinking abilities with infinite resources and information. A challenge that I give teachers teaching traditional classes is this: Do something with kids that cannot be duplicated online. That typically means face-to-face presentation, real-time discussions, sensory experiences, and hands-on material work.

Making Connections

Check out Chapter 7 on Technology and Engagement

✓ **ENCOURAGE creativity.** We should encourage creativity in our talented children. Our future society depends on these students learning how to use their knowledge in new and novel ways. Creativity is much more than the traditional "arts" but is a way of thinking innovatively and inventively in all areas (Feldman & Benjamin, 1998).

✓ **PROVIDE opportunities for advancement.** Colangelo, Assouline, and Gross's (2004) groundbreaking review of studies found that gifted students who were advanced—whether through acceleration or subject-level advancement—far exceeded their peers both in academic achievement over a lifetime and in their social benefits to students. Schools are known for being rigid in their policies, and teachers are often uncomfortable with allowing students to "move ahead." This research validates that students may indeed need, and deserve, acceleration. Make friends with your local college, and bring some of those resources over to you, or send the student over to them!

✓ **PROVIDE emotional support for being "different."** While we all know that struggling students need emotional support in order to achieve, gifted students, too, need emotional support to develop their talents and abilities. They are different, and these differences should be understood and celebrated. Conversely, research has found that when gifted kids are told how "smart" they are, they do not choose challenging work and perform less well than when they were given feedback on their use of learning strategies. So we need to stop saying they are smart and instead give them opportunities to show us.

✓ **FIND a mentor.** Students who are gifted at the secondary level are making life choices that will affect their future careers. They need to interact with someone who has experience with the content at a professional level, not merely at an academic level. Help them see where their choices can take them. Too often, gifted kids from poverty don't feel that they have the support to go beyond what they've always known.

Administrators, DO This

✓ **TRAIN teachers to understand characteristics and needs of gifted learners.** They are not all straight-A students, and not all straight-A students are gifted. Encourage teachers to create opportunities for advanced work. Some students who had previously not demonstrated motivation or interest might show their abilities when they are not bored.

✓ **ENCOURAGE the staff and teachers to focus on student strengths.** Students are more likely to show you what they can do, instead of only focusing on areas of deficit. Encourage a climate of achievement and success from everyone.

✓ **OFFER advanced classes or enrichment opportunities.** Does your school have an Odyssey of the Mind program, a chess club, or a Latin class? Do you have a partnership program with the local college? Have you thought about an IB (International Baccalaureate) program or adding another AP (Advanced Placement) class? If not, look to see what other opportunities you can give advanced learners. Start a program, such as Schoolwide Enrichment Program (Renzulli & Reis, 1985) or a cluster grouping approach to implement in your school.

✓ **CELEBRATE academic successes in addition to athletic successes.** Hold a pep rally for a Model UN program in addition to a football game.

✓ **CONSIDER "giving" high school credit for college credits.** Seek out dual-enrollment opportunities so that students can take an English 101 class and it can count for Senior year English. If a student took a class through the Talent Search Program, consider giving high school credit for these advanced classes.

✓ **ENCOURAGE parents and families to think about possibilities for their talented children.** Often, parents and families are afraid that they will "lose" their student to a broader world. Encourage them to provide opportunities for their students and how the advancement of the student can help the family. Encourage them to look at careers that challenge and interest the child. Provide parents and families with specific activities that they can do to help their student develop their abilities. Show them how to access the library and programs and opportunities available within the local and greater community. Provide childcare and transportation information to access these resources.

DO'S AND DON'TS FOR WORKING WITH GIFTED STUDENTS

Do NOT	DO
Give the same assignment to be done in the same amount of time for all students.	You can provide a series of tiered activities—all of which focus on the same objective. One strategy has been to use the • EVERYONE must do _____ • MOST should do _____ • SOME could do _____ Another option has been to provide a tic-tac-toe board for all students with directions to gifted students that they MUST use the center square and make a tic-tac-toe or an X, while other students might only have to do corners or three in a row. See page 247 for an example of how squares can be differentiated. The question in the middle requires one of the higher levels of reasoning.
Expect "good enough."	Challenge gifted kids with new content and innovative ways for them to show their understanding. They need to understand that there is always something new to learn and an infinite variety of ways to communicate the concepts. They also need to understand how content connects to other content and to see the complexity of what they're learning. • Ask "How could this be better?"
Teach content in isolation.	Focus on adapting the content connected by concepts. Make connections between math and history, such as the History of Zero (Kaplan, 2000)), or teach the history of the letters as you teach phonics (Robb, 2007). Or teach the concept of "Change" as it relates to math, language arts, science, and social studies (VanTassel-Baska, 1998).
Ask: "What/where/who."	Ask "What could happen if/Why/How did ____ happen?"
Tell the answer.	Wait for the answer.

Do NOT	DO
Just accept an answer to a higher order question.	Not all answers to higher order questions are of the same quality. Ask "Why is that the best answer? How can you prove your answer?"
Always be the one asking questions.	Encourage your gifted students to ASK questions about the content. "What do you think professional ___ asked when they were studying this?" Teach them how to ask good questions, not just provide answers.
"Wing it," or wait for a teachable moment for question-asking.	Use Bloom's Taxonomy or the Elements of Thought wheel to plan questions ahead of time. See page 248 for Elements of Thought and page 249 for ideas from Bloom's Taxonomy.
Teach what is already mastered.	Pretest. Students who get above an 85% on the pretest can focus only on the skills they don't know and can be freed up for a specified period of time. See page 250 for a Compacting Contract.
Use your gifted students as peer tutors.	Gifted students need to be able to grow as well. They should be able to either move ahead when content is already mastered or free themselves up for research and independent work.
Expect a gifted student to sit quietly when they're done with the expected work.	The use of an independent project can provide a set of "what to do when you're done" activities. EVERY student should be learning during a class period. "Free time" should not be provided only for those students who have done the expected task. They should have some activities to continue to work on • Create a PowerPoint or Prezi • Vocabulary work • Learning packets • Listening stations/Interest centers • Computer links • Journals or Learning Logs • Content-related silent reading • Artistic or creative applications to content • Investigations—independent research

(Continued)

(Continued)

Do NOT	DO
Put all of your gifted kids together in a group for the whole year.	Group according to the unit and according to their pretest scores. Not all gifted kids are gifted at everything. Using the label to justify the grouping doesn't allow other students with those strengths to engage at high levels and doesn't allow the gifted student to receive supplementary instruction in areas of more challenge.
Spread your gifted kids around the groups for "cooperative" grouping or to be the role models.	Group according to the unit and according to their test scores. A bored gifted student is an arrogant gifted student, and often, they make terrible role models because they can't explain to their peers how they got the answers. If they already know that content, they should have the opportunity to work with others who are also advanced and can work on more challenging problems together.
Use the computer to babysit gifted students.	Work with gifted students to show them new skills and expectations. Gifted students need a teacher—they cannot teach themselves.
Treat the computer as a "toy" or as a distraction.	The computer is an incredible source of information and presentation. If you are asking students to do something that they can find on the computer, you need to change your assignment so that they do something with the information that they find: Analyze it, present it, make meaning of it.
Assume the computer is only a tool.	Computer programs can help students create new knowledge and demonstrate. Page 251 also shows how different apps from an iPad can align with Bloom's Taxonomy.
Mistake creativity for silliness or as a challenge of authority.	Understand that "why" and "what if" questions from gifted students are part of their characteristics. While they should learn courtesy, they are often looking for novel solutions to old ways. If they have a good idea, listen to them and respect them.
Provide one way and only way to do something.	Provide open-ended ways to solve problems. Focus on the goal, not the way to get there. If a gifted kid asks, "Can I do this assignment this way?" decide if the student will still meet the objective of the lesson.

Do NOT	DO
Provide the problems to be solved.	Encourage students to FIND problems and figure out how to solve them. Problem-finding is one of the most critical skills in creativity (Starko, 1999).
Accept a short or incomplete answer or make a derogatory comment about their answer.	Ask for elaboration, another way of thinking about a situation, or more ideas. Increasing fluidity, flexibility, elaboration, and originality of ideas and thinking can help gifted students stretch creatively (Torrance, 1966). However, share the purpose of the questions; when students know that their creativity is being developed, they are more likely to participate. See page 252 for visuals of creativity.
He's already advanced cognitively. Don't insist that he be advanced physically and emotionally as well before you give him work that is where his mind is.	Give advanced opportunities as a student shows you that he or she can do the work. Often, a gifted student is more accepted by older students because they do not expect that student to be like them. Same-aged students may label the student as "weird" or apply pressure to achieve at their level—which means that the gifted student is underachieving.
Punish or mock a student for being "arrogant" or a "know-it-all."	Allow the student different ways to show you what they know. They can't dominate or interrupt the learning of other students, but they, too, have the right to learn something new every day. Ask them to do things like write down their ideas to share with you later, create a PowerPoint to share information, or put information on a class blog or web page.
Expect the gifted student to know everything.	• Give them instruction in what they don't know. Gifted students have strengths, but they also experience struggles and confusion while they are learning. • Teach them that making mistakes is HOW we learn. If you can already do it, you aren't learning. Understand that some gifted students are "twice-exceptional" and may have learning and social disabilities as well as gifts and talents (Hughes, 2011). Provide accommodations and modifications in their areas of challenge, and challenge their abilities at the same time.

(Continued)

(Continued)

Do NOT	DO
Tell them how smart they are and expect things to be easy for them; if it's too easy, it's too low.	Focus on their learning; emphasize the process they use to learn something. If they learn quickly, they are using effective strategies. Encourage them to try challenging things and to learn from mistakes. Gifted students sometimes feel they won't be gifted anymore if they don't "get it" and have to work hard at something.
Expect them to be like everyone else; tell them to "stop thinking so much."	It can be very lonely being the only one to make jokes that only the teacher gets or to be interested in random things. You can do the following: • Encourage connections with other people interested in a topic through the Internet. Some gifted students find university professor mentors or find groups of people interested in their topic. • Encourage the gifted students to hang out together. They should learn how to be friends with others, but they also need to find friends like themselves. They're not being exclusionary, they're finding peers. Understand that they may comprehend things that they have no control over. These are the kids who can get very upset about world hunger, war, poverty, and issues in the news. Give them outlets and opportunities to help.
Expect them to always be perfect at everything.	Gifted kids are kids, first and foremost. That means they will be silly and goofy and terrible at some things, and on occasion, make wrong choices. It doesn't make them less gifted; it means that they're kids.

TIC-TAC-TOE BOARD

Describe what _____ might have looked like.	How could you tell _____ from _____?	How might you see _____ in real life?
Restate _____ in your own words.	What is another perspective on _____?	What is the purpose of _____?
List the reasons why _____.	What evidence do you see for _____?	If _____ happened, what might have been the end?

THE ELEMENTS OF THOUGHT

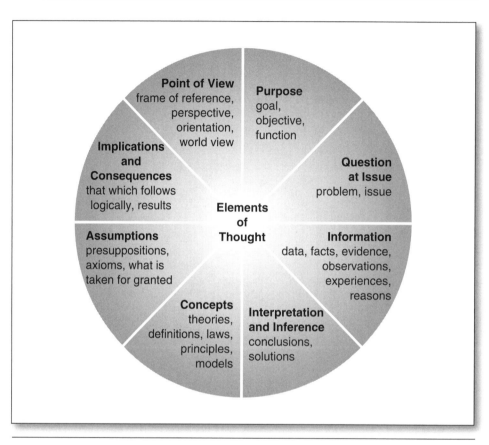

Source: Copyright © 2013 by Foundation for Critical Thinking (FCT). www.criticalthinking.org. Used with permission.

BLOOM'S TAXONOMY

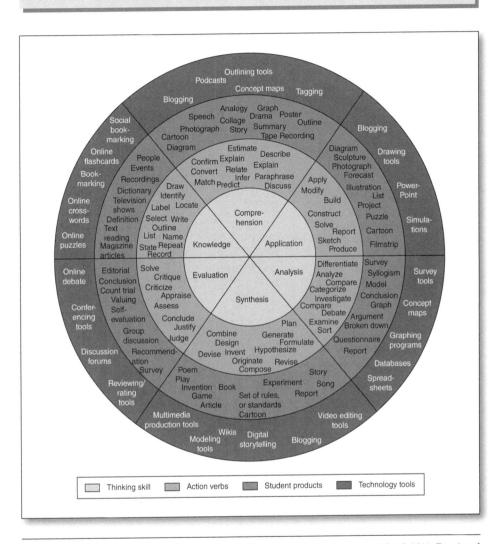

Source: Graphic created by Emily Hixon, Janet Buckenmeyer, & Heather Zamojski, © 2011. Reprinted by permission of the authors.

COMPACTING CONTRACT

Name:

Content Area:

Score on Pretest (Must be above a 90%)_____

I would like to research the following question:

I will need the following resources:

The time I will need is:

I will present my findings in this way:

To get an A, I will need to do:

If I do not use my time wisely, I understand that I will be asked to either revise my project or join the rest of the class and receive a(n) _____ for my efforts.

BLOOM'S TAXONOMY AND IPAD APPS

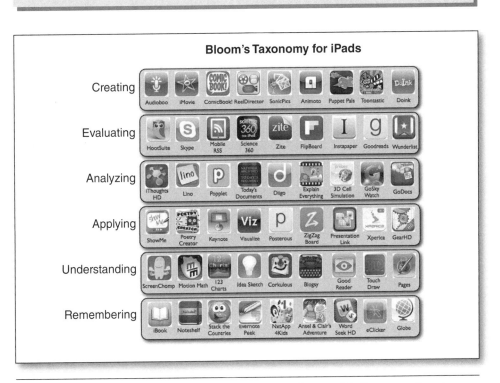

Source: Bloom's Taxonomy for iPads. Sylvia Rosenthal Tolisano. globallyconnectedlearning.com. Adapted from Dave Mileham. Used with permission.

ELEMENTS OF CREATIVITY

The Four Components of Creative Thinking

FLUENCY

FLEXIBILITY

ORIGINALITY

ELABORATION

Source: ©Jr Imagination. From "Creative Genius: How to Grow the Seeds of Creativity Within Every Child" by Marjorie Sarnat. www.jrimagination.com. Used by permission.

REFERENCES

Colangelo, N., Assouline, S., & Gross, M. (2004). *A nation deceived: How schools hold back America's brightest students.* Templeton National Report on Acceleration. Iowa City, IA: University of Iowa Press.

Feldman, D. H., & Benjamin, A. C. (1998). Letters from the field. *Roeper Review, 21,* 78–88.

Hughes, C. E. (2011). Twice-exceptional learners: Twice the strengths, twice the challenges. In J. Escalante (Ed.), *A kaleidoscope of special populations in gifted education: Considerations, connections, and meeting the needs of our most able diverse gifted students* (pp. 153–174). Austin, TX: Prufrock Press.

Hughes, C. E., & Murawski, W. W. (2001). Lessons from another field: Applying co-teaching strategies to gifted education. *Gifted Child Quarterly, 45*(3), 195–204.

Kaplan, R. (2000). *The nothing that is: A natural history of zero.* London, England: Oxford University Press.

Lavoie, R. (2004). How difficult can this be? The F.A.T. City Workshop: Understanding learning disabilities [Video]. United States: PBS Videos.

Paul, R. (1985). *Critical thinking for a rapidly changing world.* Sonoma, CA: Center for Critical Thinking.

Peterson, J. S. (1999). Gifted—Through whose cultural lens? An application of the postpositivistic mode of inquiry. *Journal for the Education of the Gifted, 22,* 354–383.

Poh, P.-S. (2008). Cognitive characteristics of the gifted. In J. A. Plucker & C. M. Callahan (Eds.), *Critical issues and practices in gifted education: What the research says* (pp. 57–83). Waco, TX: Prufrock Press.

Renzulli, J. S. (1978). What makes giftedness: Reexamining of a definition. *Phi Delta Kappan, 60,* 180–184, 261.

Renzulli, J. S., & Reis, S. M. (1985). *The schoolwide enrichment model: A comprehensive plan for educational excellence.* Mansfield Center, CT: Creative Learning Press.

Robb, D. (2007). *Ox, house, stick: The history of our alphabet.* London, England: Charlesbridge.

Robinson, A., Shore, B. M., & Enerson, D. L. (Eds.). (2007). *Best practices in gifted education: An evidence-based guide.* Waco, TX: Prufrock Press.

Spielhagen, F., & Cooper, B. (2005). The unkindest cut: Seven stupid arguments against programs for the gifted. *Education Week, 24*(31), 47–48.

Starko, A. (1999). Problem-finding: A key to creative productivity. In A. S. Fishkin, B. Cramond, & P. Olszewski-Kubilius (Eds.), *Investigating creativity in youth: Research and method* (pp. 75–96). Cresskill, NJ: Hampton Press.

Terman, L. M. (1925). *Mental and physical traits of a thousand gifted children: Genetic studies of genius.* Stanford, CA: Stanford University Press.

Torrance, E. P. (1966). *Torrance tests of creative thinking: Norms technical manual.* Princeton, NJ: Personnel.

VanTassel-Baska, J. (1998). *Excellence in educating gifted and talented learners* (3rd ed). Denver, CO: Love.

RECOMMENDED READINGS

* Castellano, J. A. (2003). *Special populations in gifted education: Working with diversi-fied learners*. Boston, MA: Allyn & Bacon.
* Csikszentmihalyi, M. (1996). *Creativity*. New York, NY: Harper.
* Gallagher, J. J. (1985). *Teaching the gifted child* (3rd ed.). Boston, MA: Allyn & Bacon.
* Gross, M. U. M. (1993). *Exceptionally gifted children*. London, England: Routledge.
* Sternberg, R. J. (1985). *Beyond IQ: A triarchic theory of intelligence*. New York, NY: Cambridge University Press.
* Tannenbaum, A. J. (1972). A backward and forward glance at the gifted. *National Elementary Principal, 51*, 14–23.

GO EVEN FURTHER WITH THIS TOPIC ON THE WORLD WIDE WEB

* www.nagc.org
* www.cectag.com/
* www.cty.jhu.edu/talent/
* www.hoagiesgifted.org
* www.prufrock.com

THE Apps WE LOVE

* Wolfram Alpha
* Mathemagics
* Night Sky
* Periodic Table
* TED
* Stick Picks
* Words with Friends
* Khan Academy

16

Engaging English Language Learners

Shartriya Collier

California State University, Northridge

WHAT REALLY WORKS WORKING WITH ELLs IN THE SECONDARY CLASSROOM

Creating Lifelong Literacy and Language Development

From the rural South to urban cosmopolitan centers, English language learners (ELLs) are becoming an increasingly larger proportion of the U.S. population. Indeed, in California, Texas, and New York, over 15% to 20% of K–12 populations are English learners. Moreover, ELLs now represent at least 10% of the population in states such as North Carolina, Minnesota, and Oklahoma (National Center for Education Statistics, 2014a). Those of you in Maine and Connecticut aren't exempt from reading this chapter though. These numbers are expected to exponentially increase over the next several decades. In fact, in the summer of 2014, the news was rampant with information regarding the 40,000 unaccompanied children who entered the United States as immigrants from Central America (Loehrke, 2014). This affects us all.

Such shifts in the demographics of the United States have profound implications for the American system of public education. While such a statement is applicable to all ELLs, it is of particular consequence for secondary schools. Many ELLs in secondary schools have years of schooling experience in their first language. Yet due to factors such as familial obligations, socioeconomic status, standardized tests, and literacy level, many do not excel in school (Collier & Auerbach, 2011). As a result of the No Child Left Behind legislation, many ELLs in secondary schools must not only pass state standardized tests but also language proficiency tests in order to graduate. Currently, in states such as California, if a student is classified as an ELL for longer than 6 years, they are considered "long term" (WestEd, 2010). Long-term ELLs can become "stuck in the ESL (English as a Second Language) track" and do not graduate on time with their English-only peers. They are sometimes seen not just as having a language difference but as having a deficit—one that is at times viewed as a disability. In fact, approximately 35% of the long-term ELLs in the Los Angeles Unified School District (the largest school district in the nation) are also identified as students with special needs. Such a classification is far from benign. Zarate and Pineda (2014) found that ELLs who spoke Spanish in the home in the elementary years, ELLs who were reclassified as fluent English proficient rather than staying in ELL tracked classes, and ELLs who attended middle schools with lower concentrations of ELLs were more likely to complete high school than those who did not meet those criteria. While there are a number of best practices to support ELLs, the most essential skills needed to excel in school and beyond are strong lifelong literacy skills. Why literacy, you ask?

Literacy is a pretty big deal. Approximately 21% of adults currently residing in the United States read below the fifth-grade level. We're not just talking about ELLs; we are talking about all U.S. adults! It has been estimated that at least 19% of high school graduates are minimally literate (National Center for Education Statistics, 2014b). Literacy development not only impacts one's ability to serve as an active citizen but also how well one does in life, the economic opportunities one has, and the impact of those opportunities on one's family and community. Yes, reading is that powerful. Current research demonstrates that children of parents with low literacy skills are more likely to (a) score lower on standards tests, (b) be placed in Special Education, and (c) drop out of school (Auerbach & Collier, 2011). ELLs have an even higher risk of such outcomes. Thus, it is urgent for educators to address the unique needs of ELLs.

So how do we do that? In order for teachers to effectively support the needs of ELLs in secondary schools, you must first understand the fundamental concepts needed to stimulate ELLs to become great readers and lifelong learners. According to the National Reading Panel (2000), fundamental literacy instruction consists of five key elements: reading comprehension skills, phonics, phonemic awareness, vocabulary, and fluency. In other words,

Making Connections

Check out Chapter 2 on Reading and Literacy

regardless of the age or English language learning status, good readers must master strategies for understanding the texts they are reading, how to sound out words, how to understand the context of the words in use, and how to read smoothly using the correct prosody and intonation (Sun-Alperin & Wang, 2011). I know! Many of you are thinking that you teach content, not reading, and secretly you are wondering what the heck prosody is. (It means the rhythm or intonation of speech.)

Seriously though, equipping ELLs with strategies to become lifelong readers is the task of *all* teachers regardless of your content area. All teachers must understand that ELLs need authentic opportunities to read engaging texts, interpret and discuss interesting topics, and experience a variety of genres that render them intrigued by the material. Let's examine research and applications for supporting ELLs and encouraging lifelong literacy skills . . . even if you teach high school math.

LITERACY DEVELOPMENT AND ENGLISH LANGUAGE LEARNERS

How does one who speaks English as a second language become literate? And what are the best practices for developing their lifelong literacy skills? Before exploring the answers, let's explore the theoretical frameworks essential for understanding literacy development in second language learners. Don't freak out! I know you bought this book because it was guaranteed to be full of practical bullet points and not tons of theory, but bear with me. Much of this theory will actually help you devise your own strategies with your students who are ELLs. Let's begin: Foundational to these theories is the need to recognize that English learners arrive with various degrees of language and literacy skills in their first language (L1). In order to more effectively address their needs in English, we as teachers must first assess their L1 literacy skills. (Relax. There are actually folks in your district trained to do just that.) We must then evaluate the foundational skills they hold in English and how these separate skill sets can be integrated in support of their overall journey toward English language skills (Krashen, 1996). According to Jim Cummins's (1991) Common Underlying Proficiency Model, the concepts and skills that students acquire in their first language will transfer to their second language *within the right instructional context*. For example, a student with eighth-grade literacy skills in Spanish will most likely understand important reading comprehension skills, such as identifying main characters and key events. Nevertheless, many secondary teachers have students from a range of countries and English language development (ELD) levels in one classroom. Thus, in a multilingual classroom where perhaps three or more languages are represented and the mode of instruction is English only, it may be difficult for teachers to support the transfer of first language skills to the development of second language competencies.

According to Chamot's (1996) Cognitive Academic Language Learning Approach, ELLs need access to *cognitive* (thinking maps, note taking skills), *social-affective* (peer interaction, cooperative grouping), and *metalinguistic* (awareness of one's own language skills and limitations) strategies to succeed in school. Don't those all sound like skills most students could benefit from? Teaching these, and making students aware of them, is especially essential due to the fact that textbooks and curricula are usually expository texts. Expository texts have more complex grammatical structures, fewer pictures, dense vocabulary, and are often detailed (Echevarria, Vogt, & Short, 2008). Those are much more difficult to grasp than books geared for elementary students! For example, Hong-Nam (2014) examined the metacognitive awareness reading strategies used by ELLs in high school and their relationship to reading proficiency and discovered that ELLs with intermediate proficiency were more likely to use more strategies when reading. Additionally, ELLs who considered themselves advanced readers also employed more reading strategies. Seifert and Espin (2012) also examined the role of text readings and vocabulary learning for ELL students. Although they focused on students with learning disabilities, they discovered that text reading, paired with vocabulary instruction, had a positive effect on vocabulary knowledge. Moreover, they concluded that consistent reading of a variety of science texts by the students and knowledge of the academic vocabulary used could be improved with direct instruction. Hey, that's certainly something all secondary teachers can do, right? Alkhawaldeh (2012) found that reading challenges included the difficulty of the reading passage, lack of familiarity with the vocabulary, lack of cooperative learning during reading, and limited background knowledge. These were all factors that impeded the reading process. Thus, this tells us we need to look at these areas when we are teaching core content. You may not have the power to change the students' background knowledge of a subject coming into your class, but you can certainly consider the reading passages you are selecting, the way in which you front-load vocabulary, the cooperative learning strategies you employ in class, and even the preassessments you use to determine what types of background knowledge they do have and how you will build upon that.

Much of the abundant body of language/literacy research incorporates a sociocultural lens of literacy (Garcia, 2005; Ramirez & Jimenez-Silva, 2014). Thus, literacy development goes beyond just decoding, phonological processing, and vocabulary development because it is not a set of discrete unconnected skills. Rather, literacy development is integrally connected to the four primary skill areas: reading, writing, listening, and speaking (Garcia, 2005). If, for example, you were teaching a history lesson on the Gold Rush, you would want to use each of these primary skill areas. As a teacher who supports ELLs' literacy needs, you should first use visuals to preview between three and five key vocabulary words that they need to know in order to understand the text. Next, take your students through the three stages of reading: prereading, reading, and postreading. Garcia (2005) argues that these stages are critical to fluency and comprehension. During prereading stages, students must be motivated to learn and attention must be paid to the preteaching vocabulary. Also, prequestions must be identified. Think about this: As teachers, we know we are supposed to have a "hook" for our lesson; we know we are supposed to frontload vocabulary and ask students questions to get them interested and critically thinking. That's all this is. You can do it in any subject, but you will find that while it is helpful for all your students, it is critical for those who are ELL. In the reading phase, the instructor may read aloud to students and/or integrate guided reading and small group discussions. As they read, students may stop to speak with their "neighbors" and use these as a tool or "brain break" to summarize key ideas. Finally, they may use a double entry (see page 268) to summarize and write key ideas. Peregoy and Boyle (2013) suggest that effective literacy instruction integrates receptive and productive skills in all lessons. In a nutshell, that means you need to have language they are listening to and language they are creating/producing. All secondary teachers can do that! In fact, Msimanga and Lelliot (2014) found that the negotiation of meaning and discourse strategies students used to discuss science concepts actually supplemented oral language and writing skills. Thus, the students were learning science while they were concurrently working on their language skills. Bam!

Ultimately, using the four skills areas—reading, writing, listening, and speaking—is key. In sum, reading supplements writing and writing supplements reading. Just as reading must occur as a process, writing should too. Want to make a middle school or high school student engaged in reading and writing? Then you had better include authentic texts in addition to your learning tasks. Matuchniak, Olson, and Scarcella (2014) examined the Pathway Project, where teachers implemented cognitive strategies to assist students in understanding, interpreting, and writing analytical essays about themes in literature. They found that students who received 2 years of instruction demonstrated significant progress in writing compared to those who only received 1 year. Doesn't sound like rocket science, but it means that the cognitive strategies and the integration of authentic literature was actually working!

Making Connections

Check out Chapters 2 and 3 on Reading and Writing Strategies

As you can see, the need for ELLs to have access to a variety of texts and textual formats is of optimal importance. What student wants to only read one type of book or be told what to read all the time? For that matter, what *person* does? Kibler (2014) discovered that providing the student access to bilingual texts increased literacy development and confidence. Do you have materials available in students' first language? If not, could you get some? It might actually help your students with their learning of your content in English.

Clearly, a variety of research-based strategies exist that may be used to help English learners in secondary schools excel and develop effective strategies for lifelong literacy development. Check out the Cognitive Academic Language Learning Approach (CALLA) website in the Plugged In box. Let's recap. First, conduct preliminary assessments to determine students' literacy levels in English and, if possible, in the first language. Second, include a variety of *cognitive* (note taking, highlighting, thinking maps), *metacognitive* (think-alouds, reflective journals), and *social/affective* (cooperative groups, positive encouragement) strategies into your instruction. Third, remember that literacy development is not a set of discrete, isolated skills. Therefore, always include reading, writing, listening, and speaking in order to increase comprehension. Fourth, provide access to authentic texts and connect those texts to writing. Finally, oral language is essential for reading and writing development. The more students discuss reading and writing, the more they develop critical analytical skills. See? This is all very doable in your secondary class. Told you so.

Plugged In

calla.ws/strategies

The following sections include myths, misconceptions, and mistakes many teachers and educators hold or make regarding ELLs in secondary schools.

WHAT TO AVOID AT ALL COSTS WHEN TEACHING ENGLISH LEARNERS IN SECONDARY CONTEXTS

Teachers

- ✗ **STOP believing that it is not your job to teach ESL, because "that's for the ESL teacher."** Whether your area of expertise is math, science, or the arts, you must integrate language skills into your instruction so that *all* learners can effectively obtain the content.

- ✗ **STOP relying solely on lecture style instruction and PowerPoint.** English learners need a variety of opportunities to use and apply language in context. If you're talking more than 60% of your instructional time, you're talking too much!

- ✗ **STOP using only textbooks and worksheets.** English learners need a variety of authentic texts in a variety of genres. Try mixing it up using magazines, newspapers, books, blogs, journals, etc. Ask your students what *they* like to read!

- ✗ **STOP labeling the parents of English learners as "people who just don't care about their children's success."** Many parents are recent arrivals to the country and are often not familiar with expectations for success in U.S. schools. Plus, they may be overwhelmed just learning our customs, ways, and policies.

✗ **STOP beginning your lesson without tapping into students' background knowledge.** Whatever you teach, keep in mind that many ELLs were not raised in the United States. Thus, it is essential that you help them connect their experiences with learning content in their home countries to learning the content in the United States.

✗ **STOP teaching without reviewing key vocabulary in advance.** If you lose your students early because they don't understand the vocabulary, the lesson was a waste. Let them know what you are talking about so the content can make sense.

Administrators

✗ **STOP isolating your English learners in separate classrooms.** The "pull-out" method of ESL instruction has been proven to be one of the least effective methods for ELLs in academic contexts. Interestingly, it is also discouraged in special education. Both areas are increasingly encouraging inclusive methods of instruction (Murawski & Spencer, 2011).

✗ **STOP believing that once ELLs have exited their sheltered (pull-out, self-contained) programs that they no longer need support.** Language learning is a lifelong process!

✗ **STOP isolating your ESL staff.** The ESL staff is a powerful resource that can provide support for content area teachers who do not know how to support instruction for their students. Help them move away from their separate classrooms and engage in collaborative or co-teaching relationships with colleagues (Honigsfeld & Dove, 2008).

✗ **STOP prohibiting "home visits."** While teachers must be safe, research by Moll, Amanti, Neff, and Gonzalez (1992) reveals that home visits are a vital tool for determining students' "funds of knowledge." This concept is talking about the many resources (values, traditions, support networks) that families have at home that can also be incorporated into school.

GO STRATEGIES FOR SUCCESS WHEN TEACHING ENGLISH LEARNERS IN SECONDARY SCHOOLS

Teachers, DO This

✓ **INTEGRATE "text sets."** Text sets are a variety of reading materials of different genres around a central topic. Thus, if you are teaching the water cycle, then gather brochures, books, articles, magazines, and stories related to the topic. This helps students see academic vocabulary in a contextualized manner, and it also helps build comprehension. (Can you connect your content to texts about vampires or video games or movies?)

✓ **PRETEACH at least five key vocabulary words prior to any lesson.** Students must have opportunities to practice reading, writing, and listening/speaking skills with the vocabulary.

✓ **TEACH academic comprehension skills when reading.** Don't assume they'll figure them out on their own. Model for students how to skim prior to reading, how to preview headings and subheadings, and how to highlight key ideas. Can't you see how these techniques will be helpful for all your students, not just those who are English learners?

✓ **INCORPORATE journals.** Journals are a great way to informally assess students' writing progress and to determine if students understand key content concepts. Begin each class with a "Quick Write" by providing a prompt or having students free write. At the end of your lessons, you can also have students respond to prompts. Try this: "Today we discussed _____," or "I really did a great job with _____," or "I was confused about _____." Review the journals often. Remember that you want students to stay engaged, so feel free to include Quick Writes that are funny, ask for strange comparisons students can make between the content they just learned and something random, or include questions to you about what they don't understand.

✓ **INCORPORATE corrective feedback.** According to Scarcella (2003), "The goal is to give feedback thoughtfully, in ways that encourage, not discourage, developing writers and language learners" (p. 131). Don't simply correct errors. Instead, explain why it is incorrect and model the correct forms. For example, the journal previously discussed could be used as an interactive journal in which you respond to students' prompts. If a student writes, "I like lrge mountain cause they pretty." You might respond, "I like large mountains as well. I agree, they are pretty!" This form of feedback can help to alleviate writing anxiety (Di Loreto & McDonough, 2013).

✓ **MODEL assignments and also provide students with samples of your desired final product.** Remember, ELLs are acquiring language and content. If you simply tell them what to do, they may not understand. Model step-by-step. This will help so many of your students!

Administrators, DO This

✓ **PROVIDE parents with a weekly or monthly newsletter in which you include a "Parent Tip" of the month** (see a sample on page 264). These tips might include strategies such as "How to help your child to become a better reader" or "How to help your child get into college." Again, many parents come from different cultural backgrounds and countries in which not interfering in school was a demonstration of respect.

✓ **ACTIVELY SUPPORT English learners, and encourage exit from the ELD program as soon as possible.** Compared to other students, long-term ELLs are more likely to drop out of school and are least likely to go to college. They need consistent support to build confidence in their learning skills and abilities. Provide incentives. You could buy books for ELLs or give awards to those who show improvement. Get creative, and think of other ways of recognizing language growth and development that would really work in your school. This said, remember that just because a student is exited from a program doesn't mean that all good teaching strategies that support language development should just stop.

✓ **CREATE a true multilingual/multicultural hub in which staff, parents, teachers, and community members feel mutually invested in academic excellence.** Have Family Nights, and develop real-world internship possibilities for students. What about offering adult literacy classes for parents? Whatever you do to create community, be sure that you celebrate all students' unique identities as essential variables in the school environment.

Making Connections

Check out Chapter 20 on Family Collaboration

COMPREHENSION STRATEGY SQP2RS

(See also SIOP MODEL, Echevarria, Vogt, & Short, 2008.)

(SQP2RS)

Surveying (Scan the text, have students preview the text for any words with which they are not familiar.)

Questioning (Have students preview the subheadings. Skim the text. Have students develop questions they have based upon the key headings.)

Predicting (Have students make predictions about what the text is about and what they will learn.)

Reading (Read the text either in small groups or as a whole class. Also, have students underline any answers they find to the questions they created.)

Responding (Have students answer the questions they created in the questioning section and/or have them formulate new ones.)

Summarizing (Have students write a summary paragraph either individually, in pairs, or in groups.)

SAMPLE PARENT TIPS

Parent Tip 1: Book Preview

Remind your son or daughter to preview the book by reading the front and back cover. Tell them to make predictions about what the book will be about before they read. This helps with comprehension once they begin reading. Remind them to ask themselves these questions as they read.

"What do you think is happening in the cover of the book?"

"What do you think the book is going to be about?"

"What do you think will happen at the end of the book?"

Parent Tip 2: Five Ws

Got a middle schooler who isn't willing to tell you what he is reading? A high schooler who says her book is "fine?" Want to know if they are actually understanding what they're reading? A good way to check basic comprehension is to ask questions and remind your son or daughter to use the five W's when they read:

Who? What? When? Where? Why?

Who are the main characters?

What are they doing?

When does the story take place?

Where does the story take place?

Why are the characters doing what they are doing?

Parent Tip 3: Reading for Fluency

Reading for Fluency:

An important part of reading is fluency. Fluency is the ability to do the following:

Recognize words automatically.

Read aloud with expression.

There are three components of fluency.

Accuracy: Also known as automaticity. It refers to the person's ability to read words without making mistakes.

Rate: The speed a person reads at.

Prosody: Refers to stress, intonation, and pauses. Commonly known as "reading with feeling."

Want your son or daughter to improve in reading? Then you need to model this with him or her. Here are three activities that you can use to improve fluency:

1. Model fluent reading. (Do this in the language that you feel most comfortable with.) When you read to your child, use expression. Use different voices for all the characters. Make it fun!

2. Pay attention to punctuation. Ask your son or daughter, "Do you see any question marks?" "Do you see any exclamation points?" Have your child point them out to you. Talk about how they change how you read the passage.

3. Give your child different ways to practice and perform. For example, you read one character and have your child read another

character. If your child is into videos or movies, let them make a video of reading that they can play for their younger sibling.

4. Have your child read his or her favorite book over and over again. It doesn't matter if it's a Calvin and Hobbes cartoon book, the Harry Potter series, or a classic like *To Kill a Mockingbird*; reading is reading.

5. Practice high-frequency words and academic vocabulary: Make word card lists. Practice using and spelling these words at the dinner table. These words are common words that cannot be sounded out when reading (in most cases). English is a difficult language! These words will eventually help your child pass the SAT and get into college!

PARENT TIPS (IN SPANISH)

Consejo del Día 1: Repasando el Libro

Recuérdele a su hijo o hija a repasar la portada y la parte posterior del libro antes de leer. Dígales que es importante de hacer predicciones sobre el libro antes de leer. Esto ayuda con la comprensión. Cuando empiezan de leer, recuérdales que es importante de hacer preguntas mientras están leyendo. Por ejemplo:

¿Qué crees que esta pasando?

¿Cuál es tu predicción sobre que va a pasar en el libro?

¿Qué crees que va a pasar al final del libro?

Si es posible leer con su hijo o hija.

Consejo del Día 2: Dos Q's C, D, P

Una buena manera de comprobar la comprensión básica es hacer preguntas. Recordarle a su hijo o hija a usar las cinco preguntas cuando leen: 5 W's (en Inglés) o "Dos Q's, C, D, P en Español:

¿Quién? ¿Qué? ¿Cuándo? ¿Dónde? ¿Por qué?

¿Quiénes son los personajes principales?

¿Qué están haciendo?

¿Cuándo se la historia?

¿Dónde tiene lugar?

¿Por qué están haciendo los personajes lo que están haciendo?

Consejo del Día 3: Fluidez de Lectura

Una parte importante de la lectura es la fluidez. La fluidez es la capacidad de:

Reconocer las palabras automáticamente.

Leer en voz alta con expresión.

Hay tres componentes de fluidez.

Precisión: también conocido como automatismo. Se refiere a la capacidad de la persona para leer las palabras sin cometer errores.

Velocidad: velocidad a la que una persona lee.

Prosodia: Se refiere al estrés, la entonación y las pausas. Comúnmente conocido como "leer con sentimiento."

Hay tres actividades prácticas que se pueden utilizar para mejorar la fluidez.

1. Modele fluidez de lectura. (Hacer esto en el idioma que se sienta más cómodo). Cuando su hijo esta leyendo, recordarle de usar expresión.

2. Preste atención a la puntuación. Pregúntele a su hijo, "¿Ve algún signo de interrogación?" "¿Ve usted alguna exclamación?" Haga que su niño le diga cuales son.

3. Dele a su hijo diferentes formas de practicar y actuar. Por ejemplo, puede leer un personaje y que su hijo juegue otro personaje.

4. Lea el libro favorito de su hijo/a una y otra vez.

5. Practique con palabras de alta frecuencia y el vocabulario académico: Haga listas de palabras. Estas palabras son palabras comunes que no se pueden sonar al leer (en la mayoría de los casos). Inglés es un idioma difícil! Estas palabras eventualmente le ayudará a niño pasa el SAT y entrar en la universidad!

SAMPLE DOUBLE ENTRY JOURNAL

Teacher Instructions: When you begin a new book, have the students take out their "Double Entry Journal." After you've provided background knowledge about the book, have them to read the first few pages silently. Then stop the students and ask them to find a good quote. Have them share the quote with their neighbor and discuss why they thought it was interesting. In the commentary section, they can write their interpretation of the quote and any clarifying questions they have. Allow them to continue reading. Continue to stop them every few pages.

Name: _____

Class: _____ Period: _____

Date: _____

Author and Reading Covered		
Page	Quotations	Commentary/Analysis

REFERENCES

Alkhawaldeh, A. (2012). High school students' challenges in English reading comprehension in Amman second directorate of education. *Journal of Instructional Psychology, 39*(3/4), 214–228.

Auerbach, S., & Collier, S. (2011). Bringing high stakes from the classroom to the parent center: Lessons from an intervention program for immigrant families. *Teachers College Record, 114*(3), 1–40.

Chamot, A. U. (1996). The Cognitive Academic Language Learning Approach (CALLA): Theoretical framework and instructional applications. In J. E. Alatis (Ed.), *Georgetown University round table on languages and linguistics, 1996* (pp. 108–115). Washington, DC: Georgetown University Press.

Collier, S., & Auerbach, S. (2011). "It's difficult because of the language": Language use and bilingual family program development in the post-proposition 227 era. *Multicultural Education, 11*(2), 9–14.

Cummins, J. (1991). Language development and academic learning. In L. M. Malavé & G. Duquette (Eds.), *Language, culture and cognition* (pp. 161–174). Clevedon, England: Multilingual Matters.

Di Loreto, S., & McDonough, K. (2013). The relationship between instructor feedback and ESL student anxiety. *TESL Canada Journal, 31*(1), 20–41.

Echevarria, J., Vogt, M., & Short, D. (2008). *Making content comprehensible for English learners: The SIOP model* (3rd ed.). Needham Heights, MA: Allyn & Bacon.

Garcia, G. G. (2005). *English learners: Reaching the highest level of English literacy*. Upper Saddle River, NJ: Merrill-Prentice Hall.

Hong-Nam, K. (2014). ELL high school students' metacognitive awareness of reading strategy use and reading proficiency. *TESL-EJ, 18*(1), 1–16.

Honigsfeld, A., & Dove, M. (2008). Co-teaching in the ESL classroom. *Delta Kappa Gamma Bulletin, 74*(2), 8–14.

Kibler, A. (2014). From high school to the noviciado: An adolescent linguistic minority student's multilingual journey in writing. *Modern Language Journal, 98*(2), 629–651.

Krashen, S. (1996). *Under attack: The case against bilingual education*. Culver City, CA: Language Education Associates.

Loehrke, J. (2014, August 6). Number of unaccompanied children released to sponsors by state. *USA TODAY*. Retrieved from http://www.usatoday.com

Matuchniak, T., Olson, C., & Scarcella, R. (2014). Examining the text-based, on-demand, analytical writing of mainstreamed Latino English learners in a randomized field trial of the Pathway Project intervention. *Reading and Writing, 27*(6), 973–994.

Moll, L., Amanti, C., Neff, D., & Gonzalez, N. (1992). Funds of knowledge for teaching: Using a qualitative approach to connect homes and classrooms. *Theory Into Practice, 31*(2), 132–141.

Msimanga, A., & Lelliott, A. (2014). Talking science in multilingual contexts in South Africa: Possibilities and challenges for engagement in learners home languages in high school classrooms. *International Journal of Science Education, 36*(7), 1159–1183.

Murawski, W. W., & Spencer, S. (2011). *Collaborate, communicate, and differentiate! How to increase student learning in today's diverse schools*. Thousand Oaks, CA: Corwin.

National Center for Education Statistics. (2014a). English learners: Fast facts. Retrieved from http://nces.ed.gov/fastfacts/display.asp?id=96

National Center for Education Statistics. (2014b). National assessment of adult literacy. Retrieved from http://nces.ed.gov/naal/

National Reading Panel. (2000). Teaching children to read: An evidence-based assessment of the scientific research literature on reading and its implications for reading instruction. Retrieved from http://www.nichd.nih.gov/publications/pubs/nrp/pages/smallbook.aspx

Peregoy, S. F., & Boyle, O. (2013). *Reading, writing, and learning in ESL: A resource book for K–12 teachers* (6th ed.). Upper Saddle River, NJ: Pearson Education.

Ramirez, P., & Jimenez-Silva, M. (2014). Secondary English learners: Strengthening their literacy skills through culturally responsive teaching. *Kappa Delta Pi Record, 50*(2), 65–69.

Scarcella, R. (2003). *Accelerating academic English: A focus on the English learner.* Oakland, CA: Regents of the University of California.

Seifert, K., & Espin, C. (2012). Improving reading of science texts for secondary students with learning disabilities: Effects of text reading, vocabulary learning, and combined approaches to instruction. *Learning Disability Quarterly, 35*(4), 236–247.

Sun-Alperin, M., & Wang, M. (2011). Cross-language transfer of phonological and orthographic processing skills from Spanish L1 to English L2. *Reading and Writing: An Interdisciplinary Journal, 24*(5), 591–614.

WestEd. (2010). What are we doing to middle school English language learners? Retrieved from http://www.wested.org/online_pubs/PD-10-02.pdf

Zarate, M., & Pineda, C. (2014). Effects of elementary school home language, immigrant generation, language classification, and school's English learner concentration on Latinos' high school completion. *Teachers College Record, 116*(2), 1–37.

RECOMMENDED READINGS

* Hurley, S. R., & Tinajero, J. V. (2001). *Literacy assessment of English language learners.* Boston, MA: Allyn & Bacon.

* Mora, J. (2000). *Metalinguistic transfer from Spanish to English biliteracy.* Retrieved from http://coe.sdsu.edu/people/jmora/Moramodules/Metalingtransfer.htm

* Roberts, C. (1994). Transferring literacy skills from L1 to L2: From theory to practice. *Journal of Educational Issues of Language Minority Students, 13,* 209–224.

* Schwinge, D. (2003). Enabling biliteracy: Using the continua of biliteracy to analyze curricular adaptations. In N. H. Hornberger (Ed.), *Continua of biliteracy and ecological framework of educational policy, research, and practice in multilingual settings* (pp. 248–265). Clevedon, England: Multilingual Matters.

* Vardell, S., Hadaway, N., & Young, T. (2006). Matching books and readers: Selecting literature for English learners. *The Reading Teacher, 59*(8), 734–741.

GO EVEN FURTHER WITH
THIS TOPIC ON THE THE WORLD WIDE WEB

- www.tesol.org
- www.cal.org
- www.ncela.us/resources
- www.webenglishteacher.com/esl.html
- www.davesESLcafe.com
- www.nabe.org
- www.everythingesl.net
- www.colorincolorado.org
- www.colorincolorado.org/educators/content/cooperative/
- www.edu-sources.org/engagement-strategies/
- www.esl.about.com
- www.onestopenglish.com
- www.breakingnewsenglish.com
- www.moramodules.com

THE Apps WE LOVE

- Mind Snacks
- FluentU
- Memrise
- Duolingo
- Sentence Builder

17

Addressing Autism Spectrum Disorder

Emily Iland

California State University, Northridge

WHAT REALLY WORKS WITH ASD IN THE SECONDARY CLASSROOM

Meeting the Unique Needs of Students With Autism Spectrum Disorder

You can't live in America without hearing about the increase in the rate of autism, unless maybe you live in a box or in the woods. Nope. Even if you live there, it's likely you know that autism cases are skyrocketing. More children are being diagnosed with Autism Spectrum Disorder (ASD) than ever before. The Centers for Disease Control (2014) reports that 1 in 68 children is now diagnosed with ASD. Because ASD is five times more common in boys than girls, 1 in 42 eight-year-old boys now meets the criteria for ASD. This astounding figure has a far-reaching impact for society in general, for the education system, and for teachers.

Most teachers now know that children with disabilities should be educated with their nondisabled peers to the greatest extent possible, and this means that more children with ASD will take their places in general education classrooms than ever before. Think about that. If 1 in 42 boys has ASD, that means a child with ASD will be part of almost every classroom. While this reality becomes more obvious year after year, it does not mean that teachers, specialists, administrators, or even classmates are prepared to understand, accept, and meet the needs of students on the spectrum. Once educators are aware of the growing need, it takes a personal commitment to help these students be successful, realize their potential, be appreciated, and truly be included at school.

Good teaching for students with ASD is no longer a mystery. What really works is becoming more and more clear. This will be discussed in detail later in the chapter, but before getting to that, it is essential to realize that students on the spectrum have multiple needs that are very closely tied to the diagnostic features of ASD. Identifying the features of autism that an individual student exhibits and then finding effective ways to address each of those areas is the key to success! With a clear understanding of the student's strengths and needs, methods, strategies, and solutions can be selected to help him or her develop skills, access their education, and be part of the school community (Doyle & Iland, 2004).

One of the most important things a teacher can do to help a student with ASD be successful in a general education classroom is to shift focus beyond academics (gasp!). Autism is a developmental disability, so prioritizing the developmental needs of a student with ASD is necessary to support the child's growth, progress, and meaningful inclusion. This chapter offers insight into the features of ASD and practical ways to meet the educational needs of students with ASD, while at the same time enhancing the educational experience of every student in the classroom. A lofty goal indeed, but a worthwhile one.

UNDERSTANDING ASD

Although teachers are not supposed to diagnose disabilities, understanding the official criteria for ASD can provide useful insight into the differences that distinguish a child on the autism spectrum from a typically developing child. Two areas of difference, social communication/interaction and behavior/sensory issues, are at the core of ASD. In 2013, new research-based criteria for Autism Spectrum Disorder were developed to create a reliable, consistent method to identify the features of the disability (American Psychiatric Association, 2013). One of the most controversial changes is that formerly separate diagnoses like Autistic Disorder, Asperger Syndrome, and Pervasive Developmental Disorder were replaced by a single dimensional category: Autism Spectrum Disorder (Iland, 2013b). As you read on to learn about the features of ASD, you may recognize features of the disorder in students you already know, and will be better prepared to understand students you will teach in the future.

Whether or not a student has a formal diagnosis, impairments in these three areas of *social communication* and *social interaction* can be noted (or have been noted) in all individuals on the spectrum, with varying levels of severity:

1. A deficit in *social-emotional reciprocity* means that the individual does not understand and engage in back-and-forth social exchanges and/or does not seem to match and reflect the emotions of others. Examples of this feature include not knowing how to have a back-and-forth conversation, problems initiating social interactions, or a lack of response to the initiations of others. People on the spectrum may seem content to be alone, but this "aloneness" is actually a symptom of the lack of reciprocity: the reduced sharing of interests, emotions, or affect with others.

2. A lack of eye contact is one of the most noticeable deficits in *nonverbal communicative behaviors used for social interaction* in ASD. Imagine the problems that can arise from difficulties or even an inability to use and read facial expressions, body language, and gestures. Someone on the spectrum may have poorly integrated verbal and nonverbal communication (matching body language and facial expression with their words) or even a total lack of nonverbal communication.

3. Deficits in *developing, maintaining, and understanding relationships* is a central feature of ASD with a significant impact. For example, the student may have difficulties making friends and may even appear disinterested in peers. The student may not know how to play (imaginative play or other games). The student may also have difficulty adjusting behavior to suit various social contexts (for example, not being deferential to authority figures).

The second area of developmental deficit in ASD is called *restricted, repetitive patterns of behavior, interests, or activities*. Of the possible four areas of impact, a person with ASD will exhibit at least two of these features (now or in the past) with varying levels of severity:

1. Examples of *repetitive (or stereotyped) motor movements, use of objects or speech* range from lining up toys, flipping objects, echoing what others say, repeating phrases or dialogue from movies, or using unusual "idiosyncratic" phrases. This criterion also includes repetitive movement of the body or hands, such as flapping, rocking, and pacing.

2. People with ASD may exhibit an *insistence on sameness, inflexible adherence to routines, or ritualized patterns of verbal or nonverbal behavior*. They may need to take the same route or eat the same food every day, repeat greetings or other rituals, have difficulties with transition, and experience extreme distress at small changes in their routine or the environment. Rigid thinking patterns, also

called black-and-white thinking, is another example of how this criterion may be manifested.

3. The *highly restricted, fixated interests seen in ASD* might look like "obsessions" to others but are actually a behavior feature of ASD (not mental illness). These interests are *abnormal in intensity* (fixated on something that others like, such as video games) or *abnormal in focus* (fixated on something that few others like, such as vacuum cleaner parts). These interests are described as "excessively circumscribed or perseverative," meaning that the person has a narrow focus of interest and wants repeated, continuous engagement with it (whether it is lizards or water towers). This feature may also include a strong attachment to, or preoccupation with, unusual objects (for example, always carrying a particular item such as a toy car or plastic spoon).

4. *Hyperreactivity or hyporeactivity to sensory input or unusual interest in sensory aspects of environment* is included for the first time in the diagnostic manual. Hypersensitivity is noted when the student has an adverse response to specific sounds, smells, tastes, or textures (or other input) and may result in avoidance. Hyposensitivity is seen when the student does not register sensation, such as under responding to heat, cold, or pain. "Sensory seeking" is seen in students who want more sensory input. Examples include excessive smelling or touching of objects and visual fascination with lights or movement.

Just as the diagnostic criteria have evolved, findings made through scientific advances are contributing to an even more complete understanding of ASD. For example, advances in neurology have led to the view of autism as a disorder of information processing (Minshew & Williams, 2008). Processing difficulties can include auditory information, language, text, social information, and even motor planning. The more complex the information is, the more difficult it is to process. This finding helps explain why people with ASD may master basic skills (such as factual memory) but struggle with more complex learning (such as higher order thinking skills). Focus on detail over the big picture, problems with time concepts and time management, disorganization, and difficulty processing multimodal input are being linked to neurological features of ASD (National Education Association, 2006). So what are you supposed to do with all this information, you ask? Read on.

MAKING THE MATCH BETWEEN NEEDS AND INTERVENTION

The Individuals with Disabilities Education Act (IDEIA, 2004, and also commonly known as IDEA) is the law that governs special education.

IDEA guides the development of the Individualized Education Program (IEP) to meet the educational needs of students with disabilities. One of the most relevant issues in considering how to effectively educate students with ASD is the fact that education is *not* just academic. According to the federal regulations that tell states how to follow IDEA law, education is academic, developmental, and functional (U.S. Department of Education, 2005); note that functional needs include skills that help the student throughout the day, including hygiene, eating, and so forth. Ignorance of this fact may be one of the greatest obstacles faced by students with ASD and their families. When schools focus only on the academic needs of a student, neglecting their developmental or functional needs, they are not only disadvantaging students with ASD, they are breaking the law!

That said, there are many competing views about *how* to effectively meet the multiple needs of students on the spectrum. It is widely agreed that no single treatment is effective for everyone (National Research Council, 2001). There is a great deal of variation among individuals with autism, so what works for one may not work for another. As autism expert Lorna Wing often said, "If you've met one person with autism, you've met one person with autism."

After having a panel of experts analyze 775 research studies, the National Autism Center published the National Standards Report (NSR; Wilczynski et al., 2009). The NSR may be a welcome tool to help educators, parents, and service providers make treatment decisions for children and adolescents on the spectrum. The NSR identified 11 interventions with sufficient empirical research behind them to be considered "Established" for addressing communication, interpersonal, play, higher cognitive functions, learning readiness, motor skills, personal responsibility and self-regulation skills, and to expand placement options. Check out page 283 for short definitions and refer to the report itself for more information.

Plugged In

www.nationalautism center.org/reports

Another category of evidence identified in the NSR is "Emerging" treatments, which may be effective but have not yet been demonstrated sufficiently. It may be reasonable to choose these interventions for a particular student, but additional studies are needed to consider whether these treatments are truly effective. Check page 284 for definitions, but again, go to the report itself for the more detailed information.

Finally, the third category of intervention identified in the NSR is "Unestablished" practices. The NSR cautions against assuming that these treatments are effective. In fact, the report states that there is no way to rule out the possibility that these treatments are actually ineffective. I've included definitions on page 285, but guess what? You're right! I'd still like to recommend you to the report itself.

Reports like the NSR are a source of guidance, not a prescription or mandate. When choosing interventions, the information about research should be integrated with individual considerations, professional judgment, values and preferences of families, and student data. The ability to implement a particular intervention faithfully should also be considered (Wilczynski et al., 2009). Even if you as the teacher prefer one treatment over another, you'll need to keep in mind that the family will need to consider what works best for them and the student.

It will also be important to refer to updates to research reports as they are published. The next update from the National Autism Center is expected to include a review and analysis of treatments for ASD based on research conducted between 2007 and 2012 and will include the evaluation of treatments for adults (age 22+). Also be on the lookout for similar reviews of the literature prepared by other organizations to help guide parents and educators, like the 2014 report from The National Professional Development Center on Autism Spectrum Disorders.

Plugged In

autismpdc.fpg.unc
.edu/sites/autismpdc
.fpg.unc.edu/
files/2014-EBP-Report.pdf

blog.mrmeyer.com

🛑 WHAT NOT TO DO

Now that you know what ASD is all about, and now that you know what the research literature suggests, here are some quick DOs and DON'Ts to help you every day.

- ✖ **STOP doubting your ability to teach and relate to students on the spectrum.** Too many teachers defer their students to the special education teacher thinking, "I don't know anything about autism." Kids on the spectrum are still kids, and they are still your students. It's your job to teach them and connect with them. You may get a happy surprise when you get to know students with ASD, who often have many endearing qualities and talents.

- ✖ **STOP thinking you already know everything you need to know about ASD.** Every kid is different; every family has information you can use to help teach that child. Take the opportunity to learn by talking to them, collaborating with specialists, attending conferences, reading articles or checking out books, films, or plays that address the human side of ASD, such as *The Curious Incident of the Dog in the Night-Time* by Mark Haddon (2004).

- ✖ **STOP focusing only on academics.** As IDEA regulations state, education must address the academic, developmental, and functional needs of the student. Students with ASD may be "uneven," with both unexpected strengths and surprising areas of need. A student who is an expert on planets may not understand how we humans get along here on earth, so be sure to take these kinds of needs into account!

- ✖ **STOP thinking of inclusion as geography (a place or a placement).** It is sad to see students with ASD in general education settings who are truly alone. Inclusion does not happen automatically or by chance by just physically putting children with and without disabilities in the same space. Real inclusion happens when students are taught to play, communicate, and interact with others. Classmates need to be "clued in" about autism in general and even be directly told about some traits of a particular child so those differences are understood and don't lead to bullying or rejection. By middle school or high school, students are often familiar with one another, but that doesn't mean they still don't need a refresher on appropriate behavior with one another, particularly if the student has become a loner. Consider also that by this age, some students with ASD are able to actually explain to their peers what they have, how it manifests itself, and how peers can be better friends.

✖ **STOP thinking that a student with ASD who is alone** *wants* **to be alone.** Solitude is more often a result of poor play and social skills than a choice. After enough failure and rejection and having few alternatives, students on the spectrum often resort to pacing the halls, seeking out the company of adults, or retreating alone into their special interest. Social isolation can only be reversed through conscious efforts of the teacher and the class.

Making Connections

Check out Chapter 19 on Social Skills

✖ **STOP assuming that a student who is not following instructions is "refusing" or defiant.** Sometimes there is a major mismatch between demands in the classroom and the social, communication, sensory, and behavior issues of ASD. When the student is frustrated or overwhelmed, he or she may just give up. A shutdown that looks like refusal can really mean the student can't cope at the moment. It is not a challenge to authority; it is more like a turtle going into its shell.

✖ **STOP ignoring what the student is trying to communicate to you through behavior.** Students who have communication challenges may resort to communicating with their actions, not words. A child who covers her ears and rocks can be signaling that she is feeling overwhelmed; a child who pushes away other kids in line for the slide may be signaling that he wants his turn. Don't wait for the child to "use his words" or insist that he do so, especially when stressed. Learning to read and respond to the student's nonverbal communication can nip all kinds of problems in the bud.

✖ **STOP ignoring/shutting out/judging the parents.** You know that when a child has a problem at school, one of the first things teachers do is blame the parents. When a child has a lot of difficulties, the parents may be on the receiving end of negativity and judgment. In fact, most parents of children with ASD have their hands full and are doing the best they can. They may also actually be experts in one particular area: their child. Their experiences often help them understand their child's needs. They may be able to tell you what worked and what didn't work in the past so you don't have to figure it out on your own.

✗ **STOP minimizing the developmental needs of bright students with ASD who don't seem to have academic needs.** While elementary school is an excellent time to build skills in socialization, communication, behavior, and self-regulation that will help the child be a more successful student and classmate, it is not too late to prioritize the same kind of developmental goals for junior high or high school students. Closing the developmental gap and the divide with a student's peer group is as important as any academic goal and will continue with them for the rest of their lives.

✗ **STOP ignoring the need to prepare high school students with life skills needed for postsecondary education or work. This is especially crucial for students on the diploma track.** As IDEA states, the purpose of a student's Free Appropriate Public Education (FAPE) is to prepare them for further education, employment, and independent living. For students with ASD, even those on the diploma track, their preparation often needs to include instruction in the area of "soft skills" like communication and socialization for work or college, along with practical (or functional skills) for independent living like money management and using public transportation. Students whose academics are strong may have a substantial need for support and development in these areas that may be overshadowed by a rushed exit from high school.

 Teachers, DO This

✓ **WORK WITH A TEAM to prioritize the developmental and functional needs of the student.** (Social communication and social interaction are key, but even toilet training, play, and eating can be goal areas—yes, in secondary school). This can be a formal team (like an IEP team) or even just a group of concerned teachers and family members. At a time when there is tremendous pressure to focus only on academics and test scores, a real child advocate can feel like he or she is swimming upstream to address nonacademic needs. In addition to the fact that educational law supports this approach, this shift in thinking can have a significant impact on the student's well-being, progress, and lifetime outcomes.

✓ **BE PROACTIVE to create true social inclusion.** The teacher's attitude about "who belongs" sets the tone for the entire class. Classmates may be concerned about differences they can see but do

Plugged In

www.autism
internetmodules.org

not understand, which can get in the way of friendships and relationships. If you can only do one thing differently than you are doing now, consider implementing a Peer Training Program that teaches nondisabled peers how to interact with, relate to, and include students with ASD in every school environment. Such programs are usually free or low cost, easy to implement, and have benefits for all students involved, not just the student with ASD. For example, the Ohio Center for Autism and Low Incidence Disabilities (OCALI) website has a free module with information, videos, and resources to help you implement a Peer Social Networking Program, a form of Peer Mediated Instruction Intervention (PMII) in which trained junior high and high school peers provide natural support to the student with ASD across settings during the school day.

✓ **MONITOR the child in all environments, and protect him or her from bullying and ostracization.** A recent study found that 63% of children with ASD from ages 6 to 15 had been bullied at some point in their lives, and 39% had been bullied in the previous month (Anderson, 2012). A student with limited social understanding, limited communication skills, and a small circle of friends can be the perfect target, especially in unstructured settings like the lunchroom or the locker room. The need for supervision will range from constant adult supervision to trained peer support and mentoring. Consider occasionally eating lunch near the students or observe students on campus to watch what goes on! Seeing the student outside the classroom is vital to a real understanding of the student's social inclusion or recreation skills. It is also important to ensure that a student with ASD does not bully others.

✓ **MAKE the learning environment tolerable.** A highly structured, sensory-friendly setting is essential for students with ASD and can benefit every student in the classroom (Mesibov & Shea, 2008). What does it mean to be tolerable? Read on for some helpful tips.

✓ **CREATE structure** so the student knows what will happen and when. Visual supports like schedules, task lists, checklists, and color coding help the student know how much work to do, when he or she is finished, where things belong, and what happens next.

✓ **CREATE sensory comfort.** An occupational therapist can help design a sensory diet of desirable input to help the student stay engaged and avoid becoming overwhelmed.

✓ **USE scales, charts, or other tools** to express types and intensity of emotions. Help the student choose, and use relaxation strategies and coping strategies to reduce stress and maintain self-control. Be sure to make these strategies age appropriate.

✓ **USE positive behavioral supports**, like the Premack principle: Alternate between preferred and non-preferred activities. Give the student two good choices to give a sense of control, like "Do you want to do your Quick Write journal first or your homework review activity?" Use favorite interests for rewards, breaks, and relaxation. Let the student shine by helping others in areas of strength, from math to passing out supplies.

✓ **ADDRESS comprehension in ASD.** Multiple features of ASD contribute to problems understanding what is read, even for individuals on the spectrum who decode very well and read with expression. Do not underestimate the impact of this issue. Check out the evidence-based and promising ways to help in *Drawing a Blank: Improving Comprehension for Readers on the Autism Spectrum* (Iland, 2011).

✓ **GET OFF THE TRACKS!** Students are typically put on the "diploma track" or the "life skills track." In fact, students with ASD are likely to have significant needs and goals in both areas. What good does it do to be a genius at math if you don't know how to communicate and interact with colleagues? These two tracks should not be mutually exclusive. To be prepared for adult life, many students with ASD are likely to need a blended track "to receive the instruction, services and supports needed for post-secondary success" (Blackmon, 2007, p. 94). Teams need to realize that the typical "one-size-fits-all" programming approach is not likely to fit students on the spectrum who have unevenly developed academic and life skills. Many teams are now moving to novel transition programming that gives students the time and supports they need to develop skills for future success, which is, after all, the purpose of education.

✓ **PRIORITIZE safety from a young age.** Picture what your student would do at the age of 18 in an encounter with the police. At any age, be sure to include goals for following instructions like "stop" and "go," answering "yes" and "no" reliably, and taking "no" for an answer. Check out www.BeSafeTheMovie.com (Iland, 2013a) for video modeling tools to teach teens and adults with disabilities how to interact safely with the police.

✓ **LISTEN to the parents and others who know the child well.** For example, ask his mom to lend you the one book she really wants you to read, ask his dad what goals he has for his child, and ask if the student has friends outside of school. These three simple questions will let the parents know that you truly care about their concerns and their child.

✓ **LISTEN to others who have experience with the child or expertise in ASD.** Ask last year's teacher the #1 thing that worked and the #1 thing to avoid. Ask educational specialists what advice they have for you. Consider important information shared by behaviorists, therapists, or team members outside of school who know what works for the child to help create consistency across environments. Collaboration is key when it comes to working with all kids, but especially those with special needs (Murawski & Spencer, 2011).

✓ **LISTEN to the child.** He or she may not be able to explain thoughts and feelings with words, so be aware of the communicative intent of things the student does. Watch for signs that the student is becoming overwhelmed, and step in to prevent a meltdown. Notice the materials and activities that the child prefers, and use these things as rewards or teaching tools. Build on the child's strengths and abilities to help with more difficult tasks.

✓ **UNDERSTAND that sometimes the student simply can't comply with instructions or keep it together.** This is not refusal or defiance; it can be called *variability of performance*. If you see it as *can't* versus *won't*, you won't take it personally! Instead, figure out what might have brought on a difficulty and how to make things go more smoothly next time. For more insights like this one, check out "Helpful Handouts" at www.barbaradoyle.com/.

✓ **ASK for help.** Sometimes teachers are reluctant to ask, perhaps fearing that they might be judged as less capable. Just like parents, however, you are likely to know very little about autism until you have a child/student who has it, and you need to learn quickly! In addition, every child with ASD is different than the one before. Take advantage of professional development opportunities so you feel more comfortable. Ask program specialists and special educators what they can do to help and support you and your student.

✓ **LOOK for resources.** There is an increasing amount of information about ASD on the web. Some of it is incredibly helpful, while others appear to be whack-a-doodle. Make sure it is from credible source! In addition to OCALI, there are readings, vignettes, and modules in a variety of other sources, like the Iris Center at Vanderbilt University.

Plugged In

http://iris.peabody.vanderbilt.edu/

AT-A-GLANCE

A Quick Guide to Established, Emerging, and Unestablished Autism Treatments (adapted from Wilczynski et al., 2009)

Established Treatments: *Treatments With Sufficient Empirical Evidence to Demonstrate Effectiveness*	
Term	*Quick Definition*
Antecedent Package	Modifying a situation that typically precedes a problematic behavior to avoid its occurrence
Behavioral Package	Applying basic principles of behavior change to reduce problem behavior and teach appropriate replacement behavior
Comprehensive Behavioral Intervention for Young Children (CBIYC)	Treating children under the age of 8 using a comprehensive combination of behavioral techniques; also known as Applied Behavioral Analysis (ABA) programs or early intensive behavioral intervention
Joint Attention Intervention	Teaching the individual to respond to the nonverbal social initiations of others or initiate interactions with shared attention
Modeling	Having an adult or child model a behavior for the individual with ASD to copy
Naturalistic Teaching Strategies	Using child-directed interactions in a natural environment to teach skills; examples include modeling play and providing a stimulating environment
Peer Training	Teaching children without disabilities how to play and interact with children with ASD; includes programs such as Integrated Play Groupsand peer-mediated social interaction (PMII)
Pivotal Response Treatment (PRT)	Building skills and producing behavior improvements by targeting key (pivotal) areas such as motivation to engage in social interaction; focus includes parental involvement in natural environments
Schedules	Presenting task lists or steps to complete a specific activity
Self-Management	Teaching individuals with ASD to regulate their own behavior by tracking when they are on-track or off-track for meeting a particular goal using such things as tokens and checkmarks; includes a reward (reinforcement system)
Story-Based Intervention	Using written descriptions of expectations for a particular situation; examples include Social Stories that explain the "who," "what," "where," when," and "why" of a situation

Emerging Treatments: *Treatments That May Be Effective, but Without Sufficient Empirical Evidence to Demonstrate This*	
Term	*Quick Definition*
Augmentative and Alternative Communication Device (AAC)	Using low-tech devices like pictures or high-tech devices like computers to facilitate communication
Cognitive Behavioral Intervention Package	Changing thought patterns that are unrealistic or negative to positively impact emotions and/or life functioning
Developmental Relationship-Based Treatment	Techniques based on developmental theory that emphasize the building of social relationships; also referred to as Denver Model, Developmental Individual-difference Relationship-based (DIR) Floortime, Relationship Development Intervention (RDI), or Responsive Teaching
Exercise	Increasing physical activity to increase positive behavior or reduce inappropriate behavior
Exposure Package	Requiring the individual to face anxiety-provoking situations while preventing the person from responding with inappropriate strategies used in the past
Imitation-Based Interaction	Teaching by having a child imitate the words and/or actions of an adult
Initiation Training	Directly teaching the individual to initiate interactions with peers
Language Training (Production or Production and Understanding)	Using techniques such as oral communication training or echo relevant word training to increase speech, or to increase both speech and comprehension of language
Massage/Touch Therapy	Providing deep tissue stimulation
Multi-Component Package	Combining more than one treatment from different fields of interest
Music Therapy	Using music, rhythm, or songs to teach skills and meet goals
Peer-Mediated Instructional Arrangement	Also called peer tutoring, involving same-age peers in teaching academic skills
Picture Exchange Communication System	Using behavioral principles and words/images to teach functional communication; also called PECs
Reductive Package	Reducing problem behaviors using materials such as water mist and ammonia without trying to teach a new "positive" behavior

Term	Quick Definition
Scripting	Developing scripts for a specific skill or situation that are practiced in advance
Sign Instruction	Directly teaching sign language as a form of communication
Social Communication Intervention	Targeting specific areas of social communication such as reading social context or choosing topics of conversation; also referred to as social pragmatic interventions
Social Skills Package	Targeting basic social responses to build social interaction skills. Examples of targeted skills range from eye contact to maintaining conversation
Structured Teaching	Modifying the environment, materials, and presentation of material to make thinking, learning, and comprehension easier for individuals with ASD; also referred to as TEACCH method (Treatment and Education of Autistic and related Communication-Handicapped Children)
Technology-Based Treatment	Using computers or technology to present instructional material
Theory of Mind Training	Developing perspective-taking and "mind reading," the ability to imagine the thoughts and mental states of others

Unestablished Treatments: *Treatments With Little or No Evidence in the Scientific Literature That Allows for Firm Conclusions About the Effectiveness of These Interventions*

Term	Quick Definition
Auditory Integration Training	Presenting modulated sounds through headphones to improve sensitivity to sound and sound distortion, retraining the person's auditory system
Facilitated Communication	Using a computer or keyboard while a facilitator supports the hand or arm
Gluten- and Casein-Free Diet	Eliminating foods containing gluten (wheat and related grain) and casein (milk protein) from the diet
Sensory Integrative Package	Addressing environmental over-stimulation or under-stimulation by challenging the individual to use all of his or her senses
Academic Interventions	Using traditional teaching methods to improve academic performance

Source: Adapted from Wilczynski et al. (2009).

INTERVENTION SELECTION CHECKLIST

Answer these questions to help select an intervention that is most appropriate to teach social skills to a particular student with ASD.	
Question	*Answer*
Which specific skills will be targeted?	
Is the intervention well matched to teach those skills?	
Is the intervention well matched to the student's developmental level (language and cognitive functioning)?	
Is the intervention appropriate to the learner's status as a beginner or intermediate?	
Is the strategy supported by research?	
If the strategy is *not* supported by research, what is the rationale or logic for using it?	
Other considerations	

Source: Adapted from Bellini (2008).

REFERENCES

American Psychiatric Association. (2013). *Diagnostic and statistical manual of mental disorders* (5th ed.). Arlington, VA: Author.

Anderson, C. (2012). IAN research report: Bullying and children with ASD. Retrieved from http://www.iancommunity.org/cs/ian_research_reports/ian_research_report_bullying

Bellini, S. (2008). *Building social relationships: A systematic approach to teaching social interaction skills to children and adolescents with autism spectrum disorders.* Shawnee Mission, KS: Autism Asperger.

Blackmon, D. (2007). *Transition to adult living: An information and resource guide.* California Services for Technical Assistance and Training (CALSTAT). Retrieved from www.calstat.org.info/html

Centers for Disease Control. (2014). Autism spectrum disorder: Data and statistics. Retrieved from http://www.cdc.gov/ncbddd/autism/data.html

Doyle, B. T., & Iland, E. (2004). *Autism spectrum disorders from A to Z.* Arlington, TX: Future Horizons.

Haddon, M. (2004). *The curious incident of the dog in the night-time.* New York, NY: Vintage Books.

Iland, E. (2011). *Drawing a blank: Improving comprehension for readers on the autism spectrum.* Shawnee Mission, KS: Autism Asperger.

Iland, E. (2013a). *Be safe teaching edition.* Saugus, CA: Camino Cinema.

Iland, E. (2013b). No more Asperger's? What educational therapists need to know about the DSM-V. *Educational Therapist Journal, 34*(1), 12–17.

Individuals with Disabilities Education Improvement Act of 2004. 20 U.S.C. §1401 *et seq.* (2004).

Mesibov, G., & Shea, V. (2008). Structured teaching and environmental supports. In K. D. Buron & P. Wolfberg (Eds.), *Learners on the autism spectrum: Preparing highly qualified educators* (pp. 114–137). Shawnee Mission, KS: Autism Asperger.

Minshew, W., & Williams, D. L. (2008). Brain-behavior connections in autism. In K. D. Buron & P. Wolfberg (Eds.), *Learners on the autism spectrum: Preparing highly qualified educators* (pp. 44–65). Shawnee Mission, KS: Autism Asperger.

Murawski, W. W., & Spencer, S. (2011). *Collaborate, communicate, and differentiate: How to increase student learning in today's diverse schools.* Thousand Oaks, CA: Corwin.

National Education Association. (2006). The puzzle of autism. Retrieved from http://www.nea.org/assets/docs/HE/autismpuzzle.pdf

National Research Council. (2001). *Educating children with autism.* Washington, DC: National Academy Press.

U.S. Department of Education. (2005). Part 300/D/300.324. Retrieved from http://idea.ed.gov/explore/home

Wilczynski, S., Green, G., Ricciardi, J., Boyd, B., Hume, A., Ladd, M., . . . Rue, H. (2009). *National Standards Report: The national standards project—Addressing the need for evidence-based practice guidelines for autism spectrum disorders.* Retrieved from http://www.nationalautismcenter.org/pdf/NAC%20Standards%20Report.pdf

RECOMMENDED READINGS

* Prizant, B. M., Wetherby, A. M., Rubin, E., Laurent, A. C., & Rydell, P. J. (2006). *The SCERTS® model: A comprehensive educational approach for children with autism spectrum disorders.* Baltimore, MD: Paul H. Brookes.

* Sargent, L. R., Perner, D., Fesgen, M., & Cook, T. (2012). *Social skills for students with autism spectrum disorders and other developmental disabilities.* Arlington, VA: Council for Exceptional Children.

* Winner, M. G. (2006). *Thinking about you thinking about me.* San Jose, CA: Author.

GO EVEN FURTHER WITH THIS TOPIC ON THE WORLD WIDE WEB

- www.autisminternetmodules.org
- www.autism-society.org
- autismnow.org
- www.cdc.gov/ncbddd/autism/index.html
- www.BeSafeTheMovie.com

THE Apps WE LOVE

- Functional Skills System
- Social Navigator
- OTs with Apps
- Moody Me

18

Developing Deaf Education

Flavia Fleischer, Will Garrow, and Rachel Friedman Narr

California State University, Northridge

WHAT REALLY WORKS IN DEAF EDUCATION IN THE SECONDARY CLASSROOM

Who Are the Deaf Students?

Oliver, a ninth-grade student, has just moved to your school from another state. Normally that wouldn't concern you at all. You know your content backward and forward, and it doesn't really matter where students come from. This time, however, you're nervous. You've just found out that Oliver is Deaf—and you don't know sign language at all! Actually, you don't even know if he signs. What if he reads lips? Or has a cochlear implant? You certainly assume he will have an interpreter with him all day. Wait. Can you make that assumption? You know you want Oliver to have the best experience in your class possible, but you're at a loss. What will you do? The first thing you will do is breathe. Next, you'll read this chapter.

Deaf students, who also include hard-of-hearing* children, constitute approximately 78,000 of the U.S. public school population in the 50 states who receive services under Individuals with Disabilities Education Act (IDEA)

Key Term

* The term Deaf is an umbrella term that includes both Deaf and hard-of-hearing people from diverse backgrounds. The authors believe that the other terms used to describe or refer to Deaf people are artificial and not how the community identifies themselves. So, avoid any issues, and just use the term Deaf.

Part B (Government Accountability Report, 2011). There are even more if you include the number of Deaf children in the District of Columbia, schools of the Bureau of Indian Education, and the U.S. territories (Government Accountability Report, 2011). Don't fret. To teach students who are Deaf, you don't need to be an expert. Leave that to specialists. You are Oliver's teacher; you just need to know how to teach *him* your content so he can be successful.

Despite varying amounts and types of hearing losses, most Deaf children are naturally attuned to information that they can access spatially in their environment using various ways of perception. Though most Deaf students access information through visual perception (their eyes), Deaf-Blind children access information spatially using tactile perception (their hands). Auditory access (getting information through their ears) for Deaf children is unnatural, limited, and exhausting, even for children who use hearing aids or cochlear implants. Let's stop there for a second. This bears repeating. *Getting information aurally is unnatural and difficult, sometimes extremely so, <u>even</u> for kids who have hearing aids or cochlear implants!* Most Deaf children with hearing aids and/or cochlear implants do not acquire an auditory language naturally. So what does that mean to you, as Oliver's teacher? Well, many studies have shown that Deaf children are better able to learn auditory languages, if they are accessible, when they have signed language(s) (Humphries et al., 2014; Johnson, 2006; Lane, 1999). So one of the things you can do is find out pretty quickly if Oliver uses American Sign Language (ASL), and then you can support a continuation of the use of ASL in addition to English.

Deaf children need access to a community that will enable them to naturally acquire knowledge and tools to capitalize upon their skills. If you don't sign and there are no other children in the ninth grade who do, where will Oliver find this community? His parents? Actually, in contrast to most families, Deaf children are primarily born into families who do not immediately have the socially based experience, knowledge, and tools to raise Deaf children who are spatially oriented. In other words, they are born into hearing families where the Deaf child is probably the first Deaf person that family has ever met. Did you know that approximately 96% of Deaf children have hearing parents (Mitchell & Karchmer, 2004)? Because our society is primarily a hearing one, and therefore has a socially constructed bias toward hearing, Deaf children are often put through various early intervention and rehabilitative programs in hopes that they can change their natural spatial inclination to become more auditorially inclined (Lane, 1999; Lane, Hoffmeister, & Bahan, 1996), but they frequently struggle in auditory-based programs, leaving them language delayed, psychologically traumatized, and unprepared for socialization and lifelong education (Komesaroff, 2007; Lane, 1999; Leigh, 2009; Schick, Marschark, & Spencer, 2006). Eek! You don't want that. So again, you struggle with what you can do for Oliver to help him be successful in your ninth-grade classroom—all while dealing with over 30 other kids with various needs *and* five other periods as well!

You look at Oliver's cumulative file and find out that, like most other Deaf students, Oliver's family is indeed hearing. You make a note to yourself to meet right away with the parents to find out what types of opportunities Oliver has to be with other people who are Deaf. You also realize that, just as you tried to learn more about Armenian culture when Ashot joined your class last year, you are going to have to pretty quickly learn more about Deaf culture and how it will impact you and Oliver. Why don't we give you a quick introduction now?

First of all, very few Deaf children are born into an environment where they can gain access to and acquire the socially based experience, knowledge, and tools to support their spatial orientation, enabling them to become successful adults. Families and schools can attain these perspectives, but it requires a commitment to understanding the world from a Deaf-centric perspective. Yep—Deaf-centric. If you are not Deaf, you are likely understanding the world from the position of a hearing-centric perspective. That's an important thing to realize right from the get-go. To provide Oliver with the valuable tools he may need, it would help if you are familiar with what is called Deaf Community Cultural Wealth (DCCW). DCCW is adapted from Yosso's (2005) work on Community Cultural Wealth, which addresses the rich knowledge, skills, and tools that minority communities possess and pass down through generations. The Deaf community has naturally developed DCCW through centuries of navigating and networking through global spaces that are not designed by, for, and of Deaf people. DCCW allows Deaf people to navigate and flourish in hearing-centric spaces and to be productive, contributing citizens in our society. Because most Deaf kids are born and raised in hearing-centric societies, most don't have access to DCCW. As a result, they are less able to acquire and develop the essential tools that will allow them to navigate through various spaces—including a mainstream school environment—successfully. To complicate matters further, we have seen the practice of placing Deaf children in general education classrooms with hearing children become more commonplace since the inception of Public Law 94-142 in the early 1970s, in what is now known as the Individuals with Disabilities Education Act (IDEA). This practice was first known as mainstreaming and later called inclusion. Although it is by far the most common educational practice for Deaf children, it rarely provides them with optimal education access. We know, we know. You are thinking, "What?! But that's why Oliver is in my general education ninth-grade math (or English or social studies or. . .) class! Does this mean he shouldn't be there? Or that I can't teach him? Isn't there another class he can go to down the hall?" Patience, our friend. Read on for more information.

As of 2002, approximately 75% of Deaf children were mainstreamed and received special education services for support in general education classrooms for at least a part of their day (Karchmer & Mitchell, 2003). The goal of a Deaf child's education tragically becomes mitigating hearing loss, rather than utilizing and optimizing their strengths as spatial beings (Johnson, 2006). We say "tragically" because this means schools are operating from a deficit perspective, rather than a strengths approach. Because we are, for the most part, a hearing-centric society, we think of being Deaf as a disability, rather than helping kids capitalize on their spatial strengths.

Furthermore, Deaf students in mainstream environments do not have access to peers and adults who are able to model, teach, and discuss with them how to navigate through society. This doesn't mean that Oliver won't have friends or adults who care; it does however mean it may be unlikely that Oliver will have other peers or adults who are Deaf to show him the way. To connect with him on a spatial level. To understand his challenges. And man, there will be challenges! Between mainstream education and the children's home environment, there are several barriers for Deaf students that prevent them from accessing, acquiring, and developing DCCW the way they might if they were in a Deaf school or Deaf environment.

The goal of this chapter is to help familiarize you with the common challenges in educating Deaf students so that YOU can facilitate a Deaf student's acquisition and access to DCCW, in this case, Oliver. Yes, we know you have 120 or so students to teach. But most of them will learn the way you already instruct—Oliver probably won't, so he does indeed deserve some additional attention.

So what's your first step—before Oliver enters your classroom? Understanding what DCCW is and then using this as a foundation for working with Oliver, or any other Deaf students you may teach in the future, will help mitigate some of their challenges. The goal, as with any of your other students, is to support their learning and socialization processes and needs.

Let's start. DCCW is comprised of six capitals: linguistic, social, familial, navigational, aspirational, and resistant (adapted from Yosso, 2005). Whoa, wait. Let's back up. What is capital? In a nutshell, capitals are socially accumulated assets and resources that can help you move forward in society. In this situation though, we are talking about those capitals that promote DCCW. Each capital constitutes an integral part of building a whole, well-rounded Deaf student with the skills and tools to flourish and succeed.

DEAF COMMUNITY CULTURAL WEALTH: THE SIX CAPITALS

Each example of capital is important for Deaf students to move forward academically, behaviorally, emotionally, and socially. Our job as teachers is to learn more about them and consider how we can maximize them in our classrooms. Here, we briefly introduce each one, but check out Six Capitals for Building Deaf Cultural Capital Wealth (DCCW) on page 301 where we offer concrete strategies for what you can do.

Linguistic Capital. Developing complex cognitive skills, socialization for positive self-development, and self-awareness are arguably the most critical aspects of development in childhood. These skills cannot be attained without linguistic capital. Deaf students routinely experience a lack of, or impoverished, linguistic capital. Even with hearing aids and cochlear implants, Deaf students do not have full and natural access to spoken languages. This means that you will want to encourage Oliver, his classroom peers, and his family members to use sign language in addition to any spoken language that is used around or with him. This may be the time to sign up for that ASL course you've always thought of taking!

Social Capital. Having access to and gaining social capital allows children to meet their social developmental milestones all the way into adulthood. Most Deaf students do not have full, natural access to language, causing linguistic delays, which frequently result in cognitive delays, thus making it very difficult for Deaf students to make sense of their social experiences and environment. Clearly then, you need to make sure that Oliver has an opportunity to communicate frequently with his grade-level peers. What interests him? If all the boys in your class are into video games, talk to Oliver's mom about hosting a party and inviting some of his classmates to play the latest video game.

Familial Capital. Familial capital involves the concept of kinship composed of a network of people who are caring, invested in, and supportive of the community and of the individuals within the community. Kinship can be fostered within and between families, friends, and through sports, school, and other social community settings (Yosso, 2005). Kinship comes from a networked support system that provides the ability and opportunity to discuss one's feelings, thoughts, and ideas in depth, and to receive supporting feedback in return. Think about how difficult it is for most tweens or teenagers to share their feelings—now compound that by being a kid who can't even communicate directly with his friends, teachers, or family without a go-between!

Aspirational Capital. Aspirational capital allows one to have dreams, hopes, and goals "in face of perceived and real barriers" (Yosso, 2005, p. 77). This ability allows a child to persevere and resist negativity, to go beyond their immediate circumstances complete with social barriers to attain higher education and better opportunities. Despite good intentions, but poor educational environments for Deaf students, current society has inherently low expectations for the Deaf. Of course, this is unfounded and has been proven to be incorrect again and over again by Deaf people who have held on to their aspirational capital. Yes, being in a Deaf school might provide Oliver with a peer group who can communicate with him more easily, but the reality is that he is with you in the typical mainstream class-room. So let's make the most of it! Never assume being Deaf means Oliver cannot do what other students do. It's just a difference—like the fact that Sarah has two moms, Gunther just moved here from Germany, and Roberto is an albino. So what? What is more important is that Oliver knows, like all of your ninth graders, that he can be whatever he wants to be—if he does his homework tonight, that is!

Navigational Capital. Navigational capital is the ability to maneuver through social institutions (Yosso, 2005). Social institutions are designed for people who have been perceived as representing the norm. Imagine you are Deaf. How would you navigate your school? How many bells ring to tell you to come in from lunch? How many teachers raise their voice to tell you to pay attention? How many videos are shown without any cap-tioning? Hmmmm. A lot, right? So what can you do to change this?

Resistant Capital. Resistant capital provides the emotional and psycho-logical ability to resist and challenge negative slights toward a person and their communities. It allows people the opportunity to maintain their dignity and to create spaces that transform negative views of themselves into an understanding of their own great potential. We all know that students can be cruel to one another. Bullying is rampant in both middle and high schools. Anyone who is different in any way has a strong chance of being a target. So knowing that, prep your class. Prep Oliver. Prep his family members. Be proactive and *teach* him how to respond. That's something you can certainly do—you're a teacher after all!

🛑 WHAT YOU SHOULD AVOID AT ALL COSTS

- ✗ **STOP thinking that the Deaf world is just the Hearing world without sound.** Go back and reread the part where we remind you that you need to try to be Deaf-centric for a bit in order to realize that your entire frame of reference is one of a hearing person. Then, when you've got the right frame of mind, come back and read the rest of our tips.
- ✗ **STOP focusing on the development of spoken language, through repetitive drills of listening and speaking skills, rather than on comprehension and analysis of content.** Instead, we should view spoken language development as a supplementary skill that may or may not provide benefits to a Deaf student. Signed language is the only fully accessible language that Deaf children, regardless of their hearing abilities, will be able to access, acquire, and learn

naturally and use to express themselves naturally. (That means without intense amounts of remediation, exhaustion, and potential frustration.) Having a high aptitude in signed languages starting at an early age has been proven to be a bona fide linguistic and cognitive foundation and platform for the acquisition of many other integral educational and life skills, such as literacy skills. Yes, being able to sign actually helps Deaf kids read too!

✘ **DON'T think that just because a Deaf student has a cochlear implant or hearing aid, he can easily hear what you are saying.** Cochlear implants and hearing aids are *not* miracle cures. More often than not, they can't understand what you are saying because the ability to hear is not the same as the ability to understand speech. Even if a kid can repeat what you've said, that doesn't mean they *understand* what you've said. The very assumption that the ability to hear equates to the ability to understand sounds often leads to late detection of actual language delays and overlooks many other learning issues.

✘ **STOP assuming that signed language is the cause of problems in developing English literacy skills.** The level of Deaf student's actual linguistic and cognitive skills is the root of the problem. Many Deaf students are linguistically and cognitively delayed because of late access, exposure, and use of a fully accessible language (spoken languages are rarely accessible to them), and the delays complicate the encoding and the decoding required to make meaning from print. Deaf people with early and robust access to signed language develop high levels of literacy.

✘ **STOP thinking that signed language can be acquired and learned by Deaf kids at any age.** Late acquisition of signed language by Deaf students is often marked by grammatical errors across all linguistic aspects. Deaf kids rarely catch up with native signers in overall linguistic competency as well as in literacy skills. Linguistic delay causes Deaf kids to struggle with acquiring spoken languages too. Ultimately, what we are saying is just like it is important for hearing kids to learn language right away, the same holds true for Deaf kids— just with signed language. That said, as a secondary teacher, don't give up. Ask your school to offer ASL as a foreign language elective, and encourage all of the Deaf and hearing students to sign up!

✘ **STOP assuming that Deaf kids struggle with socialization because they are Deaf.** Deaf kids are frequently in an environment that doesn't allow for the socialization processes to occur naturally. Again, the inaccessibility of the language used in the environment and to the misunderstandings our society has about Deaf kids lead to struggles with socialization.

✘ **DON'T assume that if Deaf kids are socializing with other kids, they are able to fully access the processes and norms to acquire**

and learn the integral social skills and strategies. Just because Deaf students may participate in sports or other activities with hearing kids, it does not mean they are able to make sense of the norms, conventions, and processes. Check to find out what is actually happening and how you might better facilitate the experience.

✘ **DON'T assume that Deaf students have opportunities to socialize outside of school.** Many Deaf kids grow up feeling isolated from their peers and, sadly, from their families. Deaf children may be able to participate in playtime together with hearing children, but as they get older, they are frequently set aside from other children because of a lack of communication and presence of social stigma that is generally associated with Deaf kids. They may have acquaintances, but they rarely develop close, deep bonds with their peers.

✘ **STOP leaving the responsibility of learning how to communicate and socialize with Deaf students to the peers.** Many teachers and administrators assume that if Deaf and hearing kids are left together to socialize, they will learn how to communicate with each other. When a situation complicates the Deaf student's ability to participate fully in groups, such as not having interpreters present, this often leads teachers to allow Deaf students to work individually. This is detrimental to Deaf students as well as to the other students as opportunities for them to learn how to work in groups are lost.

✘ **DON'T assume Deaf kids have access to familial support systems to talk about issues that concern them.** Many Deaf students struggle to communicate openly and freely with their families due to lack of language access. A vast majority of the parents of Deaf kids do not make the time to learn signed language, limiting the communication opportunities for them. It may be helpful to Deaf students if you are able to provide their families, for example, with ways to learn signed language, information on Deaf community events, contacts for counselors and psychologists who sign, or helpful videos that are captioned.

✘ **DON'T limit the potential of Deaf students.** There are so many misconceptions about Deaf kids and their abilities or potential. For instance, many adults cannot conceive Deaf kids as pilots for big airline companies or as trial lawyers. These societal-imposed limitations and barriers only serve to restrict the potential of Deaf kids and our society loses the valuable contributions that they could have made.

✘ **DON'T assume that Deaf students have an understanding of how to navigate through spaces.** Since nearly all of our spaces in our society are designed for and cater to hearing people, Deaf students must acquire a different set of tools and skills that allows them to navigate with success and without sacrificing their dignity.

Try to figure out what changes can be made to your school, curricula, processes, and rules that will enable *all* of your students, including those who are Deaf, to be successful.

✘ **STOP leaving teaching, feedback, and assessment responsibilities to the interpreters, teacher aides, itinerant teachers, and tutors.** Remember that teacher aides and interpreters do not have the extensive training to do what teachers and administrators do. Furthermore, in leaving teaching, feedback, and assessment responsibilities to others, a message is sent to Deaf students that you are not invested in them.

✘ **STOP talking to the interpreter.** They are there purely as a way for you to communicate to the student. They are not there to edit your communication, share the student's feelings without their permission, or rat on the student. Nor are they there to design curriculum, grade papers, or tutor the student. That's your job!

✘ **STOP using materials designed solely for hearing students.** Many teachers don't think in advance about how many times they rely on their voice, or the bell, or even audio in a movie. Put on headphones and see what you are missing.

✘ **STOP raising your voice when speaking to a student who is Deaf.** It doesn't help.

✘ **DON'T allow Deaf students to succumb to or accept negative views of their abilities.** Many people find it difficult to support Deaf students due to their lack of experience, knowledge, and realistic expectations, making it a challenge to turn negative views into positive ones. With all of the negativity that Deaf students face every day from others, it is very easy for them to internalize and believe in the messages.

SO . . . WHAT EXACTLY AM I SUPPOSED TO DO WITH OLIVER AND OTHER DEAF STUDENTS?

✓ **RETHINK how you introduce and teach English literacy skills to Deaf students.** Our current approaches often employ hearing-centric approaches that generally work well and consistently only for hearing students but are not applicable or beneficial for Deaf students. Instead, seek strategies that capitalize on their strengths. Ask your school to offer ASL classes for families. They will certainly be helpful to families of Deaf kids, but they may also be beneficial for those families who want to become better friends with those who are Deaf.

✓ **OFFER signed language instruction to all students.** Signed language has consistently been proven as the most accessible language and the only modality that ensures full and natural linguistic and cognitive development for Deaf students. It's guaranteed and risk-free! Deaf children with a strong foundation in signed language are better able to acquire literacy skills in their second, third (and even more!) languages. Why not offer it to all students so more students are learning this important language and learning to communicate with one another?

✓ **IMPROVE socialization processes by including signs in social situations**. To ensure a linguistically accessible social environment that is more inclusive of all students, teach them ways to communicate without requiring hearing. Football, basketball, and baseball players all have signs they use (e.g., "T" for time out), so capitalize on that and teach students ways to communicate so all can participate.

✓ **DO directly address and discuss social norms and processes with all students.** Explicit discussions of the social norms and processes in a given environment will help ensure that all children, including Deaf students, gain an understanding of the processes employed by society. How can you get Deaf students' attention without yelling at them? What are some ways we can know that it is time to clean up without a bell sounding?

✓ **PROVIDE parents with ideas and support for various socialization opportunities that are fully accessible for Deaf students to use after school.** Many parents do not know where they can find socialization opportunities for their Deaf kids after school. Develop a list of opportunities to share with them, and encourage them to be proactive in seeking out various Deaf community events as well as connecting with other parents raising Deaf kids. Often, Deaf community events will provide exposure to a wide range of peers, both Deaf and hearing, that allows for positive and accessible interactions. You may even want to attend some of these events yourself!

✓ **COMMUNICATE!** Learning how to interact and communicate with diverse people is an important skill for any kid to acquire and have. Create opportunities to expose and teach everyone different methods of communication. As an example, instead of only using spoken language for group discussions, encourage the use of gestures, writing, drawing, and other communication skills to ensure that Deaf students have direct opportunities to participate. This works well with the whole concept of differentiation and Inclusion, by the way.

Making Connections

Check out Chapter 12 on Inclusion

✓ **INCLUDE signed language lessons in your curriculum.** Lessons in signed language will allow you to create an environment where Deaf students feel valued and included, and at the same time provide wonderful linguistic and cognitive benefits to all. Not only that—think about how much more smoothly your class will run if all of your students use the hand sign to quietly ask to go to the bathroom, instead of interrupting you in the middle of an intense lecture with, "Hey teacher! Can I go to the bathroom?!"

✓ **CREATE opportunities for Deaf students to receive positive emotional and psychological support.** When needed, serve as a resource for the student's familial network to help them develop tools and skills for providing them with the appropriate, positive, and nurturing support system. It is not always transparent where a family can go to get support, so be the person who provides clear and consistent support. Call on Deaf adults to help you navigate the community and supports.

✓ **EMPOWER Deaf students to understand their great human potential, intellect, and the important role they play in our society.** Incorporate lessons and discussions about the great contributions that Deaf people have made to our society and how they accomplished such contributions. Honor Deaf Americans during Deaf Awareness Month, and regularly incorporate Deaf-centric themes in your curriculum. For example, introduce, teach, and discuss real-life role models that Deaf students can relate to in order to support their aspirations, and outline the various ways they can chase their dreams.

✓ **MODEL and foster behaviors that emphasize the value of civic responsibility to our society.** When Deaf students are valued as important contributors to our society because of their unique relationship with the world (instead of as a problem that needs to be treated and fixed), we naturally create an environment where they feel welcomed and valued. In turn, they are more emotionally and psychologically invested in our society and are more likely to make great contributions through civic engagement activities.

✓ **DO carefully gauge your expectations for Deaf students.** On this note, it is important to point out that modifying one's social environment, activity, or an assignment to ensure access and appropriateness does not automatically translate into lowering expectations as long as the skills that are to be gained by all students are the same and are equitably accessible. It may be helpful to review criteria for Universal Design for Learning (UDL) when developing a curriculum to not only ensure access to Deaf students but for all students.

Making Connections

Check out Chapter 11 on Universal Design for Learning

✓ **EVALUATE the materials, tools, and instruction provided to students to ensure they are accessible to all.** Assess what Deaf students are able to access, and learn through your teaching and what concepts are not clear to them to ensure they are able to continue to navigate through their own education. Are all of your videos captioned? Are announcements made over an intercom also provided in sign language? Are assignments given that require listening to a podcast or watching a YouTube video or making an oral presentation?

✓ **USE best practices with the interpreter.** Not sure what they are? No worries! We provided a handy checklist to use to remind yourself what to do or not do when working with an interpreter. Copy the handout on page 303 and post it near your desk in the class.

SIX CAPITALS FOR BUILDING DEAF CULTURAL CAPITAL WEALTH (DCCW)

Cultural Capital	Issues and Research	What You Can Do in the Mainstream Classroom
Linguistic	Studies show that Deaf kids with native as well as early acquisition and proficiency in signed languages are better able to learn and use spoken languages (only if it is accessible). The lack of consistent linguistic input and access can account for the majority of linguistic and cognitive delays that are found among many Deaf kids.	Use ASL signs with your whole class for letters, numbers, to show readiness, to ask to go to the bathroom, etc. Encourage Deaf students to teach signs to the class. Allow Deaf students to sign their answers, even if their interpreter then says them in English. Respond directly to the students. Encourage parents to learn sign language, and encourage their kids to find peers who sign.
Social	Deaf kids often exhibit delayed social skills development due to lack of access to their social environment and the feedback it provides. The social feedback allows kids to continue to develop and adjust their understanding of self and gain confidence in this process. As their skills develop, kids are able to learn how to positively navigate through relationships with peers.	Utilize Cooperative Learning groups, and make sure Deaf students are included and an integral part. Find out what the Deaf students like, and put them with peers who share their interests. Invite Deaf students to share with the class their interests and strengths, as well as how they can better communicate with them.
Familial/ Kinship	A struggle to develop true kinship with their own families is in many ways a unique experience for Deaf kids. Within some families and the larger community, there may be a sense that kinship is based on feelings of pity, low expectations, with a focus on what people feel they are lacking rather than on their significance and full human potential.	Encourage the Deaf students' families to come visit your class, to give you strategies, and to tell you what their Deaf kid(s) are good at. Do not view being Deaf as a problem, but merely as an important part of human variation like being Latino and speaking Spanish. Invite other Deaf people into the class to talk about their challenges, successes, and what worked for them.

(Continued)

Cultural Capital	Issues and Research	What You Can Do in the Mainstream Classroom
Navigational	Many Deaf kids lack navigational capital for one simple reason—the hearing "norm" has a completely different skill set that is often not accessible, not applicable to, or useable by, Deaf kids. Since their immediate network and community are most frequently hearing people who don't have any experience with navigational capital for Deaf kids, they don't have opportunities to acquire the skill set.	Tune out sounds one day and see if you can figure out what aspects of your class or the school rely solely on auditory cues. Does your school use bells or music for transitions? Do you rely on your voice to get attention? Once you know what they are, you can work with Deaf students to come up with alternatives.
Aspirational	Because of societal views, Deaf kids are often told explicitly and reminded repeatedly that they are limited in what they can accomplish. As a result of these repeated messages of inability and limitations, many Deaf kids do not gain aspirational capital and, more often than not, have little resilience.	Collect resources that show successful Deaf actors, scientists, ballerinas, mathematicians, professors, and other jobs; allow any student in class to read and report on these materials.
Resistant	Deaf kids experience negative slights directed at them but have not yet had opportunities to observe, acquire, and learn resistant skills and strategies in order to deflect and transform the slights.	Talk to all students about their words and actions, about bullying, and about how to respond.

Ask individuals in the Deaf community the best way to respond if someone talks about you, or to the interpreter instead of you, or says "Read my lips."

Talk to Deaf students directly about how people can be mean and what their responses can be to change others' attitudes and behaviors. |

STRATEGIES FOR WORKING WITH INTERPRETERS

- ☐ Thank the interpreter for her work. It's not an easy task.

- ☐ Ask where the interpreter should sit or stand so that the student can see the interpreter as well as you throughout the lesson.

- ☐ Ask what works best when you want to move around the room.

- ☐ Talk to the student, not the interpreter. Have eye contact with the student when you are communicating with him, even if he has to look at the interpreter's signing.

- ☐ Make sure both the student and the interpreter know you are more than willing to repeat what was not understood and come up with a word or signal that means they would appreciate a repeat.

- ☐ Avoid speaking too quickly, even when you are excited about a topic.

- ☐ Avoid making the interpreter teach the student; that's your job.

- ☐ Make sure both the interpreter and the student know that you expect the interpreter to interpret and that is it. Questions should be directed to you, and you do not want the interpreter helping with homework, giving answers to quizzes, and the like.

- ☐ Provide the interpreter with any written materials in advance when possible. The more time the interpreter has to look over materials, learn difficult words that will need fingerspelling, or concepts that will need explaining, the better.

- ☐ If there will be videos or other visual material, give the interpreter a heads-up and a chance to watch it in advance if possible. Try and get all materials captioned, but recognize that young children who do not yet read won't be accessing this material at all.

- ☐ Keep the interpreter in the loop, but avoid asking him to be the liaison with the family. Again, that is your job and you should directly communicate with the child's family members—for good news or bad.

- ☐ Find out what the process is for when the interpreter will be absent. Too often, no one thinks about this in advance, and then the student is left missing out on a whole day of instruction because there was no sub when the interpreter was home sick.

- ☐ Again, thank the interpreter for her work.

REFERENCES

Government Accountability Report. (2011). Deaf and hard of hearing children: Federal support for developing language and literacy. Retrieved from http://www.gao.gov/assets/320/318707.pdf

Humphries, T., Kushalnagaer, P., Mathur, G., Napoli, D. J., Padden, C., & Rathmann, C. (2014). Ensuring language acquisition for deaf children: What linguists can do. *Language, 90*(2), e31–e52.

Johnson, R. (2006). Cultural constructs that impede discussions about variability in speech-based educational models for deaf children with cochlear implants. *Perspectiva, 24*, 29–80.

Karchmer, M. A., & Mitchell, R. E. (2003). Demographic and achievement characteristics of deaf and hard of hearing students. In M. Marschark & P. Spencer (Eds.), *Oxford handbook of deaf studies, language, and education* (pp. 2137). New York, NY: Oxford University Press.

Komesaroff, L. (2007). *Surgical consent: Bioethics and cochlear implantation.* Washington, DC: Gallaudet University Press.

Lane, H. (1999). *Mask of benevolence: Disabling the deaf community.* San Diego, CA: DawnSign Press.

Lane, H., Hoffmeister, R., & Bahan, B. (1996). *A journey into the DEAF-WORLD.* San Diego, CA: DawnSign Press.

Leigh, I. (2009). *Identity and deafness.* Oxford, England: Oxford University Press.

Mitchell, R. E., & Karchmer, M. A. (2004). Chasing the mythical ten percent: Parental hearing status of deaf and hard of hearing students in the United States. *Sign Language Studies, 4*(2), 138–163.

Schick, B., Marschark, M., & Spencer, P. (2006). *Advances in the sign language development of deaf children.* New York, NY: Oxford University Press.

Yosso, T. (2005). Whose culture has capital? A critical race theory discussion of community cultural wealth. *Race Ethnicity and Education, 8*(1), 69–91.

RECOMMENDED READINGS

* Bahan, B., Bauman, H-D., & Montenegro, F. (Directors). (2008). *Autism unveiled* [DVD]. San Diego, CA: DawnSign Press.

* Holcomb, T. K. (2013). *Introduction to American deaf culture.* New York, NY: Oxford University Press.

* Siegel, L. M. (2008). *The human right to language: Communication access for deaf children.* Washington, DC: Gallaudet University Press.

* Through Your Child's Eyes: American Sign Language. (2011). Produced by DJ Kurs in cooperation with California State University, Northridge and the California Department of Education. Retrieved from www.through yourchildseyes.com

GO EVEN FURTHER WITH
THIS TOPIC ON THE WORLD WIDE WEB

- www.VL2.gallaudet.edu
- www.gallaudet.edu/clerc_center.html
- www.nad.org
- www.rid.org
- www.deafhoodfoundation.org/Deafhood/Home.html

THE Apps WE LOVE

- iASL
- ASL Pro
- ASL Dictionary
- Hamilton Mobile CapTel
- Subtitles
- Caption Fish
- Closed Capp

19

Superb Social Skills Instruction

Michelle Dean

California State University, Channel Islands

WHAT REALLY WORKS IN SOCIAL SKILLS INSTRUCTION IN THE SECONDARY CLASSROOM

Strategies to Help Students With Social Challenges

You're a middle school student with no one to hang out with after school. You're a high school student with no date to the prom. You're the kid last picked for teams or the one who no one wants as their chemistry partner. How does this make you feel? Pretty awful, I bet. That's the life of a student who struggles with social skills. And that's the student this chapter is about.

School is a great place to make friends—students meet in classrooms, hang out before or after school, eat together at lunch, or chit-chat in the halls. Unstructured social environments allow students to identify common interests, form peer groups, and work through disagreements (Spencer, Bowker, Rubin, Booth-LaForce, & Laursen, 2013). Making friends comes naturally to many children. Other children, however, have a difficult time making friends. What happens to the 15-year-old who still doesn't know how to join in a group conversation? Lacking social competence, they do not know what to do during unstructured periods at school. Consequently, students with social challenges struggle to make and keep friends.

It's easy to take the skills needed to socialize for granted. Think about all the skills needed to have a social conversation. We show interest in and try to understand the point of view of each other, we take turns in the conversation, we read body language and nonverbal cues (like winking, smiling, or clenching fists), and we adjust our own behavior to the interest of the group. For example, if everyone wants to watch a movie, insisting on playing hide-and-seek is not socially (or developmentally!) appropriate. Likewise, someone who is smiling is much more approachable than someone who is furrowing their brow. For some kids though, making sense of these subtle social nuances is difficult, and they do not have all the skills needed to socialize—which are actually quite sophisticated. Rather than appearing friendly, students who lack social competence come across as rude, shy, or socially awkward, and consequently, they are likely to withdraw from social experiences or to be neglected or rejected by other kids (Chronis, Jones, & Raggi, 2006; Proulx & Poulin, 2013). You've all seen these kids. They're the ones no one (sometimes not even the teachers) wants to hang with! (Insert sad face here.)

Students with social challenges often have a hard time making and keeping friends (Kasari, Rotheram-Fuller, Locke, & Gulsrud, 2011). These kids can be fairly easy to spot—they are the ones hanging out at the edge of a group or those who are alone during free time (Bauminger, Shulman, & Agam, 2003). Children who are left out of or avoid groups have less time to practice and develop their social skills. So over time, the gap widens between those who are skilled socially and those who are not. If we allow socially challenged children to continue to use their current repertoire of social skills—the skills that lead to rejection and/or neglect—they will continue to be left out of social groups as time progresses. And it will just get worse as they get older! In elementary school, children learn to understand the social world through play (Dunn, 2004). Adolescents, on the other hand, are more interested in hanging out and walking around, and not so interested in playing games (Maccoby, 2002). Not having learned to socialize through play in elementary school will make it even more difficult to learn how to hang out in a group, go to the mall, or talk about sports and movies in middle and high school. These are key aspects of every secondary school student's growing up experience!

We need to identify the students who are having a hard time making friends and getting along with others. It's more than just helping them find a buddy, however. Social challenges can interfere with cognitive, social, and emotional development (Dunn, 2004). That means that not having friends can also affect academic achievement, getting along with teachers, and developing independence. Social incompetence is also related to long-term mental health issues (Buhs, Ladd, & Herald, 2006; Mayes, Calhoun, Murray, Ahuja, & Smith, 2011). Children who are rejected in kindergarten are a lot more likely to continue to be rejected through fifth grade (Buhs et al., 2006). Experiencing years of rejection in school is difficult and, not surprisingly, can lead to school dropout, depression, and anxiety (Rutherford, Quinn, & Mathur, 2004). See why this is just as important as math and English? This stuff is serious!

Making Connections

Check out Chapters 12 and 17 on Inclusion and ASD

We can't just put socially challenged students in the same room as other students and assume a simple fix. Strategies need to be tailored to the students, their specific needs, and the context in which we expect them to be social. We need to be mindful that there are a variety of reasons that cause children to have social difficulties. For example, a child with autism may have difficulty having a back and forth conversation because he or she has difficulty with perspective taking. An English language learner may be familiar with textbook English, but finds kid-friendly social language (e.g., what up, dude; omg! for realz) very confusing. (I have to admit, sometimes I do too!) Each of these children may lack certain skills that are needed to have a social conversation, but the skills are different. Therefore, it is inappropriate to group these children together and teach one general social skills lesson and hope it fixes everyone's social dilemmas. At the same time, throwing all students with autism together in an "Autism classroom" makes absolutely no sense either; where exactly are these students supposed to learn social skills if they all struggle with it?

Schools are beginning to realize that social proficiency is as important as academic proficiency. Social skills interventions are an effective way to teach students socially appropriate behaviors. While there are excellent tools and resources out there, you don't need a specific social skills curriculum or a fancy (and expensive!) manual to teach social skills. There are evidence-based intervention strategies that have been effective in helping kids develop social skills. You are probably already using these strategies to teach academics and never thought they could apply the same strategies to social skills. Therefore, the purpose of this chapter is to discuss evidence-based social skills interventions strategies and approaches that are easy to implement at school and, of course, really work.

SOCIAL STRATEGIES

Effective social skills interventions help students make friends, keep friends, and successfully manage conflicts when they arise by targeting specific skills that are socially valid—skills that are relevant to everyday life (let's not use SpongeBob references with tenth graders. Vampires or

Beyoncé . . . maybe). I know what you are thinking: If I don't have a specific curriculum that the district provides to me, how do I know what I am
supposed to do? Research has taught us that high-quality social skills
interventions contain a combination of the following evidence-based intervention components: direct instruction, modeling, role-play, feedback,
prompting, and reward (Celeste, 2007; Chan et al., 2009). First, a social
"coach" (this could be a teacher, parent, interventionist, peer, or anyone
willing, able, and capable of engaging in the social intervention) intro-
duces the targeted social behavior. Next, the coach models how to use the
behavior appropriately. Make sure the student who needs the skill is given
opportunities to role-play or practice the behavior. Throughout the practice sessions, the coach (yes, this is probably you!) will guide the student
to use the newly learned behavior through verbal or physical prompting
as needed. Finally, the coach gives the student feedback about their use of
the behavior and rewards the student for using the behavior correctly.
Some kids will learn new skills quickly, but others may take longer
(January, Casey, & Paulson, 2011). Doesn't this all sound very similar to
how to teach academics as well? If so, great! We're in familiar territory!

Another important component of social skills intervention is the environment. Effective interventionists structure the environment to facilitate
social interaction and engagement. Think about it. It is easier to get to
know someone when you're sitting across a table from each other than it
is when you're sitting near each other at a basketball game. Environment
affects the way we socialize! Because most research on social skills interventions tends to be based in clinics or controlled environments (Kasari &
Smith, 2013), it is common to use "pull out" models for the initial stages of
social skills interventions at school. A student with social challenges meets
with a social coach (usually a teacher or school psychologist) outside the
classroom privately or in a small group. The strength of "pull out" is that
it minimizes distractions and offers a quiet setting where children can
learn a new skill in a private setting. The coach and students can move
through a series of social scenarios that introduce the topic and offer
opportunities to practice skills. Social relationships, however, are not built
in isolation. So don't limit yourself when choosing an environment. The
classroom, school clubs, or the cafeteria can also be great places to learn
and practice skills. When a skill is mastered in a small group or private
setting, the child can test out his new skills in a natural environment
(Bellini, Peters, Benner, & Hope, 2007). Keep in mind though that secondary students can be a difficult bunch; teachers and coaches need to be
hypercareful that they don't humiliate students by "practicing" social
skills in front of peers who might make fun of the student later.

Before beginning a social skills intervention, you should be clear about
what skills the child needs to learn, how you intend to teach the skills,
what practice opportunities will be available, and how you will measure
the student's progress. Therefore, formal or informal assessments should

be used to determine the child's social strengths and weaknesses, while factoring in the child's age, developmental level, and environment. There are standardized social skills survey instruments that parents, teachers, and the student can complete (Gresham & Elliott, 1990). Having multiple reporters fill out the survey provides a more comprehensive view of the student's social behaviors, with you observing the student at school, the parent observing at home, and the student describing his or her own experiences. As a middle or high schooler, the student's point of view is really important to ascertain. Often, school psychologists administer these assessments, and they should be happy to share the information with you. These formal measures compare the social skills scores of the child with social challenges to the average of a large group of children the same age.

In addition to using formal survey instruments to measure social behaviors, also watch how students socialize in natural environments like breaks or lunch. In order to prevent having your perceptions of the student's social challenges cloud your observation of what the kid is actually doing, observations should be systematic, with the student being observed in a certain location and at a certain time during the school day; the frequency, duration, or level of specific social behaviors should be recorded (Falkmer, Anderson, Falkmer, & Horlin, 2013; McMahon, Vismara, & Solomon, 2012). For example, if the target skill is social engagement, you would observe the student between classes and record the amount of time he was walking with friends, engaged in conversation, or mutually involved with other students of his age. Don't worry if this all seems overwhelming to you. There are professionals, such as special educators, school psychologists, and diagnosticians, who do this on a regular basis. Collaborate with them and you'll get the assessment data that you need.

BUILDING SOCIAL SKILLS
AT SCHOOL: WHAT NOT TO DO

Teachers

- ✗ **STOP assuming that students *want* to be alone.** Because children with social difficulties are often isolated between classes and at lunchtime, school personnel mistakenly believe that the student needs downtime, is a loner, or wants to be by himself or herself. Rather than *not wanting* to interact, they *do not know how* to interact with their peers.

- ✗ **STOP suspending students (or kicking them out of class).** Suspending students is a popular consequence for students who misbehave or break the rules at school. For students with social challenges, when we suspend them or just kick them out of class, we are taking away opportunities to practice social skills. Also, because students with social challenges are prone to isolation or withdrawal, suspensions can be viewed as a reward, and therefore inadvertently rewarding misbehavior.

- ✗ **STOP assuming proximity to peers is sufficient.** Physical inclusion, on its own, does not increase social engagement. In order to create an environment to promote social interactions, teachers need to structure the environment to increase socialization and to train peers and students with special needs to socialize with each other.
- ✗ **STOP overlooking the girls.** Because girls are typically associated with internalizing behaviors, compliant girls with learning difficulties are easier to tolerate and to overlook (Arms, Bickett, & Graf, 2008). More attention tends to be given to boys, who are associated with externalizing behaviors. Consequently, the social difficulties of girls may be more difficult to detect than boys (Dean et al., 2014). As such, girls with special needs are at risk for having unmet service needs (Bussing, Zima, Perwien, Belin, & Widawski, 1998) and negative outcomes (Arms et al., 2008).
- ✗ **STOP punishing children with social challenges for making social faux pas.** Children with social challenges are likely to misunderstand directions or to violate common social norms. Instead of punishing the student, capitalize on the teachable moment and use the faux pas to inform social skills intervention. Most of your other secondary students will start to learn that you may do different things and have different expectations for certain students; that's okay! Let them all know you will be fair by treating them differently.
- ✗ **STOP assuming social skills can only be taught in isolation.** While it is often beneficial to introduce social skills in a quiet or private setting, in order to master skills, students need to be able to practice in real-life settings. It is important to continue social training throughout the school day. Don't forget that you can use collaboration and co-teaching with a special educator to provide social skills instruction during the school day in the classroom itself.

Administrators

- ✗ **STOP minimizing the importance of teaching social skills.** Social competence is directly related to academic achievement and engagement and is an integral part in building independence. It is important to encourage school personnel to teach and encourage social development for all students, even at the secondary level. Remember that the new Common Core Standards emphasize critical thinking and collaborative skills!
- ✗ **STOP restricting access to sports and extracurriculars.** Having a variety of sports, clubs, and extracurricular activities allows students to establish a common ground, coparticipate in activities, and

identify shared common interests. Look around. Do all sports require students to try out? Do all clubs require students to be popular? Do you have options for students who do not excel socially but who may want to participate in activities with their peers?

BUILDING SOCIAL SKILLS AT SCHOOL: WHAT TO DO

Teachers, DO This

✓ **MAKE teaching social skills a priority.** Students with social deficits are more likely to have poor academic achievement, poor adjustment (Buhs et al., 2006), and increased loneliness and anxiety (Bauminger et al., 2003) as they move into adolescence and adulthood. Teaching social skills and providing opportunities to practice skills can improve outcomes for all students, but especially students with social difficulties who genuinely need that direct instruction. I know you're busy! But would it be that hard to incorporate social skills into collaborative group projects now? Teach them how to interact when they are science lab partners, when they are doing group debates in English, or when they are collaboratively solving math problems.

Making Connections

Check out Chapter 10 on Cooperative Learning

✓ **FIND ways to incorporate social skills into academics.** Be creative! Try to find social opportunities in every period you teach. For example, students could socialize during the warm-up problems in math. You can write down math problems on one piece of paper and the answers on the other. Pass out the math problems to one side of your classroom and the answers to the other. The student assignment would be to match the problem to the answer. Have fun finding the many social opportunities throughout the school day.

✓ **UNDERSTAND how specific social difficulties impact social engagement.** Social deficits vary from child to child. Teachers need to understand what the student needs to do differently in order to build relationships and make friends. How do you do this? Watch the child during free time. Ask yourself these questions: Are they initiating conversations with others? Are they hanging out in an area with other kids, or are they alone in the corner of a library? What are the other kids doing? What does the student with social challenges need to do differently in order to join in? Maybe he needs to stop playing on the computer by himself, or maybe she needs to join a club at lunchtime. Then, think about the supports that student may need in order to try new social strategies. I know this may seem like way beyond your job as a content teacher, but remember, we are there for the students. You taking this interest in even one student could make a difference for him for the rest of his life!

✓ **DO use typically developing peers.** Think about your classroom. There are always a few students who get along well with others, like to help, and are generally well liked by everyone. These students have great social skills and could be excellent peer models (Campbell & Marino, 2009). In a peer-mediated intervention, peers are trained to work with the student who has social difficulties, to socially engage, to interpret unusual social behaviors, and to accommodate interactions in a way that is inclusive. For example, a peer could help an adolescent socialize in the hallway during passing periods, be a lunch companion, or work collaboratively during a class project. Peer mediation has been used to increase social initiations, interactions, and to build play skills like taking turns, sharing, and other social engagement behaviors. Popular and empirically supported peer assistance strategies include peer modeling, role-play, verbal explanation, reinforcing, giving feedback, and the use of visual aids (Chan et al., 2009).

Plugged In

www.circleofriends.org

www.bestbuddies.org/best-buddies

✓ **DO choose peers with prosocial skills.** Less socially skilled children should be in close proximity to competent children. Students who are socially excluded are at risk of being bullied, and educators should separate victims from their perpetrators (Geiger, Zimmer-Gembeck, & Crick, 2004). That said, be aware that nice kids need breaks. Be careful to not penalize a kind student by always making him or her work with the socially difficult child; vary it up. There are many students who can benefit from working on their kindness and patience skills. Share the love. Want more ideas? Check out the websites in our Plugged In box.

✓ **THINK about developmental appropriateness.** Socializing in elementary school is very different from socializing in secondary school. In secondary school, talking and hanging out are far more important than play. Think about developmental levels and age appropriate social skills when designing social skills intervention programs. Parents aren't always as in tune with what is developmentally appropriate for their child's age; help them out!

✓ **WORK as a team with parents.** Because of their close proximity to their children, parents are an excellent resource for modeling social behavior (Hancock & Kaiser, 2006), but they may not always know what to do. This is where you come in! Teach parents how to be supportive in helping their children practice social skills and in guiding their children through social difficulties. Working with parents helps to promote generalization (the child being able to learn new skills across a variety of settings and people) by giving the student opportunities to practice targeted skills at home and in community settings. In addition, teachers and parents working together promote consistency between home and school—that's huge.

✓ **CAPITALIZE on the moment.** Use real-life experiences and teachable moments to teach new skills and to expand on previously learned skills. Manipulate the environment to give children opportunities to practice social skills within the normal school day. For example, if a social goal is asking for something appropriately (known as *requesting*), then during a cooperative learning activity, a teacher may pair the student with social challenges with another student. The student with social challenges will be given the iPad, and the assignment guidelines will be given to the typically developing child. In order to do the assignment, the child with social challenges will need to ask his peer for the guidelines. In turn, the typically developing peer can model appropriate requesting by asking for access to the iPad. Both students will receive natural rewards by having their requests fulfilled. A teacher should remain in close proximity to praise students for using the targeted skill and to prompt and give feedback as needed. They can also teach classroom peers how to give praise, feedback, and prompts.

Administrators, DO This

✓ **HAVE a positive attitude toward students with special needs.** As school leaders, administrator's attitudes toward students with special needs shape the school environment (Horrocks, White, & Roberts, 2008). When the principal has a positive attitude toward students with social difficulties, it sets the tone for the entire school.

✓ **EDUCATE your teachers about disabilities.** Just having a disability increases the probability that a child will have social challenges. When teachers' knowledge about disabilities is limited, it makes it difficult to set goals and expectations for the students. Training teachers about disabilities, how to make accommodations and modifications, and to set goals and expectations will help teachers better meet the needs of the students in their class. You don't know the information yourself? No problem. Bring in professional development and make sure you stay through the whole thing.

✓ **ENCOURAGE adults to facilitate socialization in between classes and at lunch.** Adults are an excellent resource to facilitate social engagement at school. Oftentimes, however, during lunchtime and passing periods, adults are socializing with each other in a class-room or the faculty lounge, while students with social challenges are outside struggling alone. Lunch and passing periods are the most difficult times of the day for students with social challenges. Consequently, this is the time where they really need some social supports. I know that adults need breaks too! But try to stagger adult breaks and meal times, so there is at least one adult available to prompt and offer assistance for a student in need. It could be as simple as encouraging a student to sit with a group during lunch or walking them to a club and introducing the student to the adult running the group and the other student members.

✓ **PROVIDE tabletop activities for extracurriculars.** Some students prefer hanging out with a few students rather than hanging out with the entire student body on the yard or in large groups like sports teams and social clubs. Many teachers allow children to hang out in their classroom during free periods or before and after school. It is important that students with social difficulties are socializing rather than isolating. One way to increase the engage-ment of the students who are hanging out in your classroom is to make a variety of tabletop games (think ping-pong, chess, or board games) available for students to play. Tell your students with social challenges that they are welcome to come to your classroom as long as they bring a friend and play a game together. C'mon, wouldn't you rather supervise a rugged game of chess than a chaotic game of football? This is working in your favor!

SECONDARY SCHOOL CURRICULAR RESOURCES

The PEERS Curriculum for School-Based Professionals: Social Skills Training for Adolescents with Autism Spectrum Disorder by Elizabeth A. Laugeson	This is an excellent, evidence-based intervention for adolescents with ASD.
Skillstreaming the Adolescent: A Guide for Teaching Prosocial Skills, 3rd Edition (with CD) by Ellen McGinnis	This is a great, evidence-based, easy-to-follow guide for teaching social skills. The program includes a program book, skill cards, posters, and a student workbook.
Girls in Real Life Situations, Grades 6–12: Group Counseling Activities for Enhancing Social and Emotional Development (Book and CD) by Julia V. Taylor, Shannon Trice-Black	This is a great program that is specifically designed to help adolescent girls.

FIVE QUICK STRATEGIES TO INCORPORATE SOCIAL SKILLS INTO YOUR ACADEMIC LESSON PLANNING

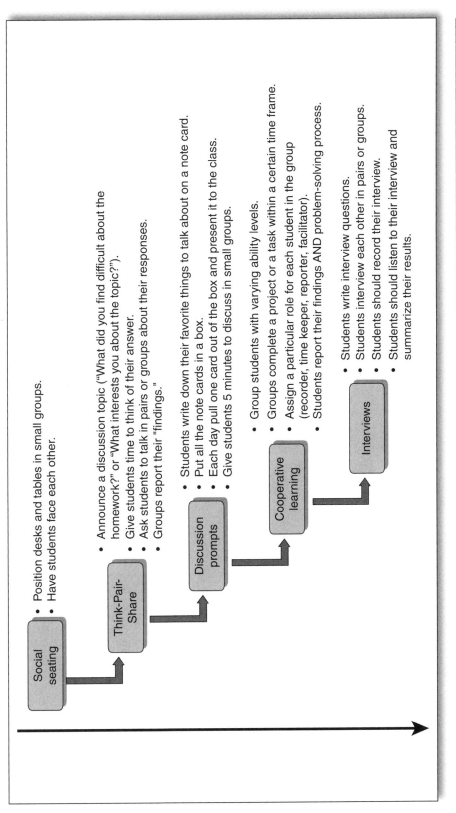

Social seating
- Position desks and tables in small groups.
- Have students face each other.

Think-Pair-Share
- Announce a discussion topic ("What did you find difficult about the homework?" or "What interests you about the topic?").
- Give students time to think of their answer.
- Ask students to talk in pairs or groups about their responses.
- Groups report their "findings."

Discussion prompts
- Students write down their favorite things to talk about on a note card.
- Put all the note cards in a box.
- Each day pull one card out of the box and present it to the class.
- Give students 5 minutes to discuss in small groups.

Cooperative learning
- Group students with varying ability levels.
- Groups complete a project or a task within a certain time frame.
- Assign a particular role for each student in the group (recorder, time keeper, reporter, facilitator).
- Students report their findings AND problem-solving process.

Interviews
- Students write interview questions.
- Students interview each other in pairs or groups.
- Students should record their interview.
- Students should listen to their interview and summarize their results.

SOCIAL CONVERSATION STARTERS FOR TEENS

What do you want to do when you graduate?	If you could travel to any place in the world what would it be?
If you had a choice of being a professional actor, musician, or athlete, which one would you choose? Why?	What is the best gift you've ever received?
What is the hardest thing you have ever done?	If you could meet anyone in the world, who would it be? Why?
What are your favorite places to eat?	What kind of music do you listen to?
If you won the lottery, what would you do with the money?	What do you do to relax?
What movie character are you most like? How so?	Where do you want to live when you move out of your parent's house?

ACADEMIC CONVERSATION STARTERS FOR TEENS

What was the hardest part of the homework assignment? Why did you think so?	What do you want to know about this topic?
How are you similar or different from the character?	What do you think the author's message is?
What do you predict will happen? Why do you think that?	What is the process you will use to complete the assignment?
What do we need to solve this problem?	What is the main idea?
Tell me how you solved that problem.	What do you think is the purpose of this assignment?
How do you think this will help you when you are an adult?	Tell me what you already know about this topic?

REFERENCES

Arms, E., Bickett, J., & Graf, V. (2008). Gender bias and imbalance: Girls in US special education programmes. *Gender and Education, 20*(4), 349–359.

Bauminger, N., Shulman, C., & Agam, G. (2003). Peer interaction and loneliness in high-functioning children with autism. *Journal of Autism and Developmental Disorders, 33*(5), 489–507.

Bellini, S., Peters, J. K., Benner, L., & Hope, A. (2007). A meta-analysis of school-based social skills interventions for children with autism spectrum disorders. *Remedial and Special Education, 28*, 153–162.

Buhs, E. S., Ladd, G. W., & Herald, S. L. (2006). Peer exclusion and victimization: Processes that mediate the relation between peer group rejection and children's classroom engagement and achievement? *Journal of Educational Psychology, 98*(1), 1–13.

Bussing, R., Zima, B. T., Perwien, A. R., Belin, T. R., & Widawski, M. (1998). Children in special education programs: Attention deficit hyperactivity disorder, use of services and unmet needs. *American Journal of Public Health, 88*(6), 880–886.

Campbell, J. M., & Marino, C. A. (2009). Brief report: Sociometric status and behavioral characteristics of peer nominated buddies for a child with autism. *Journal of Autism and Developmental Disorders, 39*, 1359–1363.

Celeste, M. (2007). Social skills intervention for a child who is blind. *Journal of Visual Impairment and Blindness, 101*(9), 521–533.

Chan, J. M., Lang, R. L., Rispoli, M., O'Reilly, M., Sigafoos, J., & Cole, H. (2009). Use of peer mediated interventions in the treatment of autism spectrum disorders: A systematic review. *Research in Autism Spectrum Disorders, 3*(4), 876–889.

Chronis, A. M., Jones, H. A., & Raggi, V. L. (2006). Evidence-based psychosocial treatments for children and adolescents with attention-deficit/hyperactivity disorder. *Clinical Psychology Review, 26*(4), 486–502.

Dean, M., Kasari, C., Shih, W., Frankel, F., Whitney, R., Landa, R., . . . Harwood, R. (2014). The peer relationships of girls with ASD at school: Comparison to boys and girls with and without ASD. *Journal of Child Psychiatry and Psychology, 55*(11), 1218-1225.

Dunn, J. (2004). *Children's friendships: The beginning of intimacy*. Malden, MA: Blackwell.

Falkmer, T., Anderson, K., Falkmer, M., & Horlin, C. (2013). Diagnostic procedures in autism spectrum disorders: A systematic literature review. *European Child and Adolescent Psychiatry, 22*, 329–340.

Geiger, T. C., Zimmer-Gembeck, M. J., & Crick, N. R. (2004). The science of relational aggression: Can we guide intervention? In M. M. Moretti, C. Odgers, & M. Jackson (Eds.), *Girls and aggression: Contributing factors and intervention strategies, perspectives in law and psychology series* (pp. 27–40). New York, NY: Kluwer.

Gresham, F. M., & Elliott, S. N. (1990). *Social Skills Rating System*. Circle Pines, MN: American Guidance Service.

Hancock, T. B., & Kaiser, A. P. (2006). Enhanced milieu teaching. In R. McCauley & M. Fey (Eds.), *Treatment of language disorders in children* (pp. 203–233). Baltimore, MD: Paul H. Brookes.

Horrocks, J. L., White, G., & Roberts, L. (2008). Principals' attitudes regarding inclusion of children with autism in Pennsylvania public schools. *Journal of Developmental Disorders, 38*, 1462–1473.

January, A. M., Casey, R. J., & Paulson, D. (2011). A meta-analysis of classroom-wide interventions to building social skills. *School Psychology Review, 40*(2), 242–256.

Kasari, C., Rotheram-Fuller, E., Locke, J., & Gulsrud, A. (2011). Making the connection: Randomized controlled trial of social skills at school for children with autism spectrum disorders. *Journal of Child Psychology and Psychiatry, 53*(4), 431–439.

Kasari C., & Smith, T. (2013). Interventions in schools for children with autism spectrum disorder: Methods and recommendations. *Autism, 17*, 254–267.

Maccoby, E. (2002). Gender and group process: A developmental account. *Current Directions in Psychological Science, 11*(2), 54–58.

Mayes, S. D., Calhoun, S. L., Murray, M. J., Ahuja, M., & Smith, L. A. (2011). Anxiety, depression, and irritability in children with autism relative to other neuropsychiatric disorders and typical development. *Research in Autism Spectrum Disorders, 5*, 474–485.

McMahon, C. M., Vismara, L. A., & Solomon, M. (2012). Measuring changes in social behavior during a social skills intervention for higher-functioning children and adolescents with autism spectrum disorder. *Journal of Autism and Developmental Disorders, 43*, 1843–1856.

Proulx, M. F., & Poulin, F. (2013). Stability and change in kindergartners' friendship: Examination of links with social functioning. *Social Development, 22*(1), 111–125.

Rutherford, R. B., Jr., Quinn, M. M., & Mathur, S. R. (2004). *Handbook of research in emotional and behavioral disorders.* New York, NY: Guilford Press.

Spencer, S. V., Bowker, J. C., Rubin, K. H., Booth-LaForce, C., & Laursen, B. (2013). Similarity between friends in social information processing and associations with positive friendship quality and conflict. *Merrill-Palmer Quarterly, 59*(1), 106–113.

RECOMMENDED READINGS

* Bukowski, W. M., Newcomb, A. F., & Hartup, W. W. (1996). *The company they keep: Friendship in childhood and adolescence.* New York, NY: Cambridge University Press.

* Hartup, W. W. (2005). Peer interaction: What causes what? *Journal of Abnormal Child Psychology, 33*(3), 387–394.

* Hartup, W. W., & Abecassis, M. (2002). Friends and enemies. In P. K. Smith & C. H. Hart (Eds.), *Blackwell handbook of childhood social development* (pp. 286–306). Malden, MA: Blackwell.

* Maccoby, E. E. (1998). *The two sexes: Growing up apart, coming together.* Cambridge, MA: Belknap Press/Harvard University Press.

* Rubin, K. H., Bukowski, W. M., & Laursen, B. (2009). *Handbook of peer interactions, relationships, and groups.* New York, NY: Guilford Press.

GO EVEN FURTHER WITH
THIS TOPIC ON THE WORLD WIDE WEB

- sociallyspeakingllc.com/my-mission-for-socially/free-pdfs/101_ways_to_teach_social.pdf
- www.cccoe.net/social/skillslist.htm
- www.socialthinking.com
- socialskillscentral.com
- www.cited.org/index.aspx?page_id=154

THE Apps WE LOVE

- Social Express
- My Sosh
- Speech Journal
- Pictello

20

Fantastic Family Collaboration

Mary Anne Prater

Brigham Young University

Nancy M. Sileo

University of Northern Colorado

WHAT REALLY WORKS IN FAMILY COLLABORATION IN THE SECONDARY CLASSROOM

Making Schools Not Just Student-Friendly, but Family-Friendly

You are teaching six high school classes with just one preparation period. An average of 30 students are enrolled in each class, and in your third week of the school year, you've learned only a few students' names. The few names that you have learned won't soon be forgotten because you've already contacted their parents to discuss their behavior. Your principal reminded you last week that fall open house is set for tomorrow, and you have been scrambling to pull together an academic overview of 180 students' progress as you prepare to meet the students' parents and other family members. Open house arrives and while you are grateful that family members have come to meet you, you simultaneously feel rushed and unprepared while being pestered by parents who want to ask you questions about their son or daughter.

Does this scenario seem familiar? Maybe you've experienced something similar. Whether you are a new teacher or a seasoned teacher, working with families can be both challenging and rewarding. Unfortunately, teacher education programs don't always prepare future teachers to work with families, particularly at the secondary level. The ability to collaborate effectively with parents and other family members is often acquired through on-the-job training during your first few years in a classroom. Correspondingly, learning to collaborate with your students' family members can be hard. You may feel that there are not enough hours in the day to do everything required to teach, let alone collaborate with family members. Or you may perceive that family members lack interest in their secondary-aged student. Or you may be upset because some family members are constantly contacting you. Many teachers selected education as their career so that they could "educate" students, not necessarily because they want to work with students' family members. Working with families is often a by-product of students' success, or more often than not, failure in school. A teacher's load at the secondary level sometimes means they teach more than 200 students in a single day. The idea of collaborating with the students' families can be overwhelming!

So what are you going to do? First, don't lose hope. Research shows that there are multiple means to successfully involve families in their child's education at all levels (Anafara, 2008; Carter & CADRE, 2003). Second, use what really works—in other words, while research can be helpful, it's the application of that research to actual practice that will most benefit you in day-to-day interactions with students, parents, and families. Third, find out what strategies your colleagues use to involve parents and families in their student's education. Finally, don't rely on one method or strategy or idea for all parents and families. What works for you with one student and his or her family members may not work for you with another student's family members.

The purpose of this chapter is to provide you with some practical ideas and strategies that can be used when working with families at the secondary level. Further, this chapter will give you an overview of current research and approaches for working with families along with some realistic thoughts on what really works and what doesn't.

WHAT THE RESEARCH SAYS ABOUT COLLABORATING WITH FAMILIES

Let's start with the basics. What exactly is a family? Families have changed greatly over time and come in a variety of configurations (Sileo & Prater,

2012). In order to count families for the census, the U.S. government considers a family to be a group of two or more people related by some facet who reside together. A less formal definition of a family is a group of persons who live in one household. A family with one mother, one father, and several children is becoming less and less the norm. Today it's not uncommon for students to come from a single parent home or to have a stepparent, two mothers, or two fathers. An older sibling may be head of the household, or the student may be living with extended family like grandparents or aunts and uncles. Thus, every student in your classroom belongs in some manner to a family.

Next, let's discuss collaboration. "Collaboration is a style of interaction: two or more people working cooperatively together toward a shared goal" (Murawski & Spencer, 2011, p. 19). Essentially, collaboration occurs in school settings between teachers and families when the two parties work toward a shared outcome. An example is a teacher and a parent working to help a student to prepare for the SAT exams. The teacher provides instruction and study skills in the classroom, and the parent provides support and structured time to study at home.

You can't collaborate if you can't communicate. In fact, genuine communication is harder to achieve than you might think! For example, non-verbal actions like where you stand, facial expressions, and whether you touch someone or not, all communicate something regardless of what you say. You could say all the right things, but unknowingly roll your eyes communicating, "I don't have time for this." Families will pick up on that even more than your words.

A lot of research supports that schools and teachers working collaboratively with their students' families makes a positive difference in the education of children (deFur, 2012; Jeynes, 2011). In many instances, family members are excited when a young child begins school. They readily attend school meetings, volunteer to work in the classroom, and support teachers in any way they can. Unfortunately, support diminishes as the child grows older. In particular, research indicates that attendance at school meetings and other traditional family involvement lessens in high schools (Harvard Family Research Project, 2007). Lack of involvement doesn't mean families don't care. Perhaps they may have been involved for years and are a little burned out; or they may view adolescents as more independent and feel they should take more personal responsibility for their schoolwork. Unfortunately, some may even have had negative experiences with schools or teachers along the way; yep, it's true. It happens, and it ends up leaving parents or families with a negative feeling about collaborating with school personnel.

A major consideration that impacts involvement is the majority cultural group of the school employees, student bodies, and families. Families who feel different from the majority culture of the school may be less inclined to participate (Dyches, Carter, & Prater, 2012). For example, if your school has only a few Latino students while all the teachers are

White, the Latino families may feel uncomfortable in the school. There may also be a language barrier. Other less traditional families, such as those headed by two moms, may also avoid the school for fear of judgment on the part of school employees. Be sensitive to these cultural and family composition differences, and find ways to welcome all families into the school and your classroom.

Making Connections

Check out Chapter 16 on Working With English Language Learners

If you have students with disabilities in your classroom (and virtually every teacher does), additional sensitivity to the family's situation and desires is necessary. Sometimes parents of students with disabilities feel isolated in the school and the community. For example, their child might not be invited by classmates to participate in weekend activities. This results in not only the student being isolated but the parents don't have opportunities to meet and interact with other parents. All students with disabilities are required to have an Individualized Education Program (IEP). You may be involved in developing students' IEPs and meeting with their family members to reach consensus on this plan. This provides a great opportunity to listen to families, share ideas on how both the school and the home can support the student, and demonstrate respect for the parents' desires for their child.

Positive collaborative attitudes benefit teachers and families when they work together toward a common goal. Perhaps most importantly, these attitudes should benefit the student. Let's take a closer look at some collaborative attitudes identified by Murawski, Carter, Sileo, and Prater (2012). When talking with family members, use descriptive messages, rather than evaluative ones. For example, say, "Joaquin hasn't been in school for a week," instead of "Why haven't you been bringing Joaquin to school?" Second, use collaborative rather than controlling messages when talking with parents. A collaborative message demonstrates to parents that you want to partner with them to find a solution to an issue, rather than telling the parent what you want them to do to fix the concern. Instead of saying, "You need to make certain Ben completes his homework before going to his sports games," say, "Let's talk about how we can both support Ben to get his homework completed."

Be honest with parents. In your honesty, however, do not blurt out accusations like, "Violet is a thief!" but rather say, "Violet seems to be taking things that don't belong to her." At the same time, take an empathetic approach when talking with families. For example, if a mother indicates that she can't work one-on-one with her son at home because of her work schedule, say, "Wow, you are doing a lot. It must be difficult to schedule all the demands on your time." Then problem solve with the mother on alternatives to help her son. Also, be sensitive to a family's response and reaction to both positive and negative news.

Always remember that you and the student's family are equal partners in the education process—in fact, you probably play a slightly lesser role in the process than the family. As a teacher, you may be the expert on educational content and knowledge, but the parent is the expert on their child! Finally, keep an open, communicative, and positive approach to collaboration. All parties need to demonstrate a willingness to work together. In some situations, family members will insist that they know what is best for the students. In most cases, however, families see you as the "expert" on their child's education. This attitude may lead them to agree to solutions or decisions because you suggested them, not because they truly believe it is the right thing for their child. So be cautious in your recommendations and how you make them to ensure family members have a say in the decisions as well.

Successful collaboration and communication with families require that teachers and family members have "the will" and "the want" to communicate; and their communication should center on openness and respect (Murawski et al., 2012). Think about how your background and values impact your day-to-day interactions with students and their families. A self-awareness of biases and dispositions will help you appreciate differences in life outlook and communication styles when working with families (Sileo & Prater, 2012). As you read the next section of this chapter on DOs and DON'Ts, remember that each family is unique and brings different skills to any collaborative partnership.

AVOID THESE CLICHÉS AND TRADITIONAL PITFALLS WHEN WORKING WITH FAMILIES

Teachers

- ✗ **STOP thinking that everyone speaks your language.** "Education speak" is often hard for family members to understand. Watch those acronyms, and help your educational colleagues stay away from them when working with families also.
- ✗ **STOP saying you teach "English/math/science/social studies" when talking with families.** You actually teach students!
- ✗ **STOP assuming that families who can't or won't meet with you during the school day or immediately after school don't care.** Many families have few resources and members may be working multiple jobs, or they may have had a bad experience with schools.
- ✗ **STOP assuming letter grades each term are sufficient for communicating with families.** Grades say nothing about what a student can do, can understand, or where a student needs help. Grades are only one aspect of the students' school experience.

- **✘ STOP using clichés** such as, "You won't be laughing after I call your parents." Enough said!

Making Connections

Check out Chapter 14 on Assessment

- **✘ STOP waiting for the student's behavior to escalate or for the student to be failing before talking to the family.** If you have concerns about a student, talk with the student and family ASAP. If you work together, you can prevent the (mis)behavior from escalating.

- **✘ STOP trying to squeeze in everything you want to communicate about a student into one 10- to 15-minute phone conversation,** especially when the parent had no idea you were going to call. Focus on the main reason for your call, and allow the parent time to respond.

- **✘ STOP asking rapid-fire questions or talking over students and family members during conferences or meetings.** You've had time to think of what you want to share with students and families. Give them time to process the information and contribute to the conversation.

- **✘ STOP avoiding talking about difficult topics (e.g., bullying) with family members.** Be sensitive in how you share information, but keep families informed about what is happening in the school environment.

- **✘ STOP assuming family members can help your students with their homework.** They may not have been taught the same way or don't have the background to help.

- **✘ STOP assuming family configurations include a traditional father, mother, several children, and a dog.** There is no longer a "typical" family configuration. You likely will be working with families headed by grandparents or families headed by two dads or two moms.

- **✘ STOP sending home forms and letters that refer to "mother" or "father."** Using "mother" or "father" or both on forms and letters doesn't take into consideration that some students have no "mother" or "father."

- **✘ STOP talking or sharing information about students and families in the teacher workroom or lounge or other public access areas in the school.** This violates confidentiality and is unprofessional.

- **✘ STOP, no actually—NEVER talk to students about other students and their families.** This is NOT acceptable, but it does occur more often than it should.

Administrators

All of the statements previously about what teachers should stop doing apply to administrators. Here are a few additional ones:

✘ **STOP thinking that you only need to communicate with families at events such as plays, concerts, and athletics.** The more you communicate with families, the more likely you are to have their support when you need it. Sit in on student/family/teacher conferences, and get to know more about your students' lives both in and out of school.

✘ **STOP assuming that all teachers know how to collaborate and communicate with families.** These skills are typically not taught as discrete subjects in secondary teacher education programs. They may need some professional development on the topic.

✘ **STOP expecting teachers to have meaningful conversations with family members during only 15- or 20-minute conferences once a year.** Student success is dependent on strong home/school bonds, so provide multiple opportunities, both formal and informal, for families to interact with teachers and school personnel.

✘ **STOP deferring responsibility to teachers for speaking with families.** Welcome family members to speak with you as well and ensure that administrators are accessible to families.

STRATEGIES THAT REALLY WORK WHEN COLLABORATING WITH FAMILIES OF SECONDARY STUDENTS

Teachers, DO This

✓ **BUILD TRUST with families by contacting them and sharing positive things about their children.** Teachers often communicate with families of students who are struggling or those who exceed expectations. Remember the students who are making average progress and communicate with their families as well.

✓ **PRAISE parents for what they are doing right.** This will help establish good relationships, and they will be more interested in your suggestions about what more they can do to help. Yes, the whole "bees to honey" analogy really does work.

✓ **DEVELOP a system to communicate something positive about EVERY student via e-mail, text, or phone with each student's family at least once per semester.** Communicate three positive comments for every one negative comment. Sharing something positive with a family member can go a long way toward strengthening your relationship. Create a list with your class rosters for each period, and mark off each student as you call home.

✓ **FIND a better way to communicate with families.** Setup a Facebook page or a class website on your school network with information about current happenings and assignments in your classroom, and encourage students and families to "friend" you. You can keep your personal Facebook information separate from your professional one, but students always like to learn some personal information about their teachers too. Consider using Edmodo as a student-safe Facebook-like application.

✓ **ASK families how they would like to receive information from you and the school.** Communicate in multiple ways such as using hard copies with some families and e-mails or websites to meet different family needs. If you are up for it, some parents are great with quick text reminders and questions.

✓ **INVITE family members to volunteer in your classroom.** Some parents haven't been in a classroom since they were students. Spending time in a classroom will help them see the challenges and opportunities their child faces each day. Plus, it can be a bonus for you as you get some adult help in the room!

✓ **ASK students to participate in discussions you have with their family members to help open communication channels with the student and families.** Secondary students are more than capable of participating in discussions that concern their education. They should have a voice in meetings about them. It's also helpful to see how your students interact with their own parents and guardians.

✓ **When you meet with students and families, GIVE THEM TIME to listen and process what you are saying.** Sometimes, in their exuberance, teachers rush through what they want to say without giving families time to process and respond. Make sure you take a breath and give the student or family member plenty of time to respond. Also, sending a short note or e-mail home on the topic of your meeting can give families a chance to prepare what they want to contribute to the conversation.

✓ **LISTEN to families without being judgemental.** It's easy to jump to conclusions and make assumptions about the family. Listen to them with an open mind. Remember that cultures and experiences can impact our frames of reference.

✓ **PROTECT families' privacy** and keep confidential any information they may volunteer that does not impact their child's education.

✓ **RECOGNIZE that family configurations vary greatly, and don't assume that every student has a mother and/or father.** Use letters and forms that say "parent or guardian." You don't want anyone to be offended or feel excluded, even if it wasn't intentional.

✓ **PROVIDE families with information about online resources** (such as Khan Academy or tutor.com or grammar-monster.com) that will support their child's school and homework. Add these resources to your website, and ask students and families for additional ideas.

✓ **ATTEND school activities that your students are involved in,** such as plays, sports events, and outside competitions. You can also go to activities where you know parents of your students may be in attendance, such as "Coffee with the Principal" or a PTA (Parent Teacher Association) meeting.

Administrators, DO This

✓ **CREATE welcome packets for families of new students.** Translate them into languages spoken by students' families, and provide them using various methods such as hard copies, e-mail attachments, and via website downloads.

✓ **SET UP a family-led community resource center in your school.** Families who may not want to talk with you or a teacher one-on-one may be more willing to take advantage of resources in a center run by family members. If a resource center is not possible, set aside one classroom as a family room for families to use. For example, while one parent is meeting with a teacher, another parent from another family can watch the younger children in the family room.

✓ **ASK family members for ideas on how to improve school climate.** Students, families, and school personnel should work together to develop and implement a shared school vision.

✓ **SET UP professional development or collaboration seminars** that teachers and families can attend together or that are family led.

✓ **SPONSOR activities that allow you and your teachers to listen to family concerns,** whether they are about individual students, policies and practices, or the school in general. This could be "Breakfast With the Principal and Teachers" or an Open Forum or a Discussion Box or even just a sign-up sheet for regular times to meet and talk.

ADVICE FOR PARENTS AND FAMILIES TO SUPPORT STUDENTS

Parent Tip	What to Do
Make sure the student has a quiet place for completing homework.	Turn off the TV, and encourage your student to put her/his cell phone on silent or out of sight when completing homework, encourage them to focus on homework and not social media sites, and minimize distractions (i.e., people, animals, Facebook, Twitter).
Provide the materials the student needs to complete homework.	Encourage your student to have paper, pencils, the computer, and other materials available when your student begins homework so time isn't wasted trying to track down materials in the middle of an assignment.
Help the student learn to manage time.	Establish routines for completing schoolwork. Help your student manage a schedule so the student has time to complete homework before other responsibilities such as after-school athletics or performing arts or a part-time job. Help the student plan how to schedule and complete large long-term projects.
Be positive about homework and help the student understand how homework is relevant to his or her life.	Discuss the importance of learning and studying outside of the school environment with your student. As your student completes work, help the student make connections between schoolwork, postsecondary education, and real life.
When the student does homework, do your own homework.	When your student is doing homework, show the student that adults learn at home as well. If the student is reading, read one of your books. If the student is completing math problems, you can pay bills or balance a checkbook.
When your student asks for help, provide guidance, not answers.	Giving your student answers may hinder the student from learning. Instead, help your student use resources such as information in books or on the Internet.
Stay informed about your student's school assignments.	Ask your student to share with you her or his different teachers' policies for attendance, in class work, and homework. If your school uses Internet programs for reporting students' progress, log onto your student's account to be informed about completed and turned-in assignments.

(Continued)

(Continued)

Parent Tip	What to Do
Encourage your student to make and keep a homework checklist.	Some students have difficulty with organization. Provide guidance on how to create an assignment checklist that helps the student determine how long an assignment will take, how to prioritize assignments, materials needed to complete work, and a schedule for work completion. Encourage your student to use an assignment planner.
Before beginning homework, encourage the student to decide which assignments are easy and which ones are hard.	Learn about your student. If it is easier for your student to complete simple assignments first, then have your student identify assignments that he or she can complete without assistance, and do those first. However, if your student fatigues easily, it may make more sense for the student to complete more difficult assignments first and to save easier assignments for later. Encourage your student to break larger tasks into achievable chunks and to take breaks when necessary.
Provide support to help a student get started with a task.	Some students encounter problems beginning tasks. Clarify directions or monitor your student as he or she completes the first problem of an assignment.
Watch for signs of frustration and failure.	Encourage your student to take short breaks. If your student is consistently frustrated with homework, discuss your concerns with the student's teachers.
Reward progress for completing assignments.	Consider different ways to reward or praise your student for working hard and for completing assignments.

Source: Adapted from Tannock, Carter, Prater, & Sileo (2012, p. 45).

REFERENCES

Anafara, V. A. (2008). Varieties of parent involvement in schooling. *Middle School Journal, 39*, 58–64.

Carter, S., & Consortium for Appropriate Dispute Resolution in Special Education. (2003). *Educating our children together: A sourcebook for effective family-school-community partnerships.* Eugene, OR: Consortium for Appropriate Dispute Resolution in Special Education.

deFur, S. (2012). Parents as collaborators: Building partnerships with school- and community-based providers. *TEACHING Exceptional Children, 44*(3), 56–67.

Dyches, T. T., Carter, N. J., & Prater, M. A. (2012). *A teacher's guide to communicating with parents: Practical strategies for developing successful relationship.* Upper Saddle River, NJ: Pearson.

Harvard Family Research Project. (2007). *Family involvement in middle and high school students' education.* Cambridge, MA: Harvard Graduate School of Education.

Jeynes, W. H. (2011). *Parental involvement and academic success.* New York, NY: Routledge.

Murawski, W. W., Carter, N. J., Sileo, N. M., & Prater. M. A. (2012). Communicating and collaborating with families. In N. M. Sileo & M. A. Prater (Eds.), *Working with families of children with special needs: Family and professional partnerships and roles* (pp. 59–90). Upper Saddle River, NJ: Pearson.

Murawski, W. W., & Spencer, S. (2011). *Collaborate, communicate, and differentiate! How to increase student learning in today's diverse schools.* Thousand Oaks, CA: Corwin.

Sileo, N. M., & Prater, M. A. (Eds.). (2012). *Working with families of children with special needs: Family and professional partnerships and roles.* Upper Saddle River, NJ: Pearson.

Tannock, M. T., Carter, N. J., Prater. M. A., & Sileo, N. M. (2012). Family members' roles and characteristics. In N. M. Sileo & M. A. Prater (Eds.), *Working with families of children with special needs: Family and professional partnerships and roles* (pp. 1–22). Upper Saddle River, NJ: Pearson.

RECOMMENDED READINGS

* Dyches, T. T., Carter, N. J., & Prater, M. A. (2012). *A teacher's guide to communicating with parents: Practical strategies for developing successful relationship.* Upper Saddle River, NJ: Pearson.

This book discusses specific skills needed to communicate effectively with families. Topics include developing caring relationships; developing general communication skills; communicating by phone, paper, and electronic means; communicating in meetings; and addressing difficult topics with families. It contains 37 pages of reproducible worksheets and forms on various related topics.

* Ridnover, K. (2011). *Everyday engagement: Making students and parents your partners in learning.* Alexandria, VA: Association for Supervision and Curriculum Development.

This book provides strategies for engaging both students and parents in students' learning. The author discusses creating positive relationships, inviting parents to engage, making inroads with resisters, and fostering participation. The book includes samples of worksheets and forms imbedded throughout the chapters.

* Sileo, N. M., & Prater, M. A. (2012). *Working with families of children with special needs: Family and professional partnerships and roles.* Upper Saddle River, NJ: Pearson.

This book focuses primarily on working with families of students with special education needs. However, many of the principles discussed apply regardless of the student population. Topics include family members' roles and characteristics, communicating and collaborating with families, working with families from diverse backgrounds, understanding the family perspective and ethical consider-ations when working with families, among other topics. One chapter is devoted to creating Individualized Education Plans (IEPs) with families and strategies for involving students. One of the most unique features of this book is a chapter in which five parents and one grandparent share their perspective of raising a child with disabilities.

GO EVEN FURTHER WITH
THIS TOPIC ON THE WORLD WIDE WEB

- www.discoveryeducation.com/parents/
- www.familyeducation.com/
- inclusiveeducationpdresources.com/collaborating-with-parents/videos.php
- www.nea.org/
- www.pta.org/
- www.php.com/

THE Apps WE LOVE

- BuzzMob
- Teacher App & Grade Book
- Collaborize Classroom
- Remind101
- TeacherKit
- HomeworkNow
- Class Messenger

Index

A SAGE Company

Corwin is committed to improving education for all learners by publishing books and other professional development resources for those serving the field of PreK–12 education. By providing practical, hands-on materials, Corwin continues to carry out the promise of its motto: **"Helping Educators Do Their Work Better."**